THE RUN OF THE MILL

THE RUN OF THE MILL

BY STEVE DUNWELL

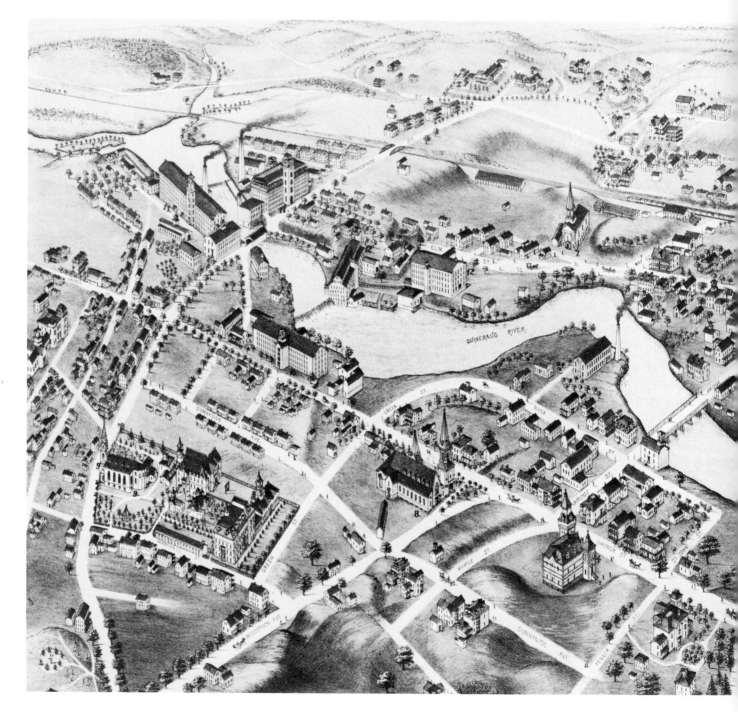

DAVID R. GODINE · PUBLISHER

A Pictorial Narrative of the Expansion, Dominion, Decline and Enduring Impact of the New England Textile Industry

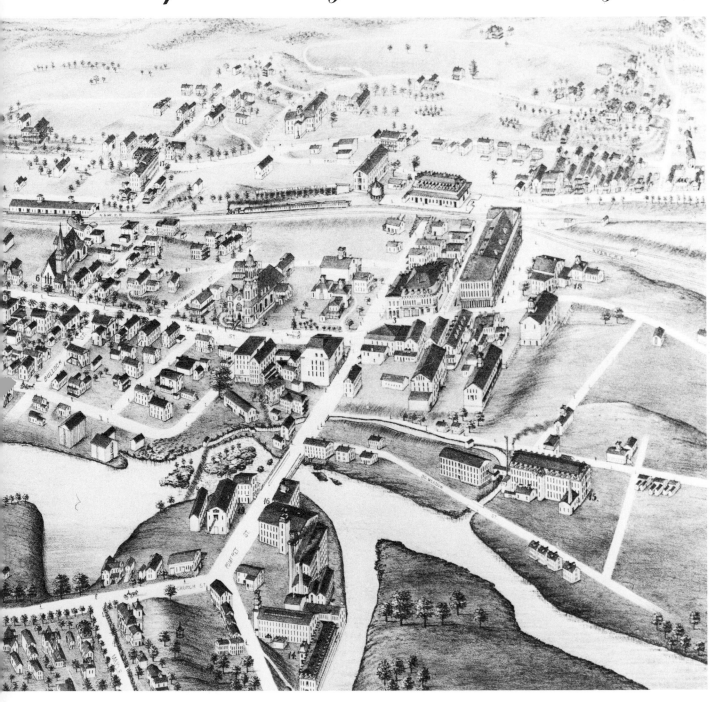

BOSTON - MASSACHUSETTS

THIS BOOK
IS DEDICATED TO
THE MILL WORKERS
OF NEW ENGLAND

EDITING AND OCCASIONAL DRAWINGS BY ANNA DUNWELL

First published in 1978 by
David R. Godine, *Publisher*
306 Dartmouth Street, Boston, Massachusetts

ISBN 0–87923–249–8

LCC NO. 78–57683

PRINTED IN THE UNITED STATES OF AMERICA

Contents

Acknowledgments

Initial work on this book was supported by a Grant-in-Aid from the Rhode Island Council of the Arts. I am especially indebted to Alan Symonds, President of Providence Pile Fabric Company, who first opened the doors of the textile mill world to me, and to Betty Bergeron and Tom Mulligan, who gave me first clues to the significance of contemporary mill towns. Several mill owners and plant managers allowed me carte blanche while photographing in their factories. Without their magnanimous and trusting cooperation the "Working" section would not have been possible: Irving Gordon, Andrews Worsted Company; Fred Bowden, Arbeka Webbing Company; Larry Jarvis, Conrad-Jarvis Company; George Thomas, Grosvenordale Textile Company and G. Thomas & Son; Frank Magnussen, Wm. Heller, Inc.; and Ted Larter, Wannalancit Textile Company. Among the many who shared their knowledge of New England mills, Chuck Boster, David Margolick, Bill Johnson, James Pye, Bob Perrault, and Dr. Alton Thomas provided crucial information and insights. Morgan Rockhill, Roger Birn, and Bill Gallery—all photographers based in Providence, Rhode Island—shared their facilities, equipment, and technical expertise. Many of the photographs presented here could not have been made without this assistance. Marsha Peters and Nat Shipton (Rhode Island Historical Society), Jerry Hess (National Archive), Robert Vogel (Smithsonian Institution), Ted Penn and Shomer Zwelling (Old Sturbridge Village), and Patrick Malone and Paul Rivard (Old Slater Mill Historic Site) all helped increase the effectiveness of my research by sharing their experience and resources. The Boston Athenaeum deserves special mention for the excellence of its collection and the courteous assistance of its staff. Without the Athenaeum my work would have been far more difficult. The Merrimack Valley Textile Museum was just as critical in bringing the book to completion: Peter Molloy, former Curator of Machinery, encouraged my photographic endeavors, and Helena Wright, Curator of Prints, especially helpful in locating elusive sources and illustrations, also added crucial encouragement when it was most needed. Paul Cook, James Conrad, Patrick Malone, Richard Candee, Helena Wright, Laurence Gross, and Michael Folsom read the preliminary manuscript and offered valuable suggestions and criticisms. I also thank David Godine, publisher of this work, who saw the possibilities of the book more clearly than I did in its early stages and encouraged me to reach far higher than I had intended. Anna, my wife, has lived with this book since its beginnings and has tolerated the four-year intrusion of the Industrial Revolution into our home with special grace. Her encouragement, insight, and editing skill helped give the book its form and point of view. Her love kept me whole during its creation.

Foreword

The spinning and weaving of natural fibers are among the most ancient and vital arts. For millennia, craftsmen have brought warp and weft together to clothe and decorate people of every description and to make utilitarian objects of every kind. In this way, textiles are truly universal. What was once a craft became an industry and today, as in antiquity, we are surrounded by its products. A T-shirt and a cashmere sweater, a fine worsted suit and a pair of double-knit polyester trousers, the sails of a racing yacht and the hawser of a super-tanker, a sheer stocking and a lace doily, an automobile's safety belt and an athlete's sneakers, a shoelace and a hardback book cover—all have two things in common. They are all textile products and they are all made by working people who live workaday lives and toil without thought of recognition or glory. Industrialization replaced the craftsmen with the machine, but it is a rare machine so automatic that it doesn't need to be programmed, tended, watched, and maintained by someone.

This is the story of textile manufacturing in New England—a story of human beings and machines and of the environment they created for each other. Textile manufacture was the first craft to be successfully mechanized. As inventive, enterprising man created new machines, his machines created a new man. The laboratory where this new alliance was tested with greatest intensity was the New England mill town. The results were at first glorious; later, disastrous. This book attempts to capture the vigor of their rise and the tragedy of their ultimate decline.

A unique invention, the mill town was a self-contained industrial community whose every component was planned and controlled to ensure the productivity of its machines. The machine was a new and demanding god; the mill town, its first American parish. Although the scope of this book is limited to the environment of the textile industry, and further restricted to its development east of the Connecticut River, general themes discussed here apply also to a wide variety of other industrial communities created throughout the eastern states during the early nineteenth century, where firearms, edge tools, furniture, clocks, instruments, shoes, heavy machinery, and other products were manufactured. Always vital, highly competitive, especially sensitive to technological evolution, the textile industry provides the best and most important example of the mill town phenomena repeated in these other manufacturing domains.

The mechanization of New England textiles set the pace for the American industrial revolution. As decisively as the gun and the plow tamed the receding western frontier, the spinning frame and the power loom changed the Northeast. The cotton mill became the symbol for all mills. The textile industry represented all industry. Major themes of industrialization were introduced here: the machine as ally and tyrant, the integrated factory, the corporation, the separation of management from labor, the woman as wage earner, the exploitation of a permanent factory class, the monopoly, the conglomerate, and even the American dream itself—all were developed or elaborated by this industry. In the mill town the farmer met the machine and the immigrant discovered America.

Like an iron hand, the textile industry gripped New England and pulled its people into a new environment. Now withdrawn, its imprint remains. Our society may now run on petroleum and electricity, but the dispersion of our villages was determined by availability of waterpower. Recently thriving, prosperous communities have become desperate, painful anachronisms. The mill town today is custodian of a bittersweet legacy—power and progress, despair and decay.

*   *   *

I grew up near the humble mill town of Wappingers Falls, New York, and often canoed down the mill stream and across the pond. But I never once saw the village or the mill itself, set down in a valley, out of sight below the falls. There was no reason whatsoever to go there.

Later, there were the countless trips between home and college, passing each time through the industrial backwater of Derby, Connecticut. I had no idea then that the site of America's first textile town was nearby; I knew only that it was one of the most stagnant and ugly communities I had ever seen. Years later, while living in Rhode Island, I knew a woman whose stepfather owned a carpet and upholstery mill in Fall River. I went to visit his factory and was overwhelmed the moment the heavy door swung open. The noise was deafening. It seemed a mechanized hell on earth, a thoroughly unwholesome place to spend a day, much less a lifetime. Yet everyone I saw there appeared fully acclimated to this bizarre, brutal environment, as if it were quite ordinary and commonplace.

Who would choose to work in such a place, and why? Certainly a person must be changed by a lifetime of mill work: in what ways? I was fascinated. I wanted to know more about the people I met. I returned with my camera and began to photograph, but the first pictures somehow missed the central truth. The lens did not catch the subtle distinctions between alienation and fatigue, pride and smugness, boredom and despair. These mill workers had more complex stories to tell. Their stories were often poignant and, like the mill story itself, spread out in myriad directions—to Canada and the Azores, to other mills in towns I had never heard of. These people lived and moved in a world with its own logic, ethic, and history; a world about which I knew I knew nothing.

For almost five years, when there have been time and money to spare, I have followed the story's thin thread from mill town to mill town, photographing, recording interviews, and noting snatches of conversation heard over the din of weave sheds and the high scream of spinning rooms. The thread was laced throughout the New England landscape, along the river banks and through the valleys. The search has taken me more than thirty thousand miles, off the thruways, down narrow roads to places that are home to a few and forgotten by or unknown to almost everyone else. What started as a curiosity soon became an obsession—to record, preserve, and understand a pervasive phenomenon that had shaped an entire region and is now fast disappearing.

Slowly, patterns and themes emerged. At the same time, it became clear that a thorough understanding of the decaying mill town present required an equivalent command of mill town history. Each village had a special destiny of its own, which reflected the interplay of economic, social, and technological forces surrounding its creation and accompanying its subsequent growth. Each village had contributed, in its own way, to the epic of New England textile history.

Starting to explore the origins of individual communities and the reasons for their widely varying success, I opened the Pandoran box of industrial history to find a vast, yet incomplete, literature. Tomes have been written about some of the most pivotal locations and events, while other crucial turning points are almost undocumented. After more than a century of analysis, the earliest years of the industry still give rise to heated controversy, for the evidence is fragmentary and many conclusions are, necessarily, conjectural. Early accounts generally reinforced the manufacturers' point of view. In many cases, these accounts were calculated misrepresentations of the industry's origins, self-serving history deliberately exaggerating the manufacturers' idealism and righteousness and camouflaging their all-too-human weaknesses. Too often, subsequent surveys have perpetuated these deceptions. Indeed, the existing literature is overburdened with secondary materials of dubious accuracy.

Recent research in industrial history and archaeology has already punctured some of these myths, yet large portions of the epic remain little explored. And with good reason: primary sources and responsible first-hand reports are exasperatingly elusive. Sometimes the truth about a particular company is buried in the hundreds of ledgers and account books left behind in New England archives, accessible only through patient, painstaking research. Other vital evidence is squirreled away in the shoe-boxes, diaries, scrap books, and memorabilia of a thousand New England attics.

For many locations, the only primary evidence is what remains of the mill structure itself. Hundreds of mill complexes survive, but few of them retain their original configuration. Fire, flood, and demolition have taken their toll. Industrial expansion has often covered the earliest structures with layers of subsequent additions, modifications, and renovations. Detailed representations of how the earliest mills and villages looked are rare, and, too often, irresponsibly fanciful.

While the original architecture and plan of many mill complexes can be reconstructed with some accuracy, the attitudes and life-styles that animated them are almost impenetrable. As mill workers have always been among the poorest and least literate classes in America, it is no surprise that they left little behind to document their experiences. Mill owners kept business records, but only rarely did they record their thoughts about the social system they engineered—an indication that motive was less important than results.

Any survey of mill history must acknowledge its limits. The industrial epic has not yet been completely reconstructed, and informed speculation must still bridge some gaps only the most exhaustive research can possibly close. A handful of scholars have already begun their laborious excavations, surfacing at intervals with dissertations that shed new light on crucial transition points. The present survey relies heavily on their achievements to date, in full acknowledgment that a wealth of insight is still to come. The field is rich and complex enough to justify many lifetimes of research, and I humbly, and gladly, leave this work to dedicated professional historians. My objective is to present this complex industrial epic, as it is now understood, to a general readership. Every effort has been made to keep this survey as rigorous, authoritative, and exhaustive as possible, within the framework of available information.

The historical treatises and dissertations that have guided me assume, al-

Wappingers Falls, N.Y., as it was in 1889. The Dutchess Company's print cloth mills occupy the lower left quadrant of this view. The river empties into the Hudson a few hundred yards below the mills.

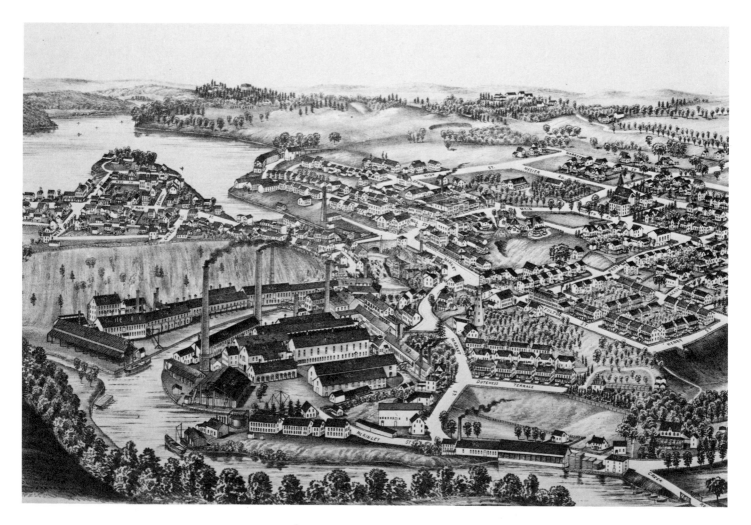

most without exception, that mill town phenomena are dead and gone—properly desiccated subjects for study and academic dissection. What I have seen and heard convinces me otherwise. The clean break between past and present is a myth. Though the industry is but a shadow of its former self, looms are still banging away throughout New England. The ordered kingdoms of over four hundred New England mill towns have become fragmented, yet these towns and villages remain unique American communities where vanishing trades are still practiced. Mill town attitudes and styles are passed from parent to child. Mills and machines were built to last, and many of them have done just that.

This book is designed to show the disturbing present in relation to the grand design of the past, for the mill town is an orphan of a powerful lineage. Mill communities are touchstones for the social landscape New England has created. There is no misty-eyed nostalgia here, only a cold, hard image of who we are and where we come from.

The photographs of people in this book are not candids. All were created with the active cooperation, or at least tacit consent, of the subjects themselves. The people are neither symbols nor archetypes, but proud individuals who can and will speak their own minds. Their words are quoted from tapes and notes, edited for greater clarity and readability.

*   *   *

Recently, I returned to Wappingers Falls. The bridge over the falls has a high wall, so a passing automobile traveler sees only blank concrete, as if the town is trying to hide its shame. I looked over the wall, and it is all still there—the steep falls, the mammoth iron penstock, and the mill nestled in the bend of the river. The mill is tenanted and dilapidated now. Its time has passed, and it crumbles slowly into industrial senility. Just as in my youth, there is no reason whatsoever to go there—except to smell the faint vapor of the past and behold what man has wrought.

Boston, Massachusetts
September 1978

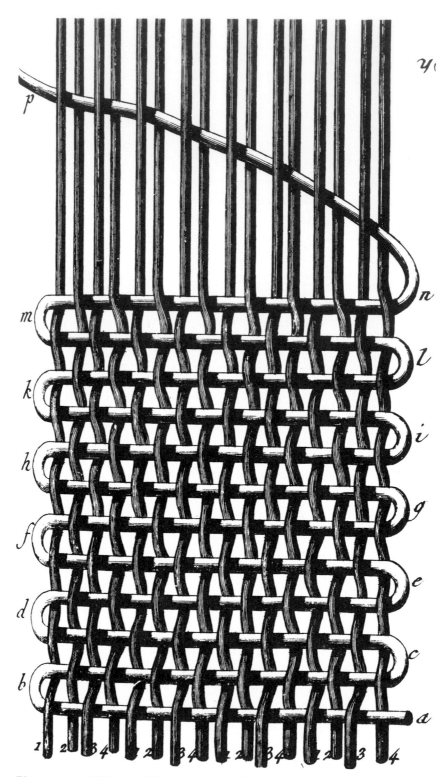

Plain weave. (Diderot, L'Encyclopédie, 1786, M V T M)

PART ONE

AS IT WAS

THE STORY

I

Birth of
the American Mill

1700-1820

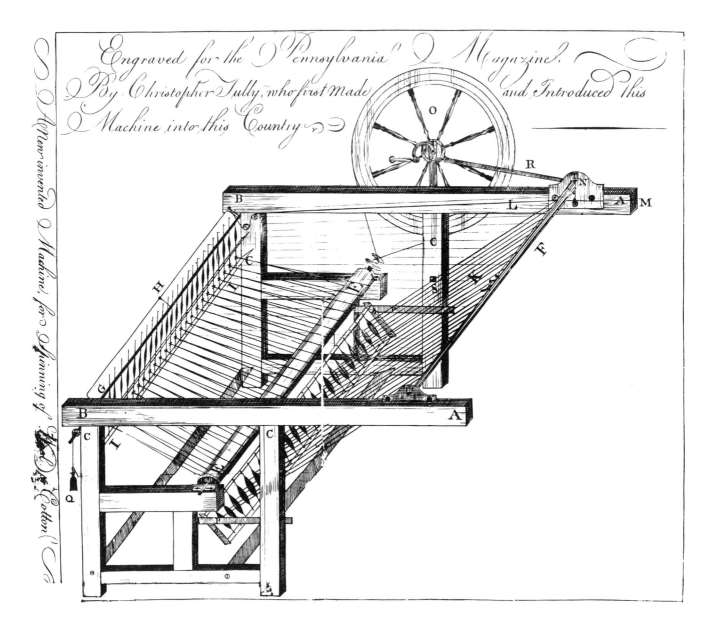

Design for a spinning jenny, imported by Christopher Tully to Philadelphia and published in Pennsylvania Magazine, 1775. (American Antiquarian Society)

Wanted: New Technology (JULY 4, 1788)

The marchers began assembling for the Grand Federal Procession at the corner of South and Third Streets in Philadelphia, each group finding its place quickly in the soft morning light. A special parade had been planned for this very special Fourth of July, the first to celebrate the new Constitution, which ten states had ratified. Every detail of the parade had been orchestrated to symbolize the hopes and potential of the fledgling nation. An infantry corps took its place at the head of the column, followed by a herald proclaiming "New Era" on his banner. A huge sculpted eagle came next, and dignitaries and patriotic standard-bearers completed the vanguard. The trade delegations took their places behind. Farmers carrying their tools and cornucopia herded their animals into line first, a tribute to their time-honored importance in a nation where nine out of ten citizens worked the land. Then a newly formed delegation—the Manufacturing Society—maneuvered its thirty-foot float into position. While other tradesmen planned to impress the gathering crowd, this society, barely a year old, intended to astonish it.

The manufacturers' float proudly featured the most advanced technology of the day: a carding machine, a spinning jenny, and a fly-shuttle loom—improved models of the basic equipment for making cloth. A calico printing display was arranged at the rear. A tent of cotton cloth produced on these machines covered the entire carriage. Eleven men and women from the society, dressed in cloth they had made, stood beside their machines, ready to demonstrate their magic: the manufacture of cotton.

The procession started moving towards the reviewing stand at Union Green. Spectators jammed the footways, windows, and rooftops along the three-mile route. While ten bay horses pulled their float forward towards the crowds, the machine demonstrators bent to their work: carding cotton, spinning it into thread, weaving jeans and lace, and printing chintz patterns onto muslin. Above them, the Society flag, showing the beehive symbol for industry, snapped in the brisk south wind. The calico printers' flag behind it declared the motto: "May the union government protect the manufacturers of America." Nearly one hundred weavers, including those from the factory, walked behind the float, following their own flag with its rampant lion holding a shuttle in its right paw.

Although the entire parade included dozens of trade groups and some five thousand participants, the manufacturers' float received special notice. It was prominently placed, near the front between the farmers and the mariners; and it was absolutely novel. One observer remarked on the "astonishment and delight" every spectator shared who watched it. Made almost entirely of wood and operated by hand, the machines on the float were primitive, even by the standards of the time. Nonetheless, they were a significant improvement on the cloth-making techniques used in most American homes. Few spectators had ever seen machines like these, for this was a time when clocks represented the zenith of mechanical sophistication, and grist mills, saw mills, and iron works marked the most advanced use of natural power.

Textile production in colonial America. Hand carding (left) aligns the fibers, which are then spun on a wool wheel (center), and woven on the loom (right). Colonists used flax and wool to make their clothing, for cotton was not suited to their methods. (Hazen, Panorama of Professions and Trades; M V T M*)

* Merrimack Valley Textile Museum

Sea Island cotton (Gossypium Hirsutum), a long-staple variety. In the colonial period, cotton was grown primarily as an ornamental plant. Alexander Hamilton, in his Report on Manufactures, noted: "There is something of this material which adapts it in a peculiar degree to the application of machines." (Ure, Cotton Manufacture)

Tench Coxe (1755–1824) of Philadelphia, the first uncompromising advocate of American industry. His winning personality and position in the Treasury gave important credibility to the quest for manufacturing. Coxe was one of the members of the United Company of Philadelphia for Promoting American Manufactures, a small group of concerned citizens active between 1775 and 1777. Recognized for his continuing devotion to manufacturing, he was asked in 1787 to organize a new group to carry on the United Company effort. He created the Pennsylvania Society for the Encouragement of Manufactures and Useful Arts, which elected him president that fall. Barely nine months later, this Society was on parade. (White, Memoir of Samuel Slater)

Emphasis on cotton further increased the novelty of the demonstration, for cotton cultivation had just begun in the States. The new fiber was difficult to process by hand, and its use was limited. The manufacturers' display substantiated the news then filtering in from Britain: cotton and machines were a splendid pair. One observer in the crowd saw in this combination "the emblems of the future wealth and independence of our country" and hoped that interstate commerce in cotton would bind the states together more firmly than any article in the new Constitution.

The whole concept of manufacturing as displayed on the float was so new that the vocabulary for describing it had not yet been coined. The word *technology* was unknown; *mechanism* had various vague meanings; and *industry* meant hand work. Few had ever heard of a *factory*. Although the float demonstrated the first stirrings of America's "Industrial Revolution," none knew quite what to call it, for this concept, too, was still unnamed. In the meantime, all manufacturing efforts were known as "Domestick Industrie," a dimly understood but highly controversial addition to the national economy.

With its demonstrators proudly at work, the manufacturers' float rolled on through the admiring crowds and finally drew up at the reviewing stand. By the time the keynote address was delivered, a crowd of seventeen thousand filled Union Green. The sun was just breaking through the clouds. Noting the "truly magnificent and irresistibly animating" spectacle of the parade, the speaker hailed the advent of a just and self-regulating democracy and invoked the blessings of the Constitution on the "arts of peace" all hoped would flourish: agriculture, manufactures and commerce, human virtue, and religion. Again, manufacturing received special mention, as the speaker counted "the industrious village"—an early statement of the mill town theme—among the "gifts of liberty."

The keynote speaker then emphasized the allegorical significance of the procession, insisting that such events should "instruct and improve, while they entertain and please." The prominence of the manufacturing float was part of the allegory, for the importance of Domestick Industrie was far larger than the number of its practitioners. The agrarian and mercantile delegations flanking it represented the poles of the controversy over the role manufacturing should play in the national drama. Although manufacturing was then only a fragile, perishable transplant needing government support for survival, many onlookers suspected it might soon threaten the purity of the pastoral American landscape and also undermine overseas trade.

The manufacturing society knew only too well how far it had come since its genesis the year before and how far it had yet to go. Tench Coxe, Assistant Secretary of the Treasury under Alexander Hamilton, and, like his superior, an ardent supporter of manufacturing, had organized the parent group known as the "Society for the Encouragement of Manufactures and Useful Arts" while he and Hamilton attended the Constitutional Convention in 1787. At that time, Coxe had addressed the founders of the society, reporting dramatic technological advances made in Britain while Americans were fighting for independence. Noting that these methods were virtually unknown in America when peace had come in 1782, he praised the progress that had been made towards competence in textile manufacture. Recent British advances would astonish even the most visionary enthusiast, he observed, adding that "strange as it may appear, they also card, spin, and weave (using waterpower) in the European factories."[1] Coxe told his colleagues of one documented example— an English factory where a few hundred women and children accomplished the work of twelve thousand hand spinners. Manufacturing, he reasoned, could be the "political salvation" of the nation, freeing it from economic bondage to England and making best use of the limited labor supply of the time. When Coxe advised his listeners to "borrow" English inventions for American use he was actually advocating industrial espionage, for Britain kept close guard on her manufacturing secrets.

Working knowledge of the spinning jenny shown on the float had arrived in Philadelphia in 1775. But the waterpowered techniques Coxe had reported —known generally as the Arkwright System—seemed more elusive and much more valuable. While none of the members of the society knew exactly how the Arkwright System operated, all realized that it was far superior to the equipment on their float. The mysterious Arkwright designs would have to be transplanted to America before manufacturing could flourish. Coxe had already tried, unsuccessfully, to import Arkwright models by way of France.

For the moment, the cotton-draped float and its simple hand-powered machines demonstrated the state of the art as it was known. As the celebrations continued on into the night under a vivid and auspicious aurora borealis, it seemed that "all was order, all was harmony and joy." No one dreamed that an Englishman named Samuel Slater had already seen the manufacturing society's advertisement for an Arkwright spinner and was planning to bring his knowledge of the Arkwright mysteries to America. Nor could anyone in the crowd have imagined that their enthusiasm for textile manufacturing, when combined with imported expertise, would breed an industry that would soon take hold in New England and change the almost-virgin landscape and their way of life forever.

The Arkwright System

To understand the significance of the English inventions America so urgently required demands a grasp of the basic operations by which natural fiber is converted into cloth. These operations form one of civilization's oldest and most fundamental technologies, and all but the most privileged Americans shared this knowledge, using it daily in the home. Textile production was divided, as it had been in antiquity, and as it is today, into two basic stages: *spinning*, the stretching and twisting of fibers into yarn; and *weaving*, the construction of fabric by the interlacement of groups of yarns at right angles to each other.

Raw fiber first had to be cleaned and foreign matter removed. When cotton was used, the seeds were laboriously picked out by hand. Wool was

The spindle and flyer mechanism. The flyer rotates on an axle that passes through the stationary spindle. The untwisted fibers of the sliver enter the mechanism from a fixed point coaxial with the spindle, then are guided to one of the flyer's legs and from there to the bobbin around which the resulting yarn is wound. (The Edinburgh Encyclopedia)

A flax spinning wheel with two flyers, ca. 1680. For its time, this was a high-production machine. Yarn distribution is semi-automatic; the spinner must move the yarn from one hook to another on the flyer leg. Spinning wheels without flyers, known as wool wheels, were also common. (Some Proposals for the Employment of the Poor, England, 1681; Smithsonian Institution)

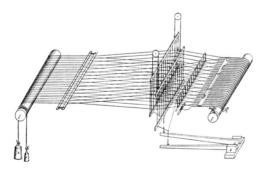

Schematic drawing of the simplest loom mechanism. From left to right: the warp beam, a pair of lease sticks for tension control, a pair of heddles hung on opposite sides of a pulley and operated by pedals from below, the reed, the finished cloth, and the cloth beam which stores the product. (Usher, Mechanical Inventions)

washed, then scoured in alkali to remove excess grease. Flax fiber had to be separated from the rest of the plant by pounding the stem and pulling it through sharp teeth. After these preparations, the carding process aligned fibers by pulling them between closely spaced teeth moving in opposite directions. The traditional carding method used a pair of hand-held boards, the cards, to carry these teeth. After carding, the fibers were rolled together into a loose tubular shape called the sliver.

Spinning itself requires three separate operations: *drafting*, in which the bundle of fibers is elongated and its diameter reduced; *twisting*, which further reduces the diameter and secures the fibers together to make yarn; and, finally, the *winding* of the yarn onto a suitable core. The basic mechanical element of spinning is the spindle—a revolving shaft that provides twist and around which the yarn can be wound. Early spindles were propelled with a flick of the wrist or the turn of a wheel. The spinner stretched the sliver by hand, twisted it by rotating the spindle, and then reversed the rotation to wind the yarn around the shaft. As the spinner alternated between twisting and winding motions, the traditional process was intermittent.

One of the major medieval contributions to technology was the flyer, a radical improvement in spinning technique described by Leonardo da Vinci. The flyer guides drafted fiber to the spindle, around which it rotates, so that twisting and winding can occur simultaneously. With the flyer propelled by a foot treadle—as in the Brunswick spinning wheel—or by an external power source, the spinner's hands are free to draft the fibers while the flyer is twisting and winding, making the three-part process simultaneous and continuous. Labor is saved and efficiency increased. Flyer-equipped spinning wheels were commonplace in colonial homes.

For spun yarn to be woven into cloth, strong yarns must be arranged in a parallel array and held in place under tension to form the warp. The primary tool for creating the warp was the warping mill, a revolving cylinder around which groups of warp yarns could be wound and held in order. After the entire warp was on the warping mill, it was unwound directly onto another cylinder, the warp beam, which fits on the rear of the loom. Once on the loom, the warp yarns are drawn in parallel off the warp beam, through the eyelets of a warp selection mechanism, the heddles, through the comb-like reed which preserves their parallel spacing, and finally wound under tension on another cylinder, the cloth beam, at the front. Each heddle raises selected warp yarns to form an opening, the shed, through which a shuttle carrying the weft, or filling, yarn can pass. Each successive weft strand is beaten into place against the cloth and a different set of warp strands then raised to form a new shed for the next weft strand.

The best hand looms included only one significant improvement over their ancient predecessors—the fly-shuttle, invented in 1733 by John Kay, an English broadloom weaver. Kay's device, while still hand-powered, increased production threefold. Eliminating the need for two shuttle-throwing assistants, it was especially valuable for broadloom work where the weaver could not reach from one side of the loom to the other. Professional weavers in

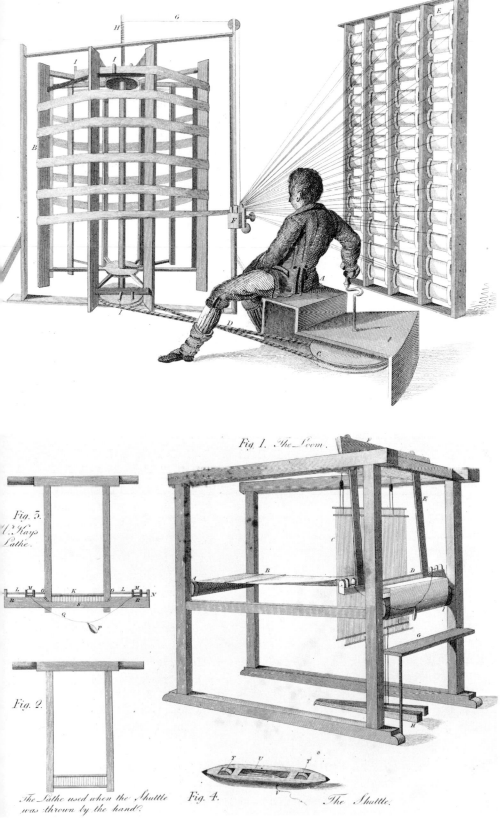

A warping mill, used for winding yarns off their spools to make portions of the warp, which will later be unwound off the revolving cage and onto the loom. Distribution of warp yarns on the cage at left is controlled automatically by the guide (F), which descends as its supporting cord (G) unwinds from the axle. (Guest, Cotton Manufacture)

Kay's fly-shuttle loom, as represented in Richard Guest's Compendious History of the Cotton Manufacture, 1823. BOTTOM LEFT: the unmodified beater, or "lathe." TOP LEFT: the beater carrying Kay's mechanism—a box on each side of the reed fitted with a plunger attached to a cord. A quick pull on the cord sends the shuttle flying out of one box and across to the other. BOTTOM CENTER: the shuttle.

The spinning jenny, designed by John Hargreaves in 1767. Drafting and twisting occur as the carriage is pulled away from the rotating spindles at left. Then a bar is lowered in front of the spindles to allow winding of the yarn as the carriage is pushed back towards them. (M V T M)

Roller drafting combined with flyer spinning for continuous yarn production. (Edinburgh Encyclopedia)

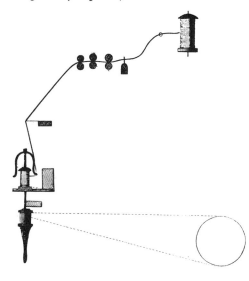

Kay's district feared unemployment and forced Kay to flee to Paris, where he died in poverty and misery. Their revolt confirmed the opposing interests of labor and invention—a theme that would assume increasing importance as the mechanization of textiles progressed.

Far simpler than weaving, spinning was more susceptible to early efforts at labor-saving mechanization. Five years after Kay's patent, John Wyatt and Lewis Paul proposed what they called "a system of machinery to supersede the artless method of spinning with the fingers." The two Englishmen used a series of paired rollers, each turning faster than the pair before, to draft sliver for spinning. A radical improvement over previous techniques, their rollers did for the spinner's hand what the wheel had done for the traveler's foot.

Roller drafting was one key ingredient for continuous mechanized spinning. The flyer was the other. Failing to bring the two together, Wyatt missed his chance for fame and fortune and died in poverty. Roller drafting languished in temporary obscurity while attention concentrated on a simpler alternative, Hargreave's spinning jenny (1767). The jenny, named after the inventor's wife, was, in effect, a series of spinning wheels, without flyers, mounted in tandem to allow intermittent, semiautomatic action. The machine was only suitable for spinning soft filling yarns, as its twist was not strong enough for warp use. Angry hand spinners smashed the early jennies, and Hargreaves, too, died in poverty. Nonetheless, the jenny enjoyed several decades of popularity.

In 1769, just two years after the jenny patent, the roller and flyer were successfully combined by Richard Arkwright, an itinerant barber and hair

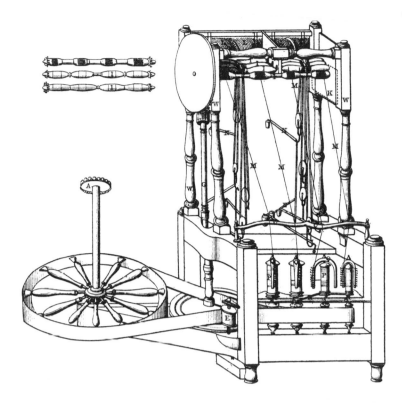

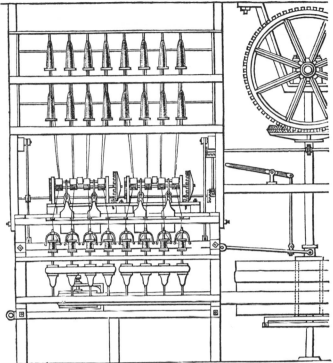

merchant who knew of Wyatt's work almost thirty years earlier. The mechanization of spinning was now complete. Drafting, twisting, and winding could now occur simultaneously and continuously in separate zones of the same machine. Arkwright built his first water-powered mill at Cromford in 1771, but it did not achieve commercial success until 1774, after he entered into partnership with Jedediah Strutt, an inventor and stocking manufacturer who provided the capital needed to perfect and exploit Arkwright's frame. Arkwright was granted a general patent on his entire carding and spinning system a year later.

Once the commercial potential of Arkwright's designs was proven, a heated controversy over the originality of his work began. Inventors and mechanics who had preceded him challenged his patents, which were finally nullified in 1785. Primacy of invention is always difficult, and sometimes impossible, to establish; Arkwright's debt to previous efforts was unmistakable. Nonetheless, his contribution to industrialization was of paramount importance. He had arranged the inventions which preceded him into a system of serial production using waterpower, and he had promoted this system as the basis for a manufacturing empire. This accomplishment earned him knighthood.

Arkwright was more notable as an opportunist than as an inventor—the right man, in the right place, at the right time. First, he made machines that worked and earned profit—something none of his predecessors had achieved. From that point on, organization and regimentation were the keys to his success. In a single stroke, Arkwright made the skilled hand spinner obsolete. His machines required a new kind of worker—the unskilled operative whose

ABOVE LEFT: The Arkwright water frame, patented 1769. This early design carried four spindles. Manual control of yarn distribution on the bobbin required the machine to be stopped frequently so that the yarn could be moved to another hook on the flyer. ABOVE RIGHT: An improved, eight-spindle model featuring semiautomatic yarn distribution. (Both: Ure, Cotton Manufacture). BELOW: Sir Richard Arkwright (1732–1792). (Baines, Cotton Manufacture)

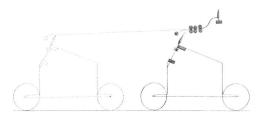

ABOVE: *Schematic side view of the carriage of Crompton's spinning mule. Mule spindles are mounted on a wheeled carriage that moves away from the frame during the twisting and drafting phase, and towards it for winding. Rollers mounted on the frame control the feed on the roving passing between them.* (Edinburgh Encyclopedia)

BELOW: *A typical English spinning mule. Turning the large hand wheel (center) moves the carriage back and forth on its rails. The mule was capable of subtle, delicate spinning, and was ideally suited for wool and fine cotton filling, or weft, yarns where tensile strength was not required. Like the jenny, it could not be used for the warp.* (Baines, Cotton Manufacture)

labor was paced, for the first time in history, by the constant demands of mechanized production. Andrew Ure, Arkwright's most fervent admirer and tireless apologist, identified Arkwright's main challenge as the training of workers "to renounce their desultory habits of work, and to identify themselves with the unvarying regularity of the complex automaton. To devise and administer a successful code of factory discipline, suited to the necessities of factory diligence, was the Herculean enterprise, the whole achievement of Arkwright." Ure went on to commend Arkwright's "Napolean nerve and ambition" and his desire "to subdue the refractory tempers of work people, accustomed to irregular paroxysms of diligence, and to urge on his multifarious and intricate constructions, in the face of prejudice, passion and envy."[2] Arkwright transformed the young and the poor—society's most vulnerable components—into a regimented cadre of machine servants and forced his industrial work ethic upon them. He also set another precedent by making the mill village at Cromford his personal kingdom, donating a chapel and a market, supporting education and charity, and living in what one early biographer called "patriarchal prosperity."

The overthrow of Arkwright's patents allowed another mechanical breakthrough, Samuel Crompton's spinning mule, to emerge. Crompton combined paired rollers with the reciprocating motion of the jenny to make his hybrid design. The mule which resulted—in effect a mechanized, semiautomatic version of the jenny—was first patented in 1779. Because of its complexity, its use of rollers, and its use of roving (a lightly twisted yarn best produced on

Arkwright machines) as a raw material, the mule did not gain general acceptance until after the Arkwright patent nullification in 1785. From that time onward, Crompton's mule and Arkwright's frame became the twin cornerstones of the spinning industry. Serving different purposes, the two machines were not direct competitors: the former was best for soft filling yarn, and the latter best for strong warp yarn.

Machines in the American Garden

England had deliberately kept its colonies ignorant of the technological advances that underlay its industrialization. Stiff fines and penalties guarded the British monopoly from espionage. Adam Smith's "nation of shopkeepers" wanted a dependent world market for its manufactured goods: the colonies could share in its progress only by consuming its products. The embargo was effective: although news of Arkwright's "water twist" was spreading, America knew very little about the process itself. As news of the English industrialization reached America, the challenge to break away from economic dependence on England became critical. True independence required economic power, and no nation that wasted its time on hand spinning could compete successfully with mechanized England.

Some Americans would have preferred a nation without industry. "For the general operations of manufacture," wrote Thomas Jefferson in his *Notes on Virginia* in 1785, "let our workshops remain in Europe." He rejected productivity as a measure of social value. Agrarian society in an unbounded land seemed the essence of democracy. Recalling this time in a letter to Benjamin Austin years later, Jefferson wrote: "We did not then believe . . . that to be independent for the comforts of life we must fabricate them ourselves. We must now place the manufacturer by the side of the agriculturalist."[3] Jefferson had come slowly to admit the undeniable importance of manufacturing independence. John Adams was another skeptic, though for other reasons; he believed that America could not attain self-sufficiency in manufacturing in a thousand years.

Alexander Hamilton and Tench Coxe were both prominent on the pro-industry side of the controversy. At first, it was Coxe who took the oratorical spotlight. In reply to those who feared industry would take scarce labor away from agriculture, he emphasized the labor-multiplying character of machinery. Prospects for employing women and children in industry were encouraging, too, for this was a hitherto untapped labor supply. Coxe was especially zealous in promoting cotton cultivation, arguing that true economic independence required self-sufficiency in both raw material and machinery. His general plan was "to *foster* and *encourage*, but not to *force* manufactures." Early industrial promoters like Coxe also looked to the factory to cure the seasonal poverty that already embarrassed the new nation. Puritanical enthusiasts eagerly awaited the "laudable spirit" that would accompany mechanization.

Hesitantly at first, then with growing conviction, America embraced

Christopher Tully's spinning jenny design, as published in 1775 in Pennsylvania Magazine, a journal edited by Thomas Paine. Tully was one of several English immigrants who received grants to make spinning machinery for American use. Tench Coxe's United Company supported Tully after his arrival in 1775, and used his jennies until 1777, when the British occupied Philadelphia. Tully's claim of "a newly invented machine" overstates his creativity, for his jenny is virtually identical to the one Hargreaves built 8 years earlier. Shown enlarged on page 2.

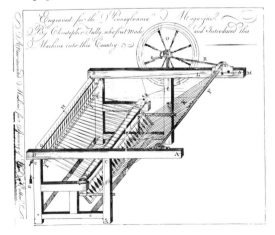

Domestick Industrie. Active efforts to transplant English technology to American soil began. Grants supported local experimenters while bounties encouraged technological espionage. Tench Coxe wondered aloud how any skilled European could resist the temptation to emigrate, with his treasure of knowledge, to this welcoming nation "so pregnant with the means of human happiness."

Between 1786 and 1790, several experimenters attempted to make textile machines in America. Efforts to duplicate the Arkwright "water frame" produced only nonworking models. The general appearance of the machine was known, but detailed understanding of its operation was lacking. The spinning jenny, however, was within America's technological reach. At least a dozen textile "manufactories" were started before 1790, using jennies powered by men or animals. Many of these experiments were sponsored by manufacturing societies like Tench Coxe's United Company at Philadelphia. Such societies usually featured the word "encourage" or "promote" prominently in their official titles, underscoring the tentative nature of their ventures. A "manufactory" was often little more than a basement or loft stocked with a few hand-operated machines. One of these early ventures, founded at Beverly, Massachusetts, in 1787, built itself a small brick building—the first textile mill. Another, the Hartford Woolen Manufactory, had the distinction of producing the woolen coat, waistcoat, and dark brown breeches that George Washington wore to his inauguration in 1789. He remarked that it was of better quality than he had expected. A modest beginning had been made.

Though the jenny furnished a significant improvement over the spinning wheel, the factories depending on it were extremely limited and primitive. The sponsors of domestic manufacturing hungered for the Arkwright designs. Attempts to import English models, plans, and experienced workers continued, while Yankee ingenuity focused on improving the nonworking models. In Rhode Island, which was the center for experimentation with the Arkwright design, repeated attempts to make the process work met with only limited success.

At this crucial point, the Rhode Island fervor for cotton manufacturing infected Moses Brown, a Quaker gentleman who had retired several years before after a prosperous mercantile career. During his retirement, he participated actively in the Quaker abolition and antipoverty movements and shared the Friends' belief that manufacturing might relieve social ills. The need to establish his son-in-law, William Almy, in a profitable business was the circumstance that brought Brown out of retirement in 1789, and his Quaker beliefs directed him to choose textile manufacturing. He converted his assets into cash, called his debts, and quickly purchased most of the available machines and prototypes in Rhode Island. The jennies he bought were placed in a Providence marketing house and hand weavers were brought in to complete the establishment. Arkwright-type machines were installed in a rented clothier's mill on the Blackstone River at Pawtucket, Rhode Island, but they could not be made to work. Oziel Wilkinson, the talented Quaker blacksmith Brown had hired to work on them, had no success.

Moses Brown (1738–1836). (Rhode Island Historical Society)

Moses Brown then set up his son-in-law and his cousin, Smith Brown, in partnership under the name Almy & Brown. The patriarch held the purse strings and made important decisions for the partners as they entered business as merchant-manufacturers. Since the roller spinning machines could not be made to work properly, the firm depended on the jennies and hand looms to make their first cloth, using cotton filling in a linen warp. Almy & Brown described their venture as "a small business in Providence at Manufacturing on lathes and jennies driven by men,"[4] and as such it was no more promising than the factories that preceded it.

The success of the firm depended on the reluctant roller machines, and Moses Brown let it be known that he was eager to employ "a person who had seen or wrought them in Europe." English spinners already knew that America wanted the Arkwright process and would reward anyone who could introduce it. Of the many who responded to the call of industrial espionage, Samuel Slater of Derbyshire was the most influential.

The educated son of a successful farmer and the heir to an appreciable estate, Samuel Slater began learning spinning at the age of fourteen as an indentured apprentice to Jedediah Strutt, Arkwright's partner. He showed promise in machine skills and mathematics and, after only three years, became an overseer of machinery and mill construction. By the time he concluded his apprenticeship in 1789, Slater had mastered all details of textile manufacturing then known in his locale. Few Englishmen understood the cotton industry as thoroughly.

Although a bright future lay ahead for Slater in the mushrooming English factories, he chose to emigrate instead. While he never recorded his own reasons, historians suggest a variety of motives ranging from altruism to a desire to reap the advantages of introducing and monopolizing the Arkwright system in America. In any case, Slater's mind was set on emigration well before he completed his indenture to Strutt. Telling no one of his destination, he left the mill. Disguised as a farmer, he passed the English customs and sailed for America on a fair September day in 1789.

Arriving in New York sixty-six days later, Slater engaged himself briefly at the New York Manufactory. Hearing from a packet boat captain of Moses Brown's desire for an Arkwright spinner, he wrote in December 1789, citing his knowledge of Arkwright designs and promising "the greatest satisfaction in making machinery." Moses Brown's reply inviting Slater to Rhode Island offered him "the credit as well as the advantage of perfecting the first water-mill in America."[5] Slater set out immediately.

Slater is commonly described as spurning the crude machines he found at Pawtucket and building entirely new ones by relying on a brilliant and unfailing memory. But scholars now view Almy & Brown's machines as so close to being workable that only small but critical modifications were necessary. Slater needed only two months and a few new parts to set the roller frames in operation, hand powered by an old Negro. In March of 1790, Almy & Brown reported that their frames were at work: "We have at last been supplied with good Cotton warps and thereby able to make all cotton goods."[6] Slater's

Samuel Slater (1768–1835). "His glory is . . . the bright, cheering, and humble halo of a well-spent life, passed in successive efforts to better the condition of our race," reported George White's Memoir of Samuel Slater in 1836. (Van Slyck, Manufacturers)

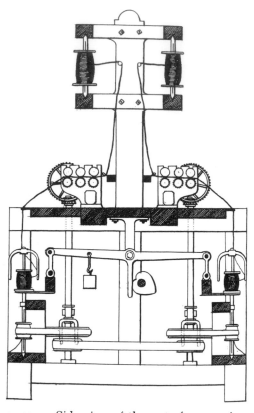

ABOVE: *Side view of the waterframe as introduced by Samuel Slater in 1790. It is a four-spindle Arkwright design with one crucial addition, the heart cam visible near the center of the machine, which Slater had developed at the Strutt works before leaving England. A pin following the surface of the rotating heart cam activates levers that raise and lower the bobbins to distribute the yarn into a perfect package. Slater used wood for the frame, bobbins, and pulleys. A clockmaker made the brass gears, and blacksmith David Wilkinson (son of Oziel Wilkinson) forged the rollers, flyers and other crucial parts of wrought iron. (Artists and Mechanics Encyclopedia; MVTM)*

The heart cam. (White, Samuel Slater)

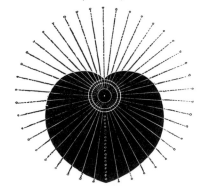

success earned him a partnership with Almy & Brown in a new manufacturing venture: Almy, Brown & Slater.

During the remaining months of that crucial year, Slater faced the more demanding task of building a perpetual cylinder card and harnessing the machinery to waterpower. On December 20, 1790, just over a year after Slater's arrival in the United States, the system was complete. Power from the lumbering undershot wheel propelled the shafts and cogs that set the frames and cards in motion. The first waterpowered cotton mill was under way. Almy & Brown soon advertised cotton yarns "spun in One of the first Manufactorys in the United States and . . . far Superior and Cheaper than that spun by Hand."[7] With Slater's success the controversy over the value of promoting industry was temporarily quieted. Within months, Alexander Hamilton delivered his Report on Manufactures to Congress, prefacing his message with the observation that "the expediency of encouraging manufactures in the United States, which was not long since deemed very questionable, appears at this time to be pretty generally admitted." He then reported that the Slater mill had "the merit of being the first in introducing into the United States the celebrated cotton mill; which not only furnishes materials for the manufactory itself, but for the supply of private families, for household manufacture."[8]

The Slater System

The continuous, automated Arkwright process Slater introduced at Pawtucket required little skill of the machine tender, whose only function was to "piece-up" or reconnect broken strands within the machine and "doff" or remove fully wound yarn packages and set empty cores in their place. Slater relied on children to perform these simple and infrequent tasks, using their finger dexterity and easy access to cramped spaces as Arkwright had done in England. The four boys he employed that first week were reinforced during the next two weeks by two other boys and three girls. All were between the ages of seven and fourteen. Wages varied between eighty cents and $1.40 per week, depending on age and size.

Although this was the beginning of an industrial child labor tradition that would eventually become a national scandal, it was introduced by Slater and his Quaker associates with untroubled conscience. Slater's future brother-in-law, ten-year-old Smith Wilkinson, was tending the breaker card during the mill's first week, an indication that neither his father Oziel—the mechanic— nor Slater saw any harm in the arrangement. As children were already accustomed to farm work, the mill simply continued a long-standing attitude that children should help their families if they could. The new, improved mill that Slater, Almy, and Brown built on the Blackstone in 1793 retained the child labor system. Within three years, the new mill had more than thirty employees. Children's names dominated the roster, with several families supplying more than one child.

The case of Roger Alexander, a contract laborer for Almy & Brown, demonstrated the economics of child labor. In 1796, four of Alexander's children were working in the new mill, receiving wages between thirty-four and sixty-nine cents a week. Altogether, the children brought home $2.30 each week; their father only made $2.72 in the same time. The children's effort almost doubled the family income, which reached $240 for the year, a respectable sum compared to the earnings in most semiskilled occupations of the time.

An immediate corollary of such arithmetic was the simple perception that child labor offered the greatest advantage to the poorest and most fertile parents. The need for children increased as the mill expanded and early recruits and apprentices fled. With increasing diligence Slater sought poor families. As he became dependent on their children, these families became dependent on his mill; each grew to need the other.

This mutual dependence forced Slater to provide services outside the mill. One of the first families he approached—a Mr. Arnold, his wife, and their twelve children—were living in a slab-roofed "den" between two rocks about a mile away from the mill. The wife agreed to come with her children on the condition that Slater supply them with "as good a house as she then lived in." Slater, Almy, and Brown constructed at least two houses for factory families before 1796. Multiple-family dwellings soon followed, including a "long house" at Pawtucket that sheltered, at one point, fifty-six people in ten families. Little is known about these early mill houses except that while they were very plain and very crowded, they were a great improvement over the housing these workers could afford on their own.

The company store resolved the conflict between the families' need for regular wages and the shortage of hard currency that characterized Almy & Brown's merchandising effort. Wages were paid in credit at the store and redeemed for basic commodities. While this system held the potential for flagrant abuse and reinforced the workers' dependence on the factory, it nonetheless provided an essential service and allowed the workers to get credit which would otherwise be unobtainable.

By the turn of the nineteenth century the primary features of the Rhode Island factory system were already established: a small riverside mill equipped with cylinder cards and Arkwright spinning frames, children working within, minimal and crowded housing nearby, and a company store. Raw cotton was cleaned by hand. Yarn was either "put out" to be woven on consignment by hand weavers or was hand woven in the mill itself. In both cases, the finished cloth was sold by the merchant-manufacturer.

The First Mill Towns

During the closing years of the eighteenth century, the several mills operated by Slater, Almy, and Brown, separately and in partnership, proved beyond doubt the profit and potential of cotton manufacturing. Slater tried in vain to monopolize the technology he had perfected, but rapid turnover of personnel made his mills a training ground for a generation of millwrights. Mechanics, overseers, and even an occasional operative went on to establish mills of their own using the system Slater had demonstrated. A continuing flow of new immigrants from English mills supplemented the Slater trainees

Conjectural view of the original Slater Mill. Although the mill's importance was recognized soon after it was built in 1793, no first-hand drawings of its original design have survived, the only primary evidence being a plasterer's bill for interior finishing tendered to Almy & Brown. This reconstruction is from the 1820s, long after the 29- by 43-foot mill had been enlarged to a T configuration with the cupola over the center wing. The "eyebrow monitor" roof design, known also as a "trapdoor monitor," lighted the attic. This distinctive feature was often used on mills built during the first decades following Slater's arrival. The mill straddled a small power canal known as "Slater's Trench," with the wheel enclosed beneath it for protection from freezing. (Slater Mill Historic Site)

This is a place very disagreeably suited being very rocky and the inhabitants appear to be poor, their homes very much on the decline. I apprehend it might be a very good place for a Cotton Manufactory, Children appearing very plenty.— Description of Marblehead, Mass., by Obadiah Brown, writing to William Almy, 1797.

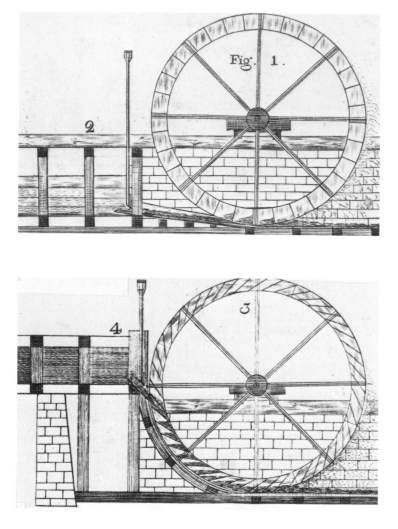

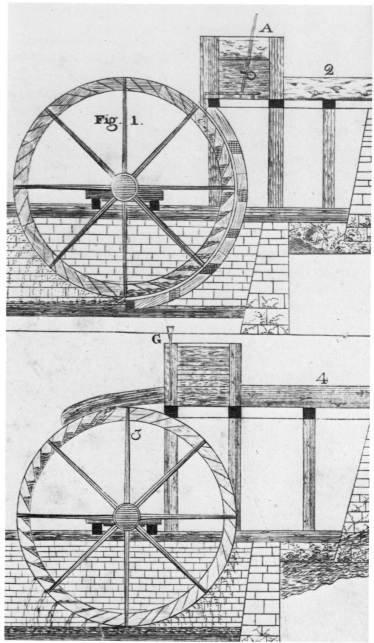

Plates from Oliver Evans's treatise, The Young Millwright and Miller's Guide (1795), showing variations in wheel design. George Washington and Thomas Jefferson were among the subscribers who helped Evans publish this first "how-to" book on American mill construction. Although Evans was concerned primarily with grist mills, his plans reflect many of the engineering conventions applied to early spinning mills. Fifteen editions of the manual were printed before 1860. (M V T M)

U P P E R L E F T : The undershot wheel, in which only the kinetic energy of the moving water is used. A vertical sluice gate regulates the flow.

A B O V E L E F T : The breast wheel. Water from the flume enters the wheel above the bottom. Both kinetic and potential energy are used. Evans describes this design as a "middling breast wheel." If the water hits the wheel below the axis it is "low breast"; above the axis it is "high breast."

U P P E R R I G H T : The pitchback wheel, actually a form of high breast design. Evans remarks: "This wheel is much recommended by some mechanical philosophers, for the saving of water; but I do not join them in opinion, [for] I think an overshot wheel with equal head and fall is fully equal in power. . . ."

A B O V E R I G H T : The overshot wheel, a simple and effective design for high waterfalls. Breast and pitchback designs became the standard of the industry at low and medium falls, Evans's opinion notwithstanding.

and added increasing awareness of advances in machine and mill design. Steady progress in machine tools and metal-working techniques led to construction of more sophisticated and efficient mechanisms. Each new mill required *waterpower*, *machinery*, *labor*, and *capital* for success.

Of these critical ingredients, only waterpower was available in abundance. New England's unique topography—a series of rising bedrock plateaus deeply eroded by glaciers—included an extensive system of fast-running streams broken by waterfalls and rapids. With numerous waterpower sites awaiting development, waterpower became the fundamental determinant for the textile industry's growth.

The first steps in starting a mill at this time were the location of a suitable waterpower site and the purchase of the land surrounding it. A "mill privilege"—the right to control all or part of the available power—had to be secured and compensation arranged for flooding land to make the millpond. Most desirable of all were the choice sites where ample water-born power could be harnessed with minimum investment in dams and waterworks. Since the early spinning mills required less than forty horsepower for operation, the ideal site was a point where a modest stream emptied a large natural pond (easy to dam) and fell sharply over a high waterfall (maximum available power equals flow times height of fall).

Scores of near-perfect sites lay scattered along New England's smaller valleys. In the classic case of Fall River, then known as Troy, a high granite ledge formed a substantial pond from which the Quequechan River fell 129

If thou dost not know a family of Children, Girles or boys, from 7 to 12 years of age with a Parent or Parents (not in affluent circumstances), a widow would be preferred, to live near by one of our Cotton Mills, that the children may work in them and the Parents may perhaps be employed in cotton wool.—*Almy & Brown to Benjamin Hedron, 1800.*

Patent drawing of David Wilkinson's screw cutting lathe, 1798. Accurate screw threads were a prerequisite for making the machinery required by the fledgling industry, whether used directly to make screws and bolts or indirectly as a means for precise measurement and shaping of machine parts. In Wilkinson's design, a reference screw guides a cutting tool along the blank stock turning in tandem beside it, thereby reproducing the screw pattern. David Wilkinson's mechanical ingenuity was invaluable to Slater, who reaffirmed his close relationship with the Wilkinson family—several of whom worked for the firm—by marrying David's sister. (National Archive)

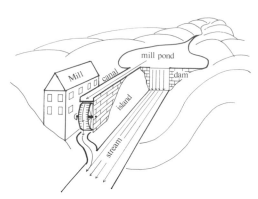

A typical mill site.

Alexander Hamilton (1755–1804), first Secretary of the Treasury and an early advocate of manufacturing. (Appleton's Cyclopedia of American Biography)

feet in steep rapids ending at tidewater, offering several possible sites that could share more than 1300 horsepower. The rapids had eroded "a deep black gulf, with high rocky sides" over which the mills could be built. All that had to be done was stick a wheel into the channel and draw off the power.

Virtually all of the best sites were deep in the unsettled wilderness. The factory village with housing and supporting services was a necessary consequence. Treasury Secretary Alexander Hamilton himself was the first to organize a large community designed for manufacturing. He set his plan in motion in 1791, soon after his enthusiastic Report on Manufactures. The site he chose was the Great Falls on New Jersey's Passaic River. He named his creation Paterson, after the governor of the state. Hamilton had seen Passaic Falls while in the field as aide-de-camp to General Washington. The fifty-foot drop in the river promised power for scores of mills, and the ease of shipping below the fall made the site even more appealing.

Hamilton organized a New Jersey chapter of the Society for Encouraging Useful Manufactures authorized to handle the five hundred thousand dollar capitalization he planned to raise for the project. The state blessed the six-mile-square site in the bend of the river below Garrett Mountain by making it tax- and draft-exempt. Hamilton envisaged a "National Manufactory" at Paterson, where a variety of mills could make everything the nation needed. L'Enfant was called in to plan wide radial avenues and boulevards for the city, but his design proved too expensive. Work began on power canals to serve the millsites, and the first mill was soon completed. But the scheme was too much, too soon. Plagued by cash shortages, the Paterson project was headed for bankruptcy. In 1796, the promoters admitted defeat and the "National Manufactory" died stillborn.

The Paterson community was barely begun when Tench Coxe proposed a similar plan for a manufacturing city on the Susquehanna River at an unspecified site upstream from Harrisburg, Pennsylvania. In an article entitled "Some ideas concerning the creation of Manufacturing Towns and Villages" dated 1793, Coxe repeated his standard arguments on the value of manufacturing as a cornerstone of independence as a prelude to describing his scheme. He emphasized that it was primarily a model for others to follow and that it was generally applicable throughout the nation, especially at those sites where rivers had a final fall near tidewater navigation. Coxe wanted his city on the west bank of the river, where it would enjoy easy commerce with frontier lands to the west. The city would become the market for frontier produce, converting these raw materials into the manufactured products needed by the pioneers.

Assuming that the river had power for at least forty mills, Coxe imagined a city that, like Paterson, would manufacture everything, from cloth to steel. The city would have sixty-foot-wide streets laid in a grid oriented to best use the wind and sun. Coxe called for eight hundred brick and stone houses of varying sizes for the citizenry and included four schools, a church, and two taverns in the plan. He estimated that a half million dollars would be required and suggested that this capital could come from a lottery, a group of stockholders, or a state subsidy. Coxe advised the owners of this and other important waterpower sites to lay out their towns first, then build the mills and sell or rent land and power to those wanting to join the venture. In this way, he reasoned, each town would mature in a manner appropriate to its natural assets. The Coxe plan, though never implemented, was an excellent preview of the corporation cities of the future. But for 1793, it was unrealistically ambitious and premature.

When Colonel David Humphreys decided in 1803 to start a manufacturing village near his home town of Derby, Connecticut, he planned a more modest and realistic venture than either Coxe or Hamilton had proposed. Humphreys's wise sense of proportion and personal attention made the scheme a success and earned him recognition as the creator of the first viable factory village built expressly for textile manufacture—the first true mill town.

Humphreys had become interested in manufacturing while serving as minister to the Court of Spain. Seeing the value of wool from the Iberian merino sheep, he brought a flock back with him when President Jefferson recalled him from his post in 1802. These sheep and their descendents made woolen manufacture practicable for the first time, and Humphreys received several citations for his "patriotic exertions." By the end of the following year, with the viability of his sheep assured, Humphreys began to organize a village to convert his merino wool into cloth. He chose a site where the Naugatuck River passed through a narrow valley and met a natural rock dam blocking two-thirds of its breadth at Rimmon Falls, just four and a half miles upstream from its confluence with the Housatonic River at Derby. The twenty-foot cascade at Rimmon Falls was already being used by a scythe works, two fulling mills, and a sawmill. The little settlement beside the mills was known locally as "Chusetown." Humphreys bought Rimmon Falls, all the mills, and all the privileges for $2,647 on the thirteenth of December, 1803. He added improved machinery to the mills and started them working while he prepared for the next stage: the creation of a small but perfect industrial paradise.

The plan for a utopian mill community may reflect Thomas Jefferson's patronage of the project. Jefferson's stand on industry was still evolving. He now hoped to temper the ill effects of industry by isolating small factories in the rural areas, where concentration of population and attendant vice would be avoided. It was Jefferson who encouraged Humphreys in 1806 to begin manufacturing cloth.

The frame for the first Humphreys woolen mill was raised on the fifth and sixth days of June. Construction began, too, on the boardinghouses where orphans brought from the almshouses of New York to tend the machines would live. Farmers' daughters may have been another component in the labor force. Once the project was under way, Humphreys left for a tour of Europe, where he visited factories and observed the rapidly changing social climate associated with the Industrial Revolution, returning the next year with an acute concern for factory conditions and a determination to make his village a model of industrial virtue. Confident of his ability to succeed where others had failed, he established a mill town precedent by naming the village after himself: Humphreysville.

David Humphreys (1752–1818), warrior, patriot, diplomat, and Renaissance man. His brilliant war career as aide de camp to General Washington was followed by a series of diplomatic posts in Europe. His negotiating skills earned Washington's special praise and confidence. Ever gallant, his last living act was to escort a lady to her carriage. Though suddenly stricken while helping her in, he politely waited until the carriage had departed before returning to the hotel, where he collapsed and died. (F. L. Humphreys, Life of David Humphreys)

Merino sheep, first imported from Spain by David Humphreys in 1802. The fibers of merino wool, shorter and finer than domestic varieties, were ideally suited for mule spinning techniques introduced in America during the same decade. The 21 rams and 70 ewes Humphreys brought from Lisbon to Derby, Conn., brought up to $3,000 on the market. This flock marked the beginning of a serious woolen industry in America. (M V T M)

Humphreysville, Conn., as drawn by John Barber in 1836. The factory is at the center of this view. Most of the 50 to 60 workers' dwellings described by Barber were situated to the left of it, with only a few shown. Barber noted "this romantic and beautiful village in which the buildings, which are mostly painted white, appear uncommonly beautiful as the village is approached from the south upon the river road."

Soon the village had a school, with Humphreys paying the schoolmaster's salary. Gardens were planted behind the factory to supply village needs. Humphreys instituted strict moral codes for his workers and discharged anyone who broke his rules. He offered prizes for scholarship and awards for job proficiency. He organized a militia company, drilling the unit himself under a handsome blue silk flag showing a merino ram and ewe holding the state seal. Always interested in literature, he wrote plays which he and his operatives performed on holidays. Ann Stephens, the daughter of his superintendent, recalled: "In fact, Col. Humphreys omitted nothing that could arouse the ambition or promote intellectual improvement among his operatives, although he did it after a grand military fashion."[9] Colonel Humphreys also encouraged the state legislature to make on-site visits to all factories to monitor conditions. The legislative committee reported favorably on his village and awarded it a ten-year tax- and draft-exemption.

The Humphreysville factory quickly gained fame as the source of America's best woolen cloth. Wanting to encourage the use of domestic products, President Jefferson ordered enough of Humphreys's finest fabric to make the coat he wore on New Year's Day, 1809. Writing to Humphreys a few weeks later, Jefferson declared the fabric did "honour to your manufactory, being as good as anyone would wish to wear in any country."[10] Jefferson ordered similar coats for Secretary Madison and other heads of departments. Madison wore Humphreysville woolen to his inauguration.

In 1805, while Humphreysville was just beginning, Samuel Slater and his younger brother, John, who had left the English mills for America three years before, considered starting a new mill at some distance from Pawtucket, Rhode Island. John took responsibility for finding a suitable site and chose a point fifteen miles away where the Branch River dropped forty feet from a series of ponds before joining the Blackstone. The remote location forced the Slater brothers to plan a mill village of their own.

Samuel and John Slater formed a new partnership with Almy and Brown to purchase 150 acres of land surrounding the falls and to finance the new mill, "a large and commodious building" when completed in 1806, just a few months after the Humphreys mill. It was the largest and most modern American mill of its time.

The mill site dominated a valley of rocky, sparsely settled farmland. Housing was needed—first for the mechanics, carpenters, and millwrights who would build the mill, then for the families who would work in it. There is no indication that the Slaters and their partners knew of Humphreysville, its orphans, or its boardinghouses. However, they were aware of a Philadelphia factory which boarded young girls, and they made cost comparisons on the feasibility of a boardinghouse plan. Deciding to retain the family labor system, they built the two tenements, each 36 feet by 28 feet and two stories high, that supplied Slatersville's first housing. John Slater moved to his village during its first year; his own home, though larger, was almost as crowded.

A spinning mill, two tenements, a house for the resident owner, and a company store—that was Slatersville. During the next few decades, scores of mill towns would be started on a similar plan. Perhaps they used Slatersville

John Slater, of Slatersville. (Van Slyck, Manufacturers)

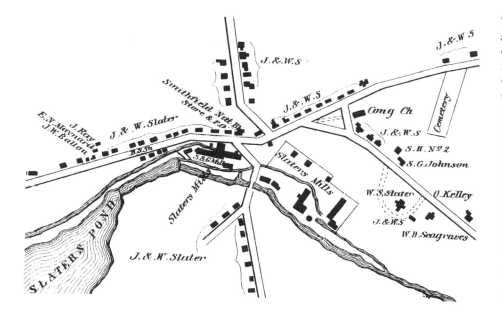

This map, showing Slatersville several decades after its settlement in 1806, is the earliest surviving representation of the community. There are two separate mill groups on either side of the bridge, each with its own power canal. The first mill, at the lower privilege, burned in 1826 and was rebuilt. The company store is opposite the upper mill. The church and Slater's house are opposite the lower one. Company housing, marked "J. & W. Slater" lines the main roads of the village. White's Memoir of Samuel Slater described the site in 1836 and concluded: "It is impossible to contemplate such a village as this without the most pleasing sensations and reflections. What a seat of wealth, a focus of activity, and a nursery of industry! What a combination and variety of operations, what diversity of employment, and what a number of distinct and curious processes are comprised in the manufacture of those fabrics requisite to supply the wants which refinements of society occasion! Who can look upon such manufacturing villages as this, without regarding them as the gems of the future Manchesters of America?" (Beers, Atlas of Rhode Island)

as a prototype, but it is equally likely that the similarity of plans demonstrates the similarity of conditions and challenges industrial pioneers were facing as they built factories at isolated waterpower sites using the limited technical and architectural vocabulary of the time.

Shortly after Slatersville began operation, trade restrictions on British imported cloth gave American textile manufacturers a competition-free market for the first time. The Embargo and Nonintercourse Acts also forced commercial interests to find new investment opportunities. An explosive proliferation of mills resulted. New England was gripped by a cotton mill fever that did not abate until the conclusion of the War of 1812. United States cotton consumption skyrocketed from one thousand to ninety thousand bales per year. Spinning mills multiplied along New England streams, displacing grist mills so fast that Moses Brown complained he no longer could find a mill to grind his corn. The first census of American manufacturing (1810) recorded 238 textile mills, including 26 in Rhode Island, 14 in Connecticut, and 54 in Massachusetts. Dozens more were under construction. By 1815, 169 mills within a thirty-mile radius of Providence had 135,000 spindles in motion.

Not a man to miss an entrepreneurial bonanza, Samuel Slater soon decided to find a site for a new factory of his own. Bela Tiffany, a young employee, had seen a "wondrous water power" in Oxford South Gore, Massachusetts, while traveling to Pawtucket to begin his apprenticeship. Tiffany returned to survey the area for Slater and confirmed the excellence of the power that could be harnessed. The mill privilege, occupied by a gristmill and sawmill, controlled the outlet of a large lake with the incredible name Chaubunagugunganaug. Tiffany added in his report that "it is the most God-forsaken place on earth."

This was just the place Slater wanted. He quickly bought a thirteen-acre plot that included the waterfall, the two earlier mills, and the only house in the area for four thousand dollars. During the two decades following, he

Locations of New England mills reported in Albert Gallatin's Census of Manufactures, 1810.

expanded his holdings to include twelve square miles of "God-forsaken" wilderness and farmland and a sizable property at nearby Dudley.

In a section of Dudley and Oxford, later renamed Webster, Slater created a village that more fully expressed the primary mill town features. The isolated location made mill housing and the company store essential. But times were changing. After the Oxford factory had been in operation only four years, the Cotton Mill Fever turned into a migraine of hard times and widespread mill failures. The local gentry, resenting the growing power of Slater and the increasing influence of the factory, did little to help it survive. Slater had to make his territory as self-sufficient as possible. Turning financier, he promoted mill banks—one at Oxford and others in Rhode Island—and helped finance turnpikes. He also cooperated with other mill owners in establishing the "generous, humane Institution" of factory mutual fire insurance in the Rhode Island area.

The mill bell scheduled the pulse of mill town life, measuring long working hours: 5 A.M. to 7 P.M. in summer, dawn to 7:30 P.M. in winter. Dividing their time between crowded tenements and the hostile interior of the factory, workers may have preferred the industrial life-style over the rigor and hardship of New England farming, but it was often only marginally attractive.

Webster, Mass., as seen in 1836. The community grew around Slater's mills near Oxford, center left, and at Dudley, about a mile downstream. It was named in honor of Daniel Webster when incorporated as a town in 1832. The petition for incorporation observed: "Said territory was rough and very thinly inhabited until the water power afforded by said river (the French) and a large natural pond invited the enterprise of manufacturers and mechanics, from which time it began to flourish vigorously." (White, Samuel Slater)

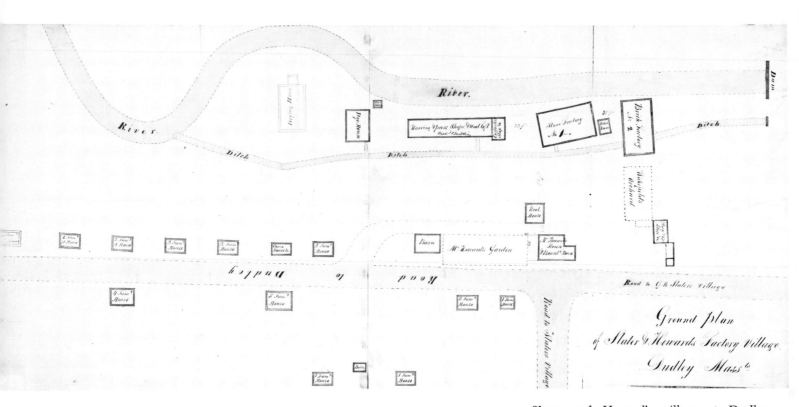

Ground plan
of Slater & Howards Factory Village.
Dudley Mass.

Slater and Howard's village at Dudley, Mass., ca. 1827–1829. This delicately rendered plan, one of the earliest of its kind, shows most clearly the simple arrangement and modest scale of the earliest factory villages. The river, flowing from right to left, is dammed and its flow diverted into the small power canal labeled "Ditch." Factories are placed on the mill island between the canal and the river. Edward Howard, Slater's partner in the venture, lived opposite the "Stone Factory" in the center of the island, with boarding facilities attached to his house and a garden beside it. An orchard and a store were opposite the upper "Brick Factory." (Baker Library)

Slater's labor force was a new American class, landless and transient, moving periodically from one mill town to another in search of the most generous employer, and Slater found it hard to keep his workers for long. The mills at Webster, Slatersville, and Pawtucket scavenged an increasingly wide area to get families for the tenements. Boston offered a steady supply; and in rare instances families were brought, at the mill's expense, directly from Liverpool.

Among Slater's efforts to stabilize this group and make them more dependable participants in factory life was the establishment, as early as 1796, of Sabbath schools. These schools, which he first taught himself, were more practical and educational than religious. Although it is questionable how much his exhausted scholars could learn after their six-day workweek, the schools did serve to reinforce habits of obedience, respect, and subservience. This early association of school and factory prepared children for the new world of repetitive indoor toil and collective industrial discipline, teaching important survival skills for a changing nation.

The manufacturer and the large, poor families he employed had developed a symbiotic relationship. Although each was dependent on the other, the mill owner held most of the trump cards. Mill town citizens generally accepted their situation—if they did not like it they could leave—but there is some evidence of occasional resistance to manufacturers' efforts to extend control. Few mill owners dared to be tyrants, for their employees were too valuable to be abused. Paternalism encompassed all that was good and bad about the system. Apologists argued that mill town life, under the "strict though mild

Wanted:
At Samuel Slater's Factory in Oxford, a MASTER FARMER, to take the lead of three of four men. One with a family to work in the mill would be preferred. Also a common LABOURING MAN with a large family, to work in the Mill. Good recommendations will be required as to industry, temperance, etc. Apply at the Mill.—Massachusetts *Spy*, Oxford, 1820.

Smith Wilkinson, Samuel Slater's brother-in-law, who started textile work at age 10 on the breaker card in Slater's first mill, later established a factory of his own at Cargill's Falls on the Quinebaug River in eastern Connecticut. The site was renamed "Pomfret Factory," and eventually became part of Putnam, Conn. Wilkinson's beliefs about mill town life are quoted in White's Memoir of Samuel Slater (1836) as part of a fascinating chapter on the "Moral Influence of Manufactories": "My settled opinion is that the natural or consequent influence of all well conducted establishments is favorable to the promotion of good morals, for the following reasons: The helps are required to labour all the time . . . consistent with what is necessary to attend to their personal wants —the usual working hours, being twelve, exclusive of meals, six days in the week— and have no time to spend in idleness or vicious amusements . . . (We) are obliged to employ poor families, and generally those having the greatest number of children, those who live in retired situations on small and poor farms, or in hired houses. . . . These families are often very ignorant, and too often vicious; but being brought together in a compact village . . . must conform to the habits and customs of their neighbors, or be despised and neglected by them." (Larned, History of Windham County)

and paternal scrutiny" of the manufacturer, exerted "a salutary influence on the character of those employed." The poor would achieve virtue through the supervised rigor of industrial labor. This puritanical reasoning led Slater's first biographer to conclude, "The introduction of manufacturing was thus, in every place, a harbinger of moral and intellectual improvement on the inhabitants of the vicinage."[11]

But profit, not human weakness, was the manufacturer's main concern. Through paternalistic control, he extended his power over as many phases of his workers' lives as they would tolerate. The mill town became an authoritarian world organized to ensure maximum stability and productivity. Although moralistic justifications may have comforted, even inspired, some mill owners, paternalism was admirably suited to serve their economic purpose.

The Early Factory

The factory, or "mill" or "manufactory" as it was once called, was one of the few new building forms added to Western architecture between the Renaissance and the nineteenth century. It grew and developed along with the Industrial Revolution, first in England, then in the United States, to provide a centralized building for large-scale cooperation of people and machines. Embodying new concepts of space, time, and work, the factory became the theater for the ongoing drama of industrialization.

In factory design, utility is paramount. Form must facilitate function, which is the organized application of power and labor to convert raw materials into finished products. It is the millwright, not the architect, who determines the mill's form. Indeed, during the first half-century of mill design, professional architects rarely contributed more than superficial decorative touches to the functional core.

Available technology determined the size and shape of the earliest mills. Hand-hewn shafts transmitted power from waterwheel to machine. If the machine was more than a few hundred feet from the wheel, a problem resulted: the shafts absorbed the power in flexing and twisting. Early metal shafting began appearing after about 1810, but it was too crude and heavy to be a significant improvement. For maximum efficiency, the machines still had to be kept as close as possible to the wheel. Interior lighting was another architectural challenge. Having only candles and oil lamps to supplement natural light, the mill relied on peripheral windows to illuminate the machines. The buildings had to be narrow enough for daylight to penetrate effectively. Then too, waterpowered mills required deep foundations to withstand vibration of the machines within and also to resist high flood waters. As the foundation was often the most expensive part of the mill, waterworks excluded, economical design was crucial.

Power transmission, lighting, and foundation economy were all maximized in the long, narrow, multi-storied design characteristic of waterpowered mills. This arrangement kept machinery as close as possible to both the wheel and the windows while minimizing the area necessary for foundations. The nar-

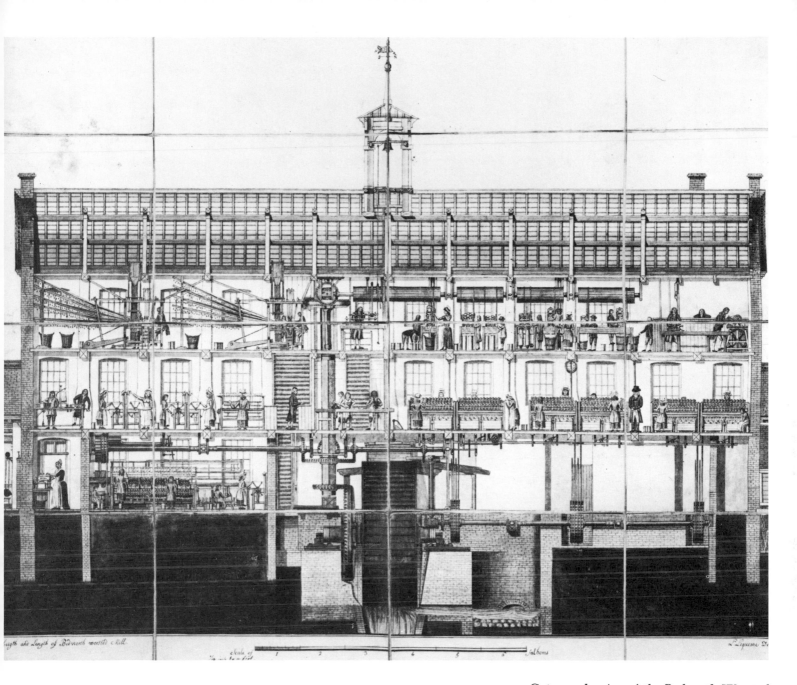

length the Length of Bedworth woostld Mill.

row profile also allowed simple, economical roof design and facilitated placement of the mill on river banks in steep-sided valleys.

This basic formula for factory design was refined in England well before Samuel Slater and others imported it to America, which itself already had extensive experience in building grist, fulling, and other mill designs. Indeed, Slater ran his first experimental machines in a fulling mill that Moses Brown had rented some years before. Once he had proven the feasibility of textile manufacturing and the wisdom of expansion, Slater built a more permanent and suitable mill. The design was a hybrid of the English tradition he grew up with and the American vernacular of the carpenters, masons, and millwrights who did the building.

Like the machinery and organization of the Slater venture, this mill became a case study for new mills built by Slater's trainees, associates, and competi-

Cutaway drawing of the Bedworth Worsted Mill, Warwickshire, England, ca. 1800. This richly detailed view provides an excellent example of English factory organization prior to the power loom and iron-reinforced construction, both introduced during the following decade. The wheel (bottom center) drives a vertical wooden mainshaft that carries power to the upper floors. Because all operations from spinning (second floor right) to handloom weaving (third floor left) proceed simultaneously under the same roof, this is an "integrated" factory. (Courtesy of Fitzroy Newdegate, Warwickshire County Record Office, No. CR136/V65)

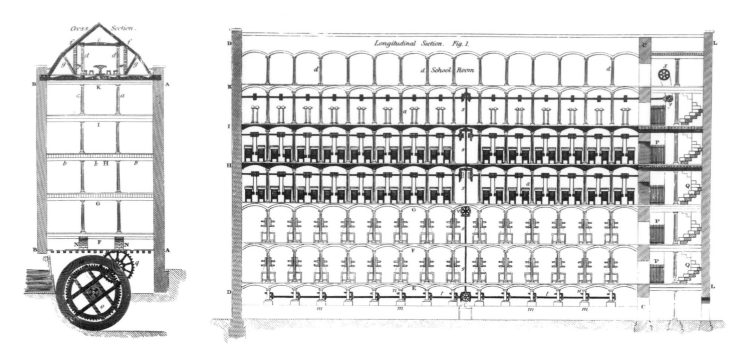

Strutt's cotton mills at Belper, Derbyshire, England, built 1808. This highly sophisticated mill—shown in longitudinal and cross section—incorporated the most modern techniques and materials of its time, setting standards that American mills would not reach for several more decades. Iron is used for shafts, gears, and pillars. A schoolroom appears in the attic. (Rees, Cyclopedia; MVTM)

tors. American manufacturers benefited from the continuing flow of English immigrants, which kept them abreast of improvements in English factory design. As the industry expanded, American factory architecture quickly evolved towards larger, more substantial structures. Bigger mills needed more efficient lighting than the trapdoor monitor allowed. The clerestory monitor, a more effective roof design, offered an alternative to the trapdoor and was used with increasing frequency after the turn of the century.

Another advance was in building materials. As the manufacturer's investment and expectation of long-range return increased, so did his preference for

ABOVE: Three dollar bill issued by the Bank of Kent, Coventry, R.I., 1819. Authentic contemporary representations of mills built before 1820 are extremely scarce. Preoccupied with more pressing concerns, manufacturers made no permanent visual record of the details of their factories. This banknote is one of the earliest and clearest images of a New England textile mill,

probably the Arkwright Manufacturing Company at Coventry. The building uses the clerestory-roof design which became popular early in the century as an improvement over the eyebrow monitor roof attributed to Slater. Clerestory roofs allowed better illumination of the attic, with more usable space and reduced fire hazard (Old Sturbridge Village)

masonry construction. The combination of highly flammable lint and spark-producing machines made fire a constant threat in all cotton mills, and to this masonry walls were a partial solution.

There were no hard and fast rules for what would work and what wouldn't in mill design. Gripped by Cotton Mill Fever, any carpenter or mason could fancy himself a millwright. The self-styled millwright could visit a few representative mills, then return to this chosen site and adapt what he had seen to his own budget, talent, and needs, and finally fit it all to the unique topography of his mill privilege. The resulting diversity of early mill architecture indicates rich, idiosyncratic variations on a few basic themes.

Simple utilitarian concepts determined the design of early mill housing as well. Since the houses were needed all at once at bargain prices, they were usually built in groups of identical units. Masonry construction was used occasionally before 1820 in southern New England, but in general each housing unit was built of wood and conceived within the vernacular of contemporary low-cost housing.

While the Cotton Fever lasted, the future of Rhode Island system cotton manufacturing seemed bright and full of promise. Small, riverside spinning mills sprouted throughout southern New England and commanded the outposts of American industrialization. Yet along the banks of the Charles River near Boston, work had already begun on new machines and mill designs that would soon present competition that earlier systems would never be able to match.

Crown and Eagle Mills, North Uxbridge, Mass., one of the finest examples of the Rhode Island system. Roger Rogerson, a friend of John Slater's, was the resident owner of the small community of brick workers' houses around the pond in front of his clerestory-roofed granite mills. Since the maximum size of each factory was limited by engineering, a larger water power such as this one on the Mumford River could be utilized fully only by increasing the number of units. Rogerson built two, and named them the Crown (left, 1825) and the Eagle (right, 1829) to honor England and America. The community was soon recognized as having "more of the quality of perfection than almost any other manufacturing village in New England." (Color lithograph by Kidder, ca. 1830; Boston Athenaeum)

II

Utopia, Inc.

1814-1845

View of Dutton Street, Lowell, Mass., showing Merrimack mills and boardinghouses.
(New England Offcring, Lowell Historical Society)

Waltham and the Power Loom

Progress in spinning technology left weaving far behind. During the decades following Arkwright's patent, thousands of hand weavers on both sides of the Atlantic laboriously converted the new machine-made yarns into a variety of plain and fancy fabrics. Many American homes had looms family members could work in their spare time. At times, Slater depended on more than six hundred hand weavers in a sixty-mile radius of his mills to weave his yarns on the "putting-out" system, paying piece rates as low as two cents per yard. Weaving agents subcontracted large commissions of yarn to be woven in more remote areas.

Since hand weavers could not keep pace with yarn production, their craft was ripe for mechanization. Yet industrialists, who lusted for the power loom, had to wait for inventors to solve the difficult engineering challenge it presented. A successful power loom must mechanically duplicate the sequence and timing of the hand weaver's cyclical motions: shed-changing, weft insertion, beating, and cloth take-up. Though straightforward in principle, these operations required great precision, timing, and delicacy.

While English inventors began as early as 1678 to experiment with "a new engine to make linen cloth without the help of an artificer,"[12] serious efforts to perfect the machine awaited the nullification of Arkwright's patents in 1785. In that year, Reverend Dr. Edmund Cartwright, a Kentish preacher who had no previous experience in either weaving or mechanical design, created the first functional power loom. It was clumsy and heavy, and so overbuilt that two strong men could hardly crank it—but it worked.

Cartwright's loom left much to be desired. It did only part of the weaver's job, and did it inefficiently. Mechanisms for advancing the warp, regulating the width, and taking up the finished cloth were still needed. Without these details, the power loom required as much labor and attention as the hand loom. A more perfect loom, patented by Horrocks in 1803, incorporated these essential functions.

That same year Thomas Johnson, "an ingenious but dissipated young man," devised a machine for "dressing" the warp with a starch coating to make it strong enough for power weaving. The combined efforts of Horrocks and Johnson made English power weaving commercially viable. The "virulent hatred" of hand loom weavers spurred machine-breaking riots; however, by 1813, acceptance had come, and some twenty-four hundred power looms of various designs were operating in England. As with the Arkwright process, England guarded its new invention closely.

Several American machinists made primitive "water looms" before 1812, but none of these designs proved practical. Credit for the introduction and

TOP: *Title page of* The Weaver's Draft Book *(1792), the first book about hand-weaving printed in America.* BOTTOM: *A pattern page from the book. Since the earliest power looms could only make "plain weave," the simplest of fabrics, all other fabrics required the handweaver's skill. Most yarn manufacturers had their product woven into specific fabrics by local handweavers paid by the yard in proportion to the difficulty of the desired patterns. This system was generally known as "putting out." (American Antiquarian Society)*

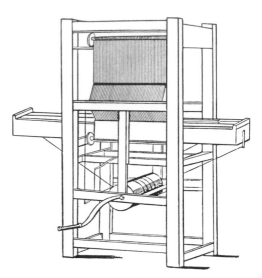

exploitation of the power loom in America belongs to a young merchant with a flair for mathematics: Francis Cabot Lowell. Lowell's mercantile career began soon after his graduation from Harvard. Born into a wealthy, well-connected family, he quickly established his importance in the Boston marketplace. India Wharf was among his creations. While the Embargo strangled Boston commerce, Lowell began considering alternate investments. In 1810, his frail health necessitated a rest cure in England and supplied an opportunity for him to investigate the possibility of cotton manufacturing.

Between 1810 and 1812, Lowell toured English factories, making careful observation of the power loom system in use. Presenting himself as a curious merchant, he easily disguised his motives and penetrated the secrecy surrounding the English machines. By 1811, he had already resolved to duplicate the loom in America and enlisted the support of a fellow Bostonian, Nathan Appleton. Lowell returned to his country in 1812 and began soliciting support for a unique new corporation—the Boston Manufacturing Company—whose success, he promised, would be built on the power loom.

Lowell's family was cautious. George Cabot, his uncle, had lost money in the nation's first textile factory at Beverly and tried to dissuade him from his "visionary and dangerous scheme." Initial support, though reluctant, was obtained, with the bulk of the stock owned by Lowell, his brother-in-law Patrick Tracy Jackson, and a handful of other relatives.

The Boston Manufacturing Company set a new standard for textile investment. Unlike the smaller family partnerships of the Rhode Island area spinning mills, the company requested an unusually large capitalization of four hundred thousand dollars; citing the "considerable risque" and "hazard" of the venture, and arguing that "great capital, always at the command of the manufacturer, is essential to his success,"[13] the company justified manufacturing as a cure for widespread unemployment, diminished trade, and inflated prices. The corporation became official in 1813.

Foundations were laid for a mill on the Charles River at Waltham. A ten-

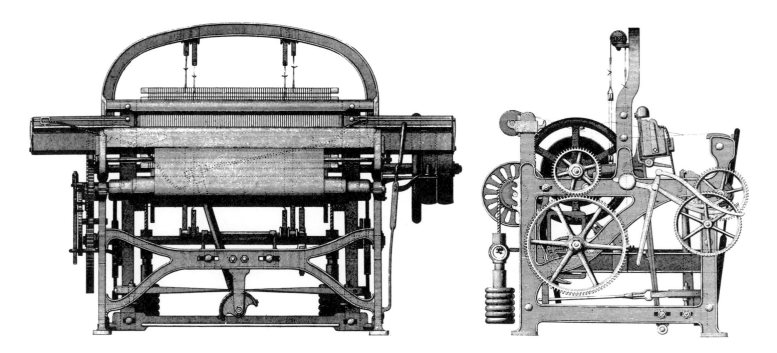

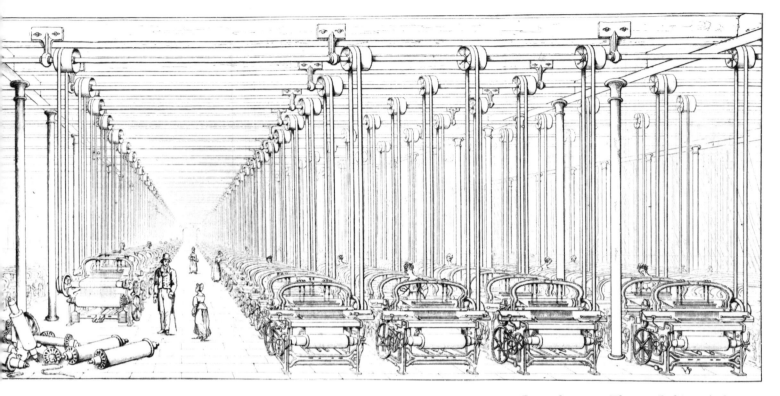

Power looms at Thomas Robinson's factory, Stockport, England. (Ure, Philosophy of Manufactures)

foot waterfall with an elbow of land jutting into the river below provided a perfect factory site. And the Great Sudbury Road lay close by, linking the factory to the port. It looked ideal!

While the mill was rising, Lowell started working to "reinvent" the power loom, aided by his English observations, his mathematical skills, and the availability of previous American versions for study. Paul Moody, an exceptional mechanic, assisted him, yet the primitive state of machine tools and metallurgy hampered their progress. In a world where the file, the hammer, and the chisel were the machinist's basic tools, where steel was unknown and ironwork still rudimentary, construction of a precise power loom was difficult.

In January of 1814, Lowell reported his progress to Jackson: "I have got our Loom up & yesterday wove several yards by Water—The Loom is excellent, tho' still susceptible for improvement. . . ."[14] That autumn, he showed the perfected machine, made almost entirely of wood, to Nathan Appleton, who later wrote: "I well recall the State of admiration and satisfaction with which we sat by the loom, watching the beautiful movement of this new and wonderful machine, destined as it was, to change the character of all textile industry."[15]

The mill was already finished and fitted with throstle spinning machines of "new and *exceedingly* improved construction." By early 1815, the "new and elegant establishment at Waltham," with its single power loom in operation, had cloth for sale in Boston.

Even in this partially equipped state, the Waltham mill earned distinction as the first fully *integrated factory* in which all processes from raw material to

Francis Cabot Lowell, 1775–1817. His eulogy noted: "He was distinguished for the clarity of his views, the clearness of his perceptions, and his power of bringing it to practical results, and perhaps, still more for the sterling purity and integrity of his character. To him, more than to any other individual is New England, or rather America, indebted for the permanent establishment of the cotton manufacture in this country." (Gibb, Saco-Lowell Shops)

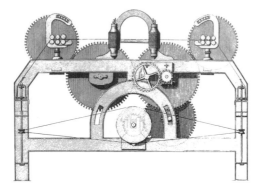

End view of the American throstle spinning frame. Each spindle is driven independently by a belt off a central drum, the throstle, named for the whistling sound it made during spinning. The design, more efficient than earlier ones, allowed attention to be paid to individual spindles while the machine continued running. (Baines, Cotton Manufacture)

Company seal of the Boston Manufacturing Company—the first modern American corporation—showing an early version of Lowell's power loom. (Gibb)

finished product were *powered* under one roof. Although many American factories had brought hand weaving into the mill alongside the carding engines and spinning frames several years earlier, the Waltham mill carried this arrangement to its logical conclusion by using the power loom. Revolutionary in concept, the integrated factory eliminated waste and middlemen and allowed coordination of production and consumption between machines. Tremendous economies resulted. Specialized for mass production of coarse cloth for the expanding frontier market, the mill was an immediate and unqualified success.

But Francis Lowell still needed a labor force. He had seen the "distress and poverty" of English manufacturing centers and held the prevailing factory system responsible for the "degradation" of labor associated with it. He still believed, however, that machine tending, properly organized, could be a respectable and virtuous occupation.

Children were well suited to Slater's machines, but Lowell's loom demanded a different kind of labor: intelligent and dexterous, though not necessarily strong. Young women matched the machine perfectly. Lowell found a previously untapped labor supply—the "well educated and virtuous" daughters of New England farmers. To entice them to work, he offered regular cash wages. To soothe prejudice against factory life, he arranged for workers to stay in respectable boardinghouses, and he saw to it that both mill and town were governed by strict moral codes. The combination made a safe, appealing alternative for young women eager to leave the farm and earn wages of their own; they quickly filled the boardinghouses, calling themselves "mill girls."

Lowell wasn't the first to employ women in industry, nor was he the first to use boardinghouses for factory labor. He was, however, the first to incorporate both women and boardinghouses into a successful factory system based on the power loom and its unique labor requirements.

A mile downstream, an earlier Rhode Island system community built around the Waltham Cotton and Wool Factory watched the Boston Manufacturing experiment. The comparison was revealing. The older firm operated a modest wooden mill equipped with four jennies, two jacks (a form of mule), and fourteen hand looms. Additional weaving was put out. One hundred and fifty workers, chiefly women and children from a few dozen families, lived in four large houses gathered around the factory. A store and a school completed the settlement. In 1815, the year of Lowell's loom patent, a local observer found the established Waltham community "free from disorder and immorality." Paternalistic control gave it "peace, order, and propriety."

This "extensive and profitable establishment" soon fell on hard times in the economic depression following the War of 1812. Rhode Island system mills throughout New England shut down. When Lowell and Appleton visited Pawtucket, Rhode Island, in 1816 they found "all was silent, not a wheel in motion. . . . All was dead and still."[16] The Waltham Cotton and Wool Factory, with its obsolete machines and inadequate financing, was desperate.

But nearby Boston Manufacturing, with its large capital reserves, expanded

The Boston Manufacturing Company Mills at Waltham, a detail from an anonymous painting ca. 1830. Mill No. 1 (1814–1816) is at left, with Mill No. 2 (1815–1819) and the three-story machine shop beside it. All buildings were made of brick and used the full clerestory-roof design. Mill No. 2, the larger of the pair, measuring 150 by 40 feet, established the prototype scale and design for many mills in the following three decades. It was equipped with 3,584 spindles. One "Mill Power" was later defined as a quantity of water power sufficient to operate this mill, equivalent to a flow of 25 cubic feet per second over a 30-foot fall, or approximately 60 horsepower. Niles Register reported in 1821: "The Waltham manufactory is the largest, and probably the most prosperous in the United States. . . . It is a magnificent and truly national establishment. . . . There is not an objection to the encouragement of manufacturing . . . that is not put down in an inspection of this establishment." (Lowell Historical Society)

during the same depression years. All responsibility for on-site management was delegated to P. T. Jackson, who built himself a home near the factory and became the company's resident "Agent." Under his direction, a second factory rose beside the first. The company went on to build family houses for the superintendents. Existing roads were improved and new ones added; all were lined with newly planted shade trees. The company added a fire engine, a school, a library, and a lyceum. Some years later, an English visitor commented favorably on the workers' houses, "some with piazzas, and green venetian blinds, all neat and sufficiently spacious."[17] By then the community had a town common, too, overlooked by a church.

Both of these factory villages had much in common with the Slatersville prototype. Yet the Boston Manufacturing enclave at Waltham was more modern, ambitious, and adventurous—and much more profitable—than the Cotton and Wool village downstream. Within a few years, the upstart company bought and absorbed its predecessor for use as a bleachery. As if to underscore this triumph of new over old, a brick mill was built around and over the obsolete wooden factory. Once the outer shell was complete, the **earlier mill was dismantled and its pieces thrown out the windows "so that there was but little disruption of the business"**!

Other Rhode Island system manufacturers—whose depressed business was further strangled by an unfavorable tariff cunningly promoted by Francis Lowell to protect *his* coarse goods but not *their* finer fabrics—were slow to answer his challenge. They had a power loom of their own in production two years after Lowell's, but few mill owners used it. Their power loom used a "Scotch" or crank motion vastly superior to Lowell's cam-operated mechanism. Yet to use it to best advantage, fresh investment capital was needed for new factories, machines, and power systems. This was beyond the resources of most of the small partnerships and family-owned enterprises of southern New England. They had the technology, but only the largest firms could afford to exploit it.

Rhode Island system firms watched the burgeoning factory on the Charles with considerable bitterness. The *Manufacturers and Farmers Journal* accused Lowell of "a disposition to monopolize the business," and alleged that "the mammoth Waltham establishment [was] designed to keep the country poor by reducing the costs of labor and agricultural goods."[18] While Waltham had much in common with the Rhode Island system, the smaller mill owners of southern New England claimed that their factories "embodied opportunity, morality, and democracy" and damned the northern competitor as "aristocratic and old world."

Nonetheless, Waltham surged ahead and cornered a vast new market for cheap, plain, mass-produced goods. Dividends averaged 18¾ percent. Expansion and modernization were almost continuous. No other textile company would ever do as well as the Boston Manufacturing Company did in its first ten years.

El Dorado on the Merrimack

The sluggish waters of the Charles River restricted expansion at Waltham. Continued growth required a new location with more potential waterpower. In 1821, four years after Francis Lowell's death, P. T. Jackson and Nathan Appleton began to search the Merrimack River for a new factory site.

They chose Pawtucket Falls,* where the Merrimack River drains a basin of over four thousand square miles and crashes thirty-two feet through abrupt, rocky rapids as it makes a wide quarter-turn around a corner of East Chelmsford, Massachusetts. Even a primitive wooden wing dam across the top of the rapids could draw off as much as three thousand potential horsepower—enough for fifty mills on the Waltham scale.

The sparsely populated site was serviced by two barge canals: the Pawtucket Canal, one of the nation's first, had been dug in 1792 to bypass the falls and facilitate river trade; a second canal, the Middlesex (1804), connected the river just above the falls with Boston. As this later canal had

Company seal of the Merrimak Manufacturing Company, 1822, featuring a breast wheel design. (Gibb)

---

* Pawtucket Falls and the Pawtucket Canal (archaic spelling, Patucket) are on the Merrimack River at East Chelmsford, Massachusetts. They should not be confused with Pawtucket, Rhode Island, the city on the Blackstone River where Samuel Slater built his first mill.

forced its predecessor close to bankruptcy, the Pawtucket Canal was available at a bargain price for immediate conversion to a power canal for the projected mills. Although the topography of the site and the placement of the canal were not ideal, Pawtucket Falls still offered the most impressive and accessible waterpower site at the shortest distance from Boston. It was an almost perfect location for industry.

The Waltham team moved swiftly and discreetly to buy up the Pawtucket Canal and all the land enclosed by the bend of the river. They secured control over the entire power of the Merrimack and the farms adjoining it for seventy thousand dollars. In 1822 the enterprise was incorporated as the Merrimack Manufacturing Company and capitalized at six hundred thousand dollars. The principal Waltham stockholders, Jackson and Appleton, restricted stock ownership to themselves, their relatives, and close associates.

The placement of the Pawtucket Canal and the topography of the site determined the basic plan for development. The first group of mills would be placed along the river bank at the shortest distance from the highest locks of the canal to get the greatest possible "head" of water while minimizing the length of the feeder canal that had to be dug to reach it. Housing would be grouped near the mill, as always. Additional feeder canals radiating from the lock would connect subsequent mills to the main canal. This was the most obvious, direct, and economical scheme for converting the canal to industrial use.

Although the investors foresaw eventual growth of the community to over twenty thousand inhabitants, they had no comprehensive city plan in mind when work began on the canals in 1822. At most, they anticipated a series of adjoining industrial units, each comprising a group of mills and its associated housing, all arranged for maximum hydraulic efficiency.

Yet this aggregation of manufacturing units would soon become the most

Lowell in 1825. The first machine shop is at left, the Merrimack Mills, their housing, and St. Anne's Church at center, and agent Kirk Boott's mansion on the right. In the same year, the editor of the Essex Gazette wrote: "It is indeed a fairy scene. Here we beheld an extensive city, busy, noisy, and thriving, with immense prospects of increasing extent and boundless wealth. Everything is fresh and green with the vigor of youth, yet perfect in all the strength of manhood. . . . It seems as if the imagination is transported into the regions of antiquity among the Asiatic monarchs, who commanded cities to rise up and be built in a day. What cannot a combination of genius, wealth, and industry produce!" (Painting by Benjamin Mather; copied by Coggeshall, in Kengott, Record of a City)

RIGHT: *The Lowell site at Chelmsford as purchased
in 1821, showing "Patucket Falls" at upper left and
the "Patucket Canal" at bottom. High rocky land
southeast of the falls made the curving canal path to
the Concord River the most economical for transportation. Unfortunately, it was not an ideal layout for
waterpower use; a complex canal system was required
to distribute waterpower to factories at a variety of optimal locations which would develop as separate communities within the city.* BELOW: *Map of Lowell,
1832, showing the canal system nearing completion.
Factory sites at the confluence of the Merrimack and
Concord rivers are still unoccupied.* (Both, Semi-
Centennial of Lowell) OPPOSITE: *Four stages in the
growth of the system. First, a power canal leading to the
Merrimack Mills, the only factories at Lowell to use the
full 30-foot head of the dam. Second, a two-level power
canal system is begun: a 13-foot head of water is used
by an upper level of factories, then passed on to lower
factories with a 17-foot head above the river. Flow rates
would be adjusted so that all factories received the
number of mill powers they had rented. Third, the
Western Canal is added to power the Tremont and
Suffolk Mills (upper level) and the Lawrence Mills
(lower level). The Eastern Canal feeds the Boott Mills*

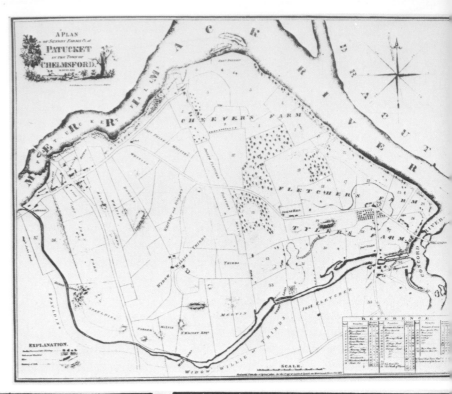

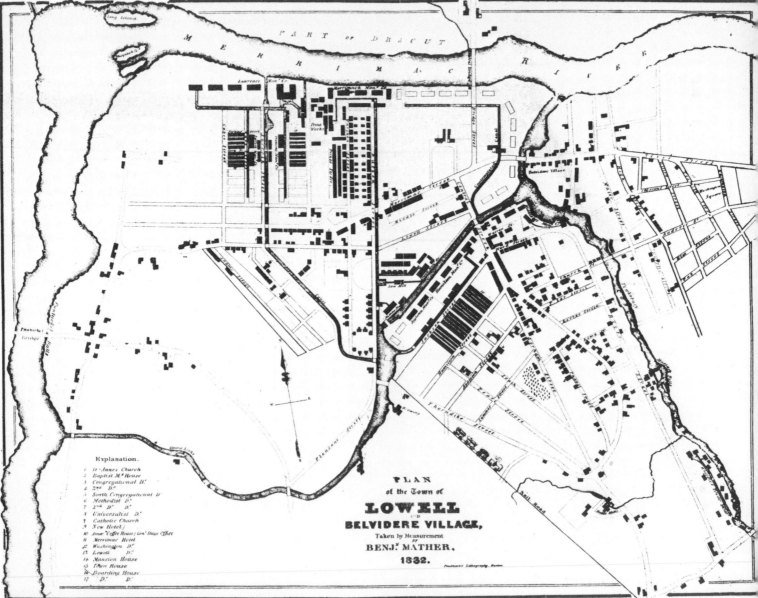

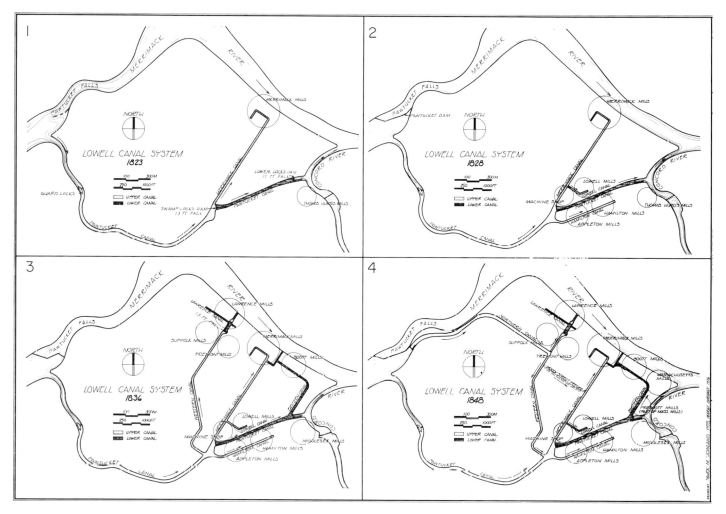

astonishing industrial city in American history and take the name *Lowell* in memory of the Waltham promoter who proved the feasibility of a large-scale integrated factory system. The enterprise would be applauded at home and abroad as a planned city, and Francis Lowell would be credited as the "informing soul, which gave direction and form to the whole proceeding."[19] In reality, the new city was neither visionary nor novel, being a limited dream of limited men desiring maximum corporate profit on a long-term investment. Manufacturers deliberately promoted accounts of their city that overstated their creativity, camouflaging serious flaws that were built in from the start. The plan showed no awareness of the organic community relationships that are the heart of a true city.

Francis Lowell never saw Pawtucket Falls, and it is unlikely that his "informing soul" had any effect on a man he never met: Kirk Boott, who was appointed resident agent by the company in 1822 to oversee every aspect of industrial and community development. From this time until his death in 1837, the history of Lowell was entwined with the biography of Kirk Boott. Boott's military background and authoritarian sensibilities suited the respon-

on the lower level. Finally, the completed system showing the Northern Canal bringing additional power to the entire Network. (Malone, Historic American Engineering Record)

Kirk Boott (1790–1837), first agent of the Merrimack Company and chief architect of the city plan. Mill girl Harriet Robinson called him "a grand potentate in the early history of Lowell who exercised almost absolute power over the mill people." (Illustrated History of Lowell; MVTM)

View of the Merrimack Mills (rear) and boardinghouses (left) on Dutton Street, the grand boulevard running parallel to the Merrimack Canal, behind the trees at right, as rendered in 1849 for the cover of the New England Offering. The arrangement created a baroque plaza focusing attention on the mill at the end. Shown enlarged on page 28.

Seal of the City of Lowell, chartered 1836. (Gibb)

sibilities of his agency. Admirers praised his "commanding manner." Less partial observers cited his "tyranny" and "autocratic ideas" and suggested a "warped" personality.

With Boott in command, the first building campaign was begun and "prosecuted with utmost vigor." Five hundred laborers, most of them Irish, widened and deepened the canals, laid the brick courses of the first mills of the Merrimack Company, and built its first two wooden boardinghouses.

Mechanics installed two huge breast wheels thirty feet in diameter and twelve feet long beneath the mills and began to equip each floor with the best machinery built at Waltham. In September of 1823, barely twenty months after incorporation, Kirk Boott recorded in his diary:

> After breakfast, went to the factory, and found the wheel moving round his course, majestically and with comparative silence. Moody declared that it was "the best wheel in the world." Appleton became quite enthusiastic. In the afternoon, he spent an hour looking at the wheel, after which returned home by Andover.[20]

By the close of the year the mill was in full operation, and the new looms wove their first cloth, a coarse brown shirting fabric. A new age of textile manufacturing had begun.

As at Waltham, the Lowell mills relied on farm women for their labor force. The Merrimack Manufacturing Company elaborated on the Waltham plan by building boardinghouses for these women. With a characteristic sense of order and proportion, Boott arranged the boardinghouses in three rows along one side of the tree-shaded canal and placed the school and the church on the other side. At the northern end of the canal, behind the counting houses, rose the three Waltham-size mills, each with a central stair tower topped by a cupola.

Boott created a rigid, feudal, militaristic community to support the mills. Known on occasion as "His Imperial Mightiness," he reigned from the apex of a social pyramid. Below him was a small aristocracy of superintendents and high officials. A gentry of overseers watched over the yeomanry of predominantly female machine operatives. At the bottom were the Irish day laborers who dug the canals and built the mills. This social stratification was repeated in Boott's hierarchic arrangement of housing: boardinghouse blocks for the operatives; modest single dwellings for the skilled workers, overseers, and superintendents; and a suitably elegant mansion for himself, set apart from the clustered housing. All others had to fend for themselves.

Shut out of the ordered universe of mill housing, the Irish day laborers encamped on vacant land nearby and set up a shantytown known as New Dublin. For housing they made "cabins, from seven to ten feet high, built of slabs and rough boards, a fireplace made of stone in one end, tapped out with two or three flour barrels or wine casks."[21] The corporations had no prior experience with immigrants and apparently did not realize that, unlike the mill girls, the Irish had no farms to return to once the job was done.

Starting operation during a time of general business recovery, the venture was an immediate success. Its stock traded at high premiums, and eager new

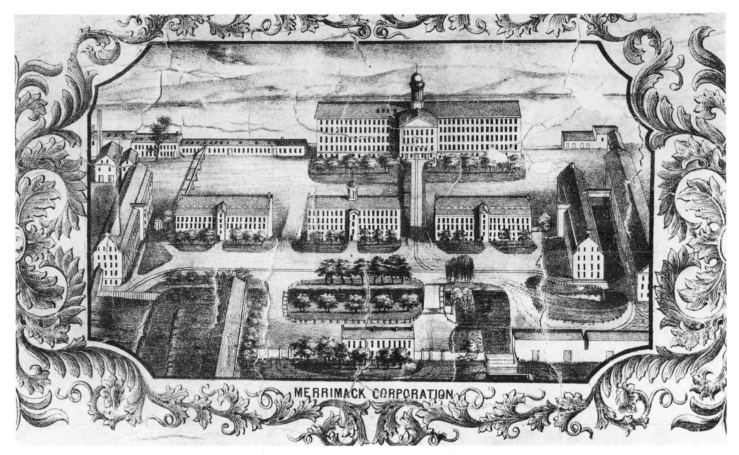

MERRIMACK CORPORATION

The Merrimack Manufacturing Company, shown in a border vignette of an 1850 map. (Lowell Historical Society)

investors clamored to share the profits. Jackson and Appleton had initially planned to simply expand their Waltham system at a more suitable privilege. Seeing the investment opportunity available at Pawtucket Falls, they switched to a more grandiose scheme. They decided to monopolize both power and real estate, augmenting their manufacturing profits by organizing new mills, selling them land, and leasing them waterpower. The location was too potent to waste on another one-company town.

The Merrimack Manufacturing Company was reorganized in 1825 to take full advantage of these new investment opportunities. The parent company transferred control of the waterpower, real estate, and machine shop to the Proprietors of the Locks and Canals, a wholly owned subsidiary that had previously administered the Pawtucket Canal. While Merrimack Manufacturing continued to make cloth, Locks and Canals was now free to reap tremendous profits by organizing and outfitting new mills, leasing power, and manipulating real estate.

The Proprietors of the Locks and Canals held Lowell's most valuable assets and completely controlled its economic growth. Investment capital poured in. Seven new corporations were formed within five years after the reorganization. Locks and Canals built seventeen mills for them. Soon, the Locks and Canals machine shop, one of the nation's largest, could build and equip a mill in a year or less. As predicted, Locks and Canals earned glorious profits.

ABOVE: *Lowell, 1834, from Dracut Heights—a popular viewpoint on the north bank of the Merrimack River. From left to right: the Concord River joins the Merrimack, with the Middlesex Mills marking the entrance to the Pawtucket Canal; the land between the two rivers and the canal is undeveloped, being reserved for future mills. Central Bridge crosses the Merrimack near the center of this view, with the Dutton St. boarding houses shown above and to the right. Then the Merrimack Mills and, at far right, the Tremont, Suffolk and Lawrence Mills. (Pendleton Lithograph; Boston Athenaeum).* OPPOSITE/BELOW: *A later view of Lowell from Dracut, slightly west (right) of the viewpoint above. Eight new factories are shown—the four to the right of Central Bridge are the Boott Mills, and the four to the left are part of the Massachusetts Mills. (Clothing sample folder, MVTM)*

Waterpower leases alone brought in one-half million dollars a year, and one investor, William Appleton, estimated he had made two million dollars on Locks and Canals stock transactions.

Lowell's phenomenal decade of expansion was unmatched in America. The city bloomed more quickly than its most optimistic promoters could have imagined. Mills and boardinghouses multiplied along the canals. Farmers' daughters poured into the city and took their places at the machines. This seemingly magical growth astonished all observers. John Greenleaf Whittier, who resided briefly in Lowell, called it "a city springing up, like the enchanted palaces of the Arabian tales, as it were in a single night—stretching far and wide its chaos of brick masonry and painted shingles" and felt himself "thrust forward into a new century." Lowell seemed the prelude to a "millennium of steam engines and cotton mills,"[22] and Whittier, though impressed, was troubled by the prospect.

Yet Lowell had no monopoly on New England textiles. As it grew, sister cities were begun at other prominent waterpower sites. Many of these mill cities followed the Lowell model, leasing waterpower to tenant mills surrounded by boardinghouses for young women. Some of these cities, including Chicopee, Manchester, and Nashua, would soon rise to prominence on their own merits. In many cases their stock was largely owned by the same Boston elite that had invested heavily at Lowell. As competition mounted and they lost their monopoly on modern machinery and profitable mill sites, the Lowell promoters looked for new ways to attract additional mills and fresh

MERRIMACK PRINTS

LOWELL, MASS.

capital. Their unceasing publicity campaign was part of the plan, as was the admission of two wealthy merchants, Amos and Abbott Lawrence, to the inner circle of heavy investors. These brothers organized three Lowell corporations in 1830—the Tremont, Suffolk, and Lawrence companies—and extended their investments in the years that followed. Meanwhile, they persuaded many of their friends and associates to follow their example. Fresh capital poured in.

Then P. T. Jackson proposed the most daring scheme of all—a railroad between Lowell and Boston. Beginning service in 1835, the Boston and Lowell railroad was the second in the Northeast. A marvel of its time, it augmented Lowell's image as the showcase of American industry. Lowell had become the "shock city" of Jacksonian America, the breaking wave of the industrial age. As such, it received more attention than any other city of its size before or since. It was scrutinized, applauded and occasionally damned by an unending stream of local and foreign observers, who judged it to be "one of the most extraordinary towns in this extraordinary country."

Life and Work: The Mill Girls

Among the many astonishing features of early Lowell, the enchanted city of America's first industry, its dependence on the labor of Yankee women was most remarkable of all. While the demands of machinery, hydraulics, real estate, and capital determined the city's structure, the mill girls gave it warmth and humanity. Within what people considered the rigid roles of the times, a fertile synthesis had occurred between the masculine forces of power and engineering and the feminine graces of virtue and culture.

Lowell was created during a period of labor shortage, when Yankee women were the only abundant source of skilled, conscientious workers. As at Waltham, their availability was conditional. Mill work had to become respectable. To achieve this, every detail of the city was designed to reinforce the twin pillars of Puritanism: work and virtue. Each hour of the mill girls' lives was subject to the strictest moral supervision.

Lured by regular cash wages, assured of acceptable working conditions and rigorously supervised boardinghouses, and tantalized by the excitement of city life, rural women packed their bandboxes and left their dreary homesteads. Their personal motives covered a wide spectrum of hope and discontent. Some worked to pay off the family mortgage or support a brother in college. Many came to earn money of their own; some spent it on fashionable clothes and accessories, while others saved for their education.

For more than two decades the city needed no advertisement. Mill girls spread its reputation, and "fabulous stories were told of the new town and the high wages offered to all classes of work people." Later, when the need for new recruits increased, labor agents began to circulate throughout the eastern states and Canada, promising "the work is so neat, and the wages such, that they can dress in silks and spend half their time reading," and bringing New England's daughters back to Lowell in their long, low black wagons.[23]

Two mill girls attend a power loom. One is apparently teaching the other. (Eighty Years of Progress; M V T M)

Few of the recruits intended to stay long. During Lowell's first decades, the average mill girl stayed less than three years. When they had achieved their goals or grown tired of the factory, they left. This mobility was a central tenet of the Lowell dogma. It ensured that the mill girls suffered no lasting harm from their long hours of machine tending. Equally important, it prevented formation of "a helpless caste, clamouring for work, starving unless employed, and hence ready for riot, for the destruction of property, and repeating here the scenes enacted in the manufacturing villages of England."[24]

Yet while the mill girls were on the payroll, the mills demanded strict obedience and total commitment. Residence in factory boardinghouses was mandatory, although each girl was free to choose among them. A room and board charge of $1.25 was deducted from the two to four dollars a girl could expect to earn in a seventy-hour work week. Above all, a diligent attitude was required, as the first article of the Lawrence company rules (1833) detailed:

All persons in the employ of the Company, are required to attend assiduously to their various duties, or labor, during working hours; are expected to be fully competent, or to aspire to the utmost efficiency in the work or business they may engage to perform, and to evince on all occasions, in their deportment and conversation, a laudable regard for temperance, virtue, and their moral and social obligations; and in which the Agent will endeavor to set a proper example. No persons can be employed by the Company, whose known habits are or shall be dissolute, indolent, dishonest, or intemperate, or who habitually absent themselves from public

A mill girl posed beside a Fales & Jenks spinning frame, ca. 1845. (Geldard, Cotton Manufacture)

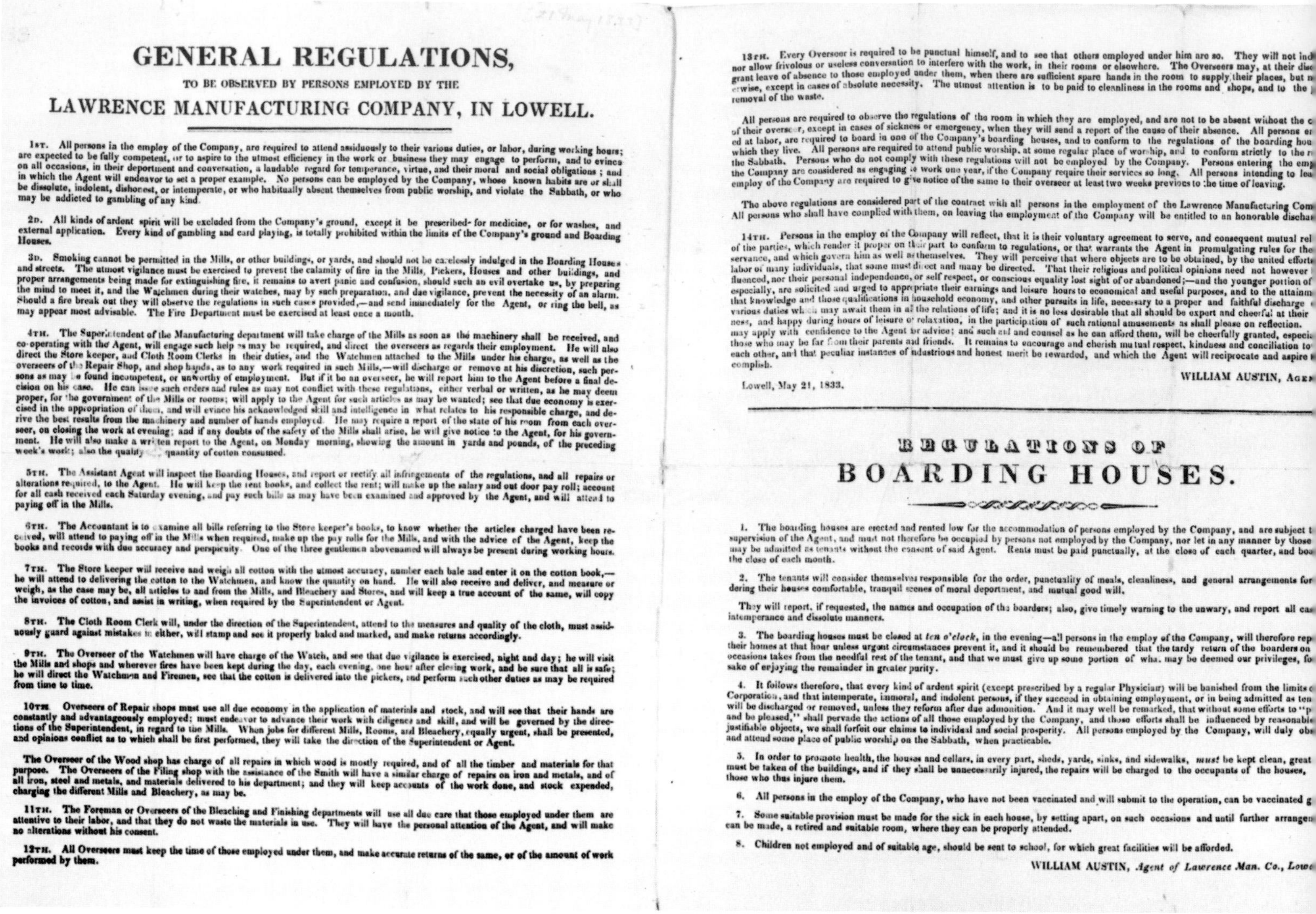

GENERAL REGULATIONS,

TO BE OBSERVED BY PERSONS EMPLOYED BY THE

LAWRENCE MANUFACTURING COMPANY, IN LOWELL.

1ST. All persons in the employ of the Company, are required to attend assiduously to their various duties, or labor, during working hours; are expected to be fully competent, or to aspire to the utmost efficiency in the work or business they may engage to perform, and to evince on all occasions, in their department and conversation, a laudable regard for temperance, virtue, and their moral and social obligations; and in which the Agent will endeavor to set a proper example. No persons can be employed by the Company, whose known habits are or shall be dissolute, indolent, dishonest, or intemperate, or who habitually absent themselves from public worship, and violate the Sabbath, or who may be addicted to gambling of any kind.

2D. All kinds of ardent spirit will be excluded from the Company's ground, except it be prescribed for medicine, or for washes, and external application. Every kind of gambling and card playing, is totally prohibited within the limits of the Company's ground and Boarding Houses.

3D. Smoking cannot be permitted in the Mills, or other buildings, or yards, and should not be carelessly indulged in the Boarding Houses and streets. The utmost vigilance must be exercised to prevent the calamity of fire in the Mills, Pickers, Houses and other buildings, and proper arrangements being made for extinguishing fire, it remains to avert panic and confusion, should such an evil overtake us, by preparing the mind to meet it, and the Watchmen during their watches, may by such preparation, and due vigilance, prevent the necessity of an alarm. Should a fire break out they will observe the regulations in such cases provided,—and send immediately for the Agent, or ring the bell, as may appear most advisable. The Fire Department must be exercised at least once a month.

4TH. The Superintendent of the Manufacturing department will take charge of the Mills as soon as the machinery shall be received, and co-operating with the Agent, will engage such help as may be required, and direct the overseers as regards their employment. He will also direct the Store keeper, and Cloth Room Clerks in their duties, and the Watchmen attached to the Mills under his charge, as well as the overseers of the Repair Shop, and shop hands, as to any work required in such Mills,—will discharge or remove at his discretion, such persons as may be found incompetent, or unworthy of employment. But if it be an overseer, he will report him to the Agent before a final decision on his case. He can issue such orders and rules as may not conflict with these regulations, either verbal or written, as he may deem proper, for the government of the Mills or rooms; will apply to the Agent for such articles as may be wanted; see that due economy is exercised in the appropriation of them, and will evince his acknowledged skill and intelligence in what relates to his responsible charge, and derive the best results from the machinery and number of hands employed. He may require a report of the state of his room from each overseer, on closing the work at evening; and if any doubts of the safety of the Mills shall arise, he will give notice to the Agent, for his government. He will also make a written report to the Agent, on Monday morning, showing the amount in yards and pounds, of the preceding week's work; also the quality and quantity of cotton consumed.

5TH. The Assistant Agent will inspect the Boarding Houses, and report or rectify all infringements of the regulations, and all repairs or alterations required, to the Agent. He will keep the rent books, and collect the rent; will make up the salary and out door pay roll; account for all cash received each Saturday evening, and pay such bills as may have been examined and approved by the Agent, and will attend to paying off in the Mills.

6TH. The Accountant is to examine all bills referring to the Store keeper's books, to know whether the articles charged have been received, will attend to paying off in the Mills when required, make up the pay rolls for the Mills, and with the advice of the Agent, keep the books and records with due accuracy and perspicuity. One of the three gentlemen abovenamed will always be present during working hours.

7TH. The Store keeper will receive and weigh all cotton with the utmost accuracy, number each bale and enter it on the cotton book,—he will attend to delivering the cotton to the Watchmen, and know the quantity on hand. He will also receive and deliver, and measure or weigh, as the case may be, all articles to and from the Mills, and Bleachery and Stores, and will keep a true account of the same, will copy the invoices of cotton, and assist in writing, when required by the Superintendent or Agent.

8TH. The Cloth Room Clerk will, under the direction of the Superintendent, attend to the measures and quality of the cloth, must assiduously guard against mistakes in either, will stamp and see it properly baled and marked, and make returns accordingly.

9TH. The Overseer of the Watchmen will have charge of the Watch, and see that due vigilance is exercised, night and day; he will visit the Mills and shops and wherever fires have been kept during the day, each evening, one hour after closing work, and be sure that all is safe; he will direct the Watchmen and Firemen, see that the cotton is delivered into the pickers, and perform such other duties as may be required from time to time.

10TH. Overseers of rooms must use all due economy in the application of materials and stock, and will see that their hands are constantly and advantageously employed; must endeavor to advance their work with diligence and skill, and will be governed by the directions of the Superintendent, in regard to the Mills. When jobs for different Mills, Rooms, and Bleachery, equally urgent, shall be presented, and opinions conflict as to which shall be first performed, they will take the direction of the Superintendent or Agent.

The Overseer of the Wood shop has charge of all repairs in which wood is mostly required, and of all the timber and materials for that purpose. The Overseers of the Filing shop with the assistance of the Smith will have a similar charge of repairs on iron and metals, and of all iron, steel and metals, and materials delivered to his department; and they will keep accounts of the work done, and stock expended, charging the different Mills and Bleachery, as may be.

11TH. The Foreman or Overseers of the Bleaching and Finishing departments will use all due care that those employed under them are attentive to their labor, and that they do not waste the materials in use. They will have the personal attention of the Agent, and will make no alterations without his consent.

12TH. All Overseers must keep the time of those employed under them, and make accurate returns of the same, or of the amount of work performed by them.

13TH. Every Overseer is required to be punctual himself, and to see that others employed under him are so. They will not indulge nor allow frivolous or useless conversation to interfere with the work, in their rooms or elsewhere. The Overseers may, at their discretion grant leave of absence to those employed under them, when there are sufficient spare hands in the room to supply their places, but not otherwise, except in cases of absolute necessity. The utmost attention is to be paid to cleanliness in the rooms and shops, and to the removal of the waste.

All persons are required to observe the regulations of the room in which they are employed, and are not to be absent without the consent of their overseer, except in cases of sickness or emergency, when they will send a report of the cause of their absence. All persons engaged at labor, and which govern him as well as themselves. They will perceive that where objects are to be obtained, by the united efforts and labor of many individuals, that some must direct and many be directed. That their religious and political opinions need not however be influenced, nor their personal independence, or self respect, or conscious equality lost sight of or abandoned;—and the younger portion of them especially, are solicited and urged to appropriate their earnings and leisure hours to economical and useful purposes, and to the attainment of that knowledge and those qualifications in household economy, and other pursuits in life, necessary to a proper and faithful discharge of those various duties which may await them in all the relations of life; and it is no less desirable that all should be expert and cheerful at their business, and happy during hours of leisure or relaxation, in the participation of such rational amusements as shall please on reflection. They may apply with confidence to the Agent for advice; and such aid and counsel as he can afford them, will be cheerfully granted, especially those who may be far from their parents and friends. It remains to encourage and cherish mutual respect, kindness and conciliation to each other, and that peculiar instances of industrious and honest merit be rewarded, and which the Agent will reciprocate and aspire to accomplish.

Lowell, May 21, 1833.   WILLIAM AUSTIN, Agent.

REGULATIONS OF BOARDING HOUSES.

1. The boarding houses are erected and rented low for the accommodation of persons employed by the Company, and are subject to the supervision of the Agent, and must not therefore be occupied by persons not employed by the Company, nor let in any manner by those who may be admitted as tenants without the consent of said Agent. Rents must be paid punctually, at the close of each quarter, and board at the close of each month.

2. The tenants will consider themselves responsible for the order, punctuality of meals, cleanliness, and general arrangements for rendering their houses comfortable, tranquil scenes of moral deportment, and mutual good will.

They will report, if requested, the names and occupation of the boarders; also, give timely warning to the unwary, and report all cases of intemperance and dissolute manners.

3. The boarding houses must be closed at ten o'clock, in the evening—all persons in the employ of the Company, will therefore keep their homes at that hour unless urgent circumstances prevent it, and it should be remembered that the tardy return of the boarders on occasions takes from the needful rest of the tenant, and that we must give up some portion of what may be deemed our privileges, for the sake of enjoying the remainder in greater purity.

4. It follows therefore, that every kind of ardent spirit (except prescribed by a regular Physician) will be banished from the limits of the Corporation, and that intemperate, immoral, and indolent persons, if they succeed in obtaining employment, or in being admitted as tenants will be discharged or removed, unless they reform after due admonition. And it may well be remarked, that without some efforts to "please and be pleased," shall pervade the actions of all those employed by the Company, and those efforts shall be influenced by reasonable and justifiable objects, we shall forfeit our claims to individual and social prosperity. All persons employed by the Company, will duly observe and attend some place of public worship on the Sabbath, when practicable.

5. In order to promote health, the houses and cellars, in every part, sheds, yards, sinks, and sidewalks, must be kept clean, great care must be taken of the buildings, and if they shall be unnecessarily injured, the repairs will be charged to the occupants of the houses, or those who thus injure them.

6. All persons in the employ of the Company, who have not been vaccinated and will submit to the operation, can be vaccinated gratis.

7. Some suitable provision must be made for the sick in each house, by setting apart, on such occasions and until further arrangements can be made, a retired and suitable room, where they can be properly attended.

8. Children not employed and of suitable age, should be sent to school, for which great facilities will be afforded.

WILLIAM AUSTIN, Agent of Lawrence Man. Co., Lowell.

Regulations of the Lawrence Mills at Lowell, 1833. Article 1 of this document is transcribed in the text. The folds and wrinkles in the paper suggest it was carried around in a worker's pocket for some time following employment. (Kress Collection, Baker Library, Harvard University)

worship, and violate the Sabbath, or who may be addicted to gambling of any kind.[25]

Disobediance brought dismissal, which was often followed by blacklisting.

In any industry, management and labor are by nature interdependent. So it was at Lowell. The manufacturer required a dependable work force for efficient operation. The girls, in their turn, expected steady employment and good wages. It was in everyone's best interest that the mills run smoothly and profitably. Company officials justified the arrangement in almost religious tones. A paymaster at the Hamilton Manufacturing Company preached:

Entire independence ought not to be wished for. . . . We are abundantly more happy for our being bound together by our mutual dependencies. . . . Let those who fill subordinate states be in due and quiet subjection

REGULATIONS

TO BE OBSERVED BY ALL PERSONS EMPLOYED IN THE FACTORIES OF THE

MIDDLESEX COMPANY.

The overseers are to be punctually in their rooms at the starting of the mill, and not to be absent unnecessarily during working hours. They are to see that all those employed in their rooms are in their places in due season. They may grant leave of absence to those employed under them, when there are spare hands in the room to supply their places; otherwise they are not to grant leave of absence, except in cases of absolute necessity. Every overseer must be the last to leave the room at night, and must see that the lights are all properly extinguished, and that there is no fire in the room. No overseer should leave his room in the evening while the mill is running, except in case of absolute necessity.

All persons in the employ of the Middlesex Company are required to observe the regulations of the overseer of the room where they are employed. They are not to be absent from their work, without his consent, except in case of sickness, and then they are to send him word of the cause of their absence.

They are to board in one of the boarding-houses belonging to the Company, unless otherwise permitted by the agent or superintendent, and conform to the regulations of the house where they board. They are to give information at the counting-room of the place where they board when they begin; and also give notice whenever they change their boarding place.

The Company will not employ any one who is habitually absent from public worship on the Sabbath, or whose habits are not regular and correct.

All persons entering into the employment of the Company are considered as engaged for twelve months; and those who leave sooner will not receive a regular discharge.

All persons intending to leave the employment of the Company are to give two weeks' notice of their intention to their overseer; and their engagement is not considered as fulfilled unless they comply with this regulation.

Smoking within the factory yards will in no case be permitted.

The pay-roll will be made up to the end of every month, and the payment made in the course of the following week.

These regulations are considered a part of the contract with persons entering into the employment of the MIDDLESEX COMPANY.

Samuel Lawrence, *Agent.*

Lowell, July 1, 1846.

Joel Taylor, Printer, Courier Office.

Regulations of the Middlesex Woolen Mills at Lowell, 1846. (Kress Collection, Baker Library)

A midcentury cloth label for Merrimack Manufacturing Company, showing vignettes of weaving and calico printing. (MVTM)

to those who have the charge over them and let those who are placed to rule and direct, do with prudence and discretion. . . .[26]

Similar backgrounds eased relations between management and labor. Both came from solid Yankee stock, although management represented a more privileged class. Both shared a common Yankee ethic and a deep-seated belief in the sanctity of work. "Who among us thought of hard work as a trial or a curse?" asked Lucy Larcom several years after she had left the mills. "It was the New Englander's natural inheritance—it was the law of the universe—and as such was recognized and welcomed."[27]

One Lowell minister insisted that "to labor is to pray," while another found the city distinguished by "a love of work. Perhaps more than any other of the large cities of this country, Lowell is a municipality of labor.... The very air seems full of honest toil."[28] Whittier found Lowell "dedicated, every square rod of it, to the Divinity of Work. The Gospel of Industry."[29]

This sanctification of work surprised foreign visitors, who could find no European counterpart. Astonished by the work ethic rampant at Lowell, Michel Chevalier, a perceptive French traveler who had once been imprisoned for advocating free love, saw its origin in the Yankee habit of constant labor and competition. "The Yankee is the laborious ant," he wrote. "He is industrious and sober, frugal and, on the sterile soil of New England, niggardly. . . . He is individualism incarnate. . . ." Chevalier found that "the rigid spirit of Puritanism has been carried to its utmost at Lowell." He concluded: "Lowell is not amusing, but it is neat and decent, peaceful and sage."[30]

Aided by the work ethic, the factory could require a seventy-hour week and still keep factory conditions within the limits of genteel tolerance. Harriet Robinson, one of the early mill girls, reported:

Though their hours of labor were long, yet they were not overworked. They were obliged to tend no more looms and frames than they could easily take care of, and they had plenty of time to sit and rest. . . . They were not driven. They took their work-a-day life easy. They were treated with respect by their employers; and there was a feeling of respectful equality between them.[31]

The spacious layout and beautiful surroundings of early Lowell helped to ease the factory routine. The mill girls said they enjoyed a life of "Arcadian simplicity," picking flowers on the way to the mill and admiring sunrises and sunsets from the windows of their workrooms. The factories were "light, well-ventilated, and moderately heated, each factory stood detached, with pleasant sunlit windows, cheerful views, and fresh air from all points of the compass."[32] Rural land still surrounded the city. Never far from view, natural beauty softened the rough edges of industry.

After their twelve-hour workday, the mill girls returned to their boarding-houses, where matrons selected for their high moral standards continued company surveillance. This was hardly necessary. The girls brought their own righteous breeding with them and watched over each other. Boardinghouse life allowed little privacy: five or six mill girls shared each bedroom and there were rarely enough beds for each. In such physically and psychologically cramped quarters, "if any gives indication of irregularity and impropriety, it cannot but be known to the rest; who, for the sake of their own character, give information themselves, and insist on the exclusion of the intruder."[33]

The gregarious boardinghouse environment was a cosmopolitan experience for girls from small, isolated farms and villages. Each boardinghouse was a social center where the girls made new friends and explored new ideas. Intent on self-improvement, they stocked the parlors with books, magazines, and literary journals. Somehow, after their long hours at the machines, some of the mill girls found time to attend lyceums, to read, to study poetry, and to write. Tenure at Lowell was more than just a job, it was an education.

A small number of mill girls were passionately committed to literature. Their study groups and literary circles, often under the direction of a local minister, consumed limited leisure time. The most influential product of these small study groups was *The Lowell Offering*, promoted by management as the house organ of the factory workers.

In his preface to the first edition, the editor, Reverend Abel C. Thomas, described *The Offering* as "not only the first work written by the factory girls, but also the first magazine or journal written exclusively by women in the whole world." He emphasized that "the articles are all written by the girls and *we do not* revise or rewrite them."[34]

Believing that the mill girls "were all self-made in the truest sense" one writer for *The Offering* remarked "that it was natural that such a thoughtful life should bear fruit" and saw its poems and articles as "the natural outgrowth of the mental habit of the mill girls." The inexperienced writers were "full of hopes, desires, aspirations; poets of the loom, spinners of verse, artists of factory life."[35] Replete with classical allusions, their immature poems and self-justifying essays seem quaint and occasionally even bizarre today. In 1840, they were quite an achievement.

The Offering reflected the controversy of the time over the alleged degradation of factory labor. It tried to prove that, at least at Lowell, "intellect and intelligence might be found even among factory operatives."[36] Although it had only fifty-four regular contributors and was subscribed to by barely two percent of the factory workers, it was promoted as the mill girls' mouthpiece and hailed as a vindication of the factory system.

Mill owners saw *The Offering* as a public relations bonanza, the ultimate proof of the uplifting capability of mechanical industry. With its poems and articles that "sounded as if written by people who never worked at all," *The Offering* was a perfect advertisement for factory life. Mill agents and superintendents were generous subscribers, sometimes taking as many as twenty-five copies of each issue. With their financial help, *The Offering* ran for five years. Although mill owners promoted similar publications at Chicopee, Newmarket, Exeter, and Fall River, *The Offering* remained preeminent.

The Lowell Offering served better as propaganda than communication, finding its most impressionable audience in the stream of visitors who came to Lowell to witness the possibilities of the industrial future. Charles Dickens praised *The Offering*, adding: "I will only observe, putting entirely out of sight the fact of the articles having been written by these girls after the arduous labors of the day, that it will compare advantageously with a great many English annuals."[37] Selections were reprinted in England, under the title *Mind Among the Spindles*. In France, Georges Sand hailed *The Offering*, and Auguste Thiers read selections from his bound edition to the French Chamber of Deputies.

Lowell's first two decades stand out prominently in the panorama of industrial history. Never again would life and work be so completely and benignly merged. Yet the idyll, and *The Offering*, were both short-lived.

Conditions at Lowell began declining years before *The Offering* came off the press. Wage cuts and increasing work loads had brought on Lowell's first inconclusive strike in 1834. *The Offering* was indeed looking back nostalgically at idyllic labor conditions fast eroding away. On rare occasions, the truth

Cover of the Lowell Offering. The beehive at left symbolizes industry. The editor, Rev. Abel Thomas, recalled that "each number consisted of sixteen pages small quarto, double columns, in small pica solid, and was sold at retail for six and one-fourth cents." (M V T M)

came closer to the surface, as in "The Spirit of Discontent," an article in the 1841 *Offering:*

> *I am going home, where I shall not be obliged to rise so early in the morning, nor be dragged about by the factory bell, nor confined in a close noisy room from morning to night. I shall not stay here. . . . Up before day, at the clang of the bell,—and out of the mill by the clang of the bell— into the mill, and at work in obedience to that ding-dong of a bell—just as though we were so many living machines.*[38]

When *The Offering* folded in 1845, factory life was neither novel nor attractive. Lowell had changed, reflecting profound changes in the industrial environment that surrounded it.

A mill girl draws warp yarns through the reed prior to mounting the warp on the loom, *ca. 1845.* (History of Wonderful Inventions; M V T M)

III

Adolescence

1820-1860

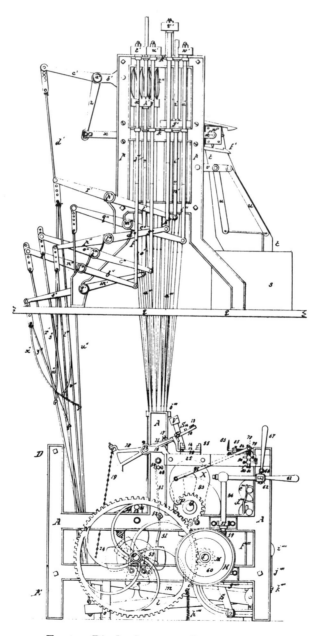

Erastus Bigelow's carpet loom, side view.
(National Archives)

Setting

During the four decades preceding the Civil War, the New England textile industry evolved from adolescence to maturity. By every standard, this period marked its most dramatic and portentous growth. Production increased fifteenfold. Employment expanded to include over one hundred thousand workers. Factories multiplied along New England's rivers. By 1850, 896 mills were in operation. Throughout this period, textile manufacture was the vanguard of industrialization, bearing the brunt of resistance to factory life and providing the best and worst examples of American mechanization.

This industrial growth was part of a rapid and decisive evolution of American society as the liberal spirit of the eighteenth century gave way to the exploitative drive of the nineteenth. Social and intellectual ferment produced a succession of movements—utopianism, transcendentalism, millennialism, temperance, phrenology, abolition, and others—all of which mill towns shared through the press and the lyceum. Emerson, Thoreau, Whittier, Poe, Horace Mann, and many others had their moment on the lyceum stage.

America teetered on the edge of industrialization, made wary by graphic reports of the "disgusting exhibition of human depravity and wretchedness" in Britain's manufacturing cities. Disturbing reports of similar conditions in New England now began to surface. A widening controversy over the rights of labor and the obligations of capital surrounded the factory. The period began with industrialists insisting that "we can have no Manchesters on this side of the Atlantic"; yet, ironically, before long new cities in several states adopted that name to glorify their intended destiny.

Accelerating industrial expansion produced geometric changes in the complexity of manufacturing. A wide spectrum of individual enterprises resulted, each with its own story of creation, growth, and decay reflecting the ability of its management to respond to changes in the world around it. Competition rapidly became intense. Profit margins shrank, linking success more closely than ever to unpredictable fluctuations in raw material prices and market demand. Boom or bust conditions prevailed, prompting one mill worker to warn his uncle who was considering acquiring a factory:

> Manufacturing is a very unsteady business, sometimes up, and sometimes down, some few gets Rich, and thousands are ruined by it. . . . Manufacturing breeds lords and Aristocrats, Poor men and slaves.[39]

The general economic climate set the tempo for industrial growth. Prosperity in the early twenties, thirties, and forties encouraged successive waves of investment and mill construction. Conversely, serious depressions in 1827, 1837, 1848, and 1857 crushed scores of mills, both old and new. Those who knew the industry survived. Inexperienced investors often suffered disastrous losses, leaving empty, bankrupt mills behind to be reorganized and reequipped in the next boom period. In success and failure, textile manufacturing transformed New England during these four decades. Although the industry was still experimental, its effects were to be lasting.

RHODE ISLAND STYLE   WALTHAM STYLE

Crown and Eagle Mills, North Uxbridge, Mass., ca. 1830.

Lowell, Mass., ca. 1833. (Both, Boston Athenaeum)

From the 1820s to the present, histories of New England textile mills have attempted to distinguish between two general patterns of development: the Rhode Island system and the Waltham system. Although the distinction does bring some order to the profusion of different mills built between 1820 and 1860, it is also a dangerous oversimplification of a highly diversified industry. The terminology itself is misleading: Rhode Island system mills flourished throughout New England, and Waltham system mills in fact used Lowell, more than Waltham, as their model. Moreover, each system was perceived differently by mill promoters in different regions and different decades. Nonetheless, the comparison is worth perpetuating, for the two systems did serve as benchmarks for manufacturers during the four pre-Civil War decades of industrial expansion.

CLASSIC FEATURES	RHODE ISLAND SYSTEM	WALTHAM SYSTEM
ownership	families and partnerships	joint stock corporations
capitalization	often minimal	large
power at site	less than 1,000 HP, often less than 100 HP	more than 1,000 HP; often much higher
power distribution	arranged independently by each mill	power canal system shared by several mills or companies, often leasing power from a promotional agency such as Locks & Canals
on-site management	owner	agent
labor	children and families preferred	young women preferred
housing	family houses and tenements	boardinghouses
product	emphasis on diversity	emphasis on mass production
sales	manufacturer sold direct	commission sales agency
community form	village	city
example	Crown and Eagle Mills	Lowell

Technological Evolution

MACHINE SHOPS

Machine building is a specialized art requiring tools, materials, skills, and designs American machinists acquired slowly during the first decades of the century. America's first machines were crude and primitive, built largely of wood, and laboriously shaped by hand or turned on simple lathes. Growing up during a continuing embargo on machine exports from England, in a young nation without proper machine shops, early American mills had to provide their own. As soon as the basement of an early mill was completed, a machine shop was installed and set to work making the machines to equip the floors above.

Advanced machines are made by other machines—machine tools, the only family of machines capable of reproducing itself. Since machine tools are also precision machines in their own right, the early shops were restricted to a frustrating, chicken-and-egg evolution until a critical point was reached in the 1820s, when machine tools achieved an appreciable level of sophistication.

The primitive metallurgy of the time also restricted mechanical progress. Until steel became available in the late 1850s, brass, wrought iron, and cast iron were the main alternatives to wood for machine construction. Each had its uses: brass for delicate gears and bearings, wrought iron for parts requiring flexibility but not strength, and cast iron for frames and parts where its weight, brittleness, and resistance to milling did not matter.

Competent machinists were needed to build the new designs. At first, only a handful of Americans cultivated this skill. Mill owners hired the best. Both Samuel Slater and Francis Lowell owed their success to able mechanics who could translate their designs into wood and metal: David Wilkinson at Pawtucket and Paul Moody at Waltham. Their workshops trained America's first generation of professional machine builders.

The Lowell Machine Shop, shown in a border vignette on Sidney & Neff's map. This shop bought out its predecessor at Waltham. The machines, the patterns, and Paul Moody himself were all transferred to Lowell. The shop was built like a textile mill to allow conversion at a later date. (Lowell Historical Society)

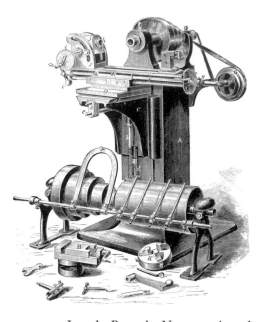

By their nature machines evolve towards increased efficiency, automation, and versatility. Squeezed between increasing competition and rising labor costs, manufacturers encouraged mill machinists to create machines that were bigger, faster, and simpler to operate. Invention served the manufacturer by minimizing his dependence on expensive skilled laborers and maximizing productivity of the unskilled operatives who took their places.

As the vanguard of mechanical progress, the early mills shaped the nation's perception of technology. The machinists' creations seemed "gifted with intelligence." Americans beheld the mechanized mill interior with "admiring wonder" and judged it "one of the marvels of the world." The machine promised to liberate humanity from needless toil and drudgery, joining its hum with the roar of the waterfall to sing "a song of triumph and exultation at the successful union of nature with the act of man."[40]

While celebrating the machine's ability to harness nature for human liberation, Americans slowly became aware that the machine had an antithetical mandate of its own. An ideally mechanized mill would be staffed entirely by unskilled labor tending as many machines as humanly possible, running at maximum theoretical speed. Mechanization opened the door to labor exploitation as manufacturers urged inventors to make this ideal a reality.

ABOVE: *Joseph Brown's No. 1 universal milling machine, patented 1862 and manufactured by the Brown & Sharpe tool company of Providence, R.I. Measuring instruments made by the company established new standards of precision for all machine shops. The milling machine allowed mechanics to cut complex metal parts with an accuracy justified by the new instruments.* (Slater Mill Historic Site)

BELOW: *The Mason Machine Works, at Taunton, Mass., founded in 1829 by William Mason. Manufacturing a variety of textile machinery, the firm was most famous for the self-acting mule Mason patented in 1842 and for the elegant locomotives he produced after 1853. Mason learned machine building at the Colt pistol factory.* (Van Slyck, Manufacturers)

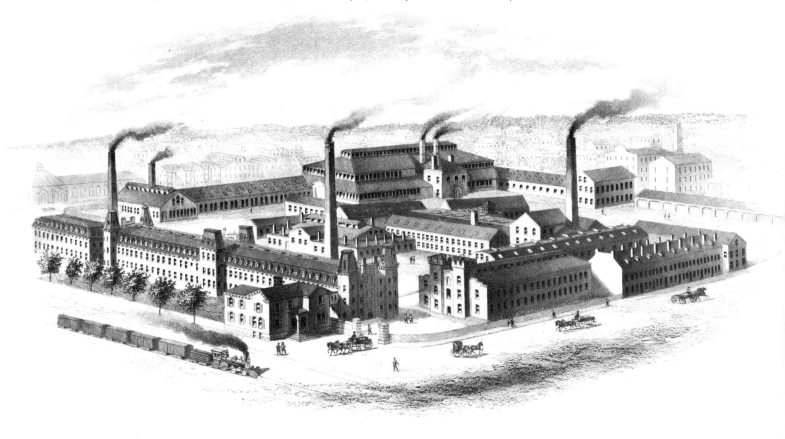

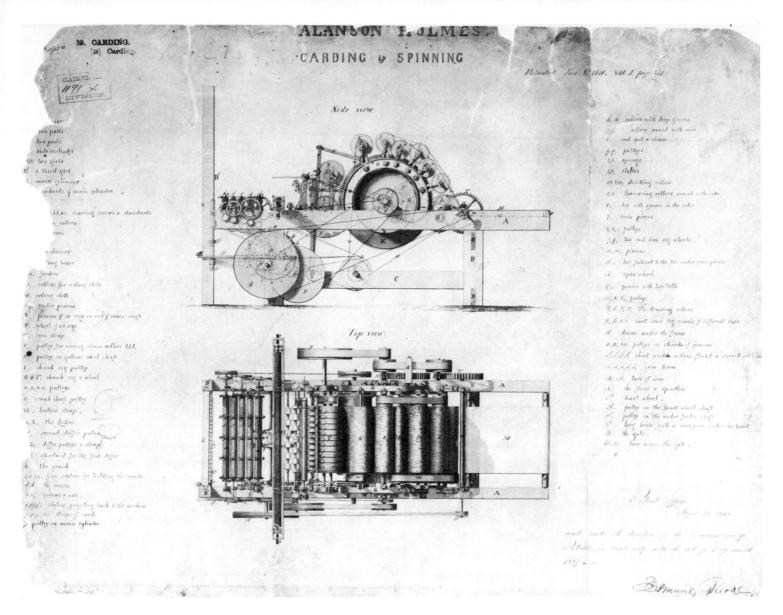

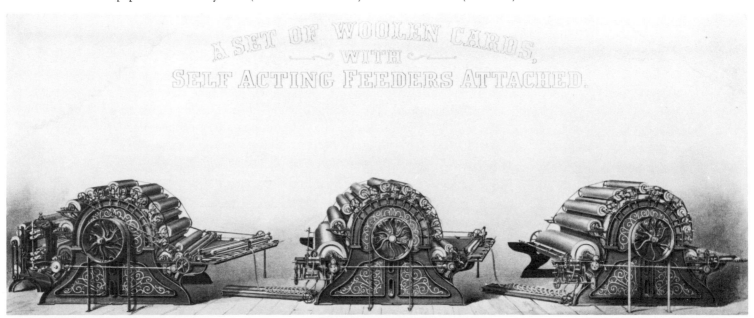

ABOVE: Patent drawing for a carding machine by Alanson Holmes, 1810, a complex machine for the time when it was designed. Its intricacy represents well the norm of the industry a decade later. This and all other patent drawings dated before 1836 are reconstructions made after the fire that destroyed the patent office and all its papers in that year. (National Archives)

BELOW: Carding machines by Harwood & Quincy, ca. 1865. Both the decorative design of the frames and the precise engineering of the cylinders are indicative of the tremendous advances in machine design which separate these machines from their predecessor above. (M V T M)

SPINNING

Mule spinning was an ongoing headache for mill owners: only the cantankerous, inefficient mule could spin delicate filling yarns. Woolen mills were totally dependent on it. Rhode Island style cotton mills relied on it for making sophisticated fabrics. Waltham style mills used it less frequently, preferring throstle-spun yarns for both warp and filling in their coarse fabrics.

The mule required a strong, skilled, male operator to move its carriage back and forth. As the skill was very difficult to acquire, mill owners depended on trained English mule spinners who were notoriously independent—"the most troublesome class of operators in the mill." Mule spinners brought two other English traditions with them: the craft union and an arrogant attitude towards management. They demanded, and received, high wages for their skill. Mill owners bemoaned their "disorderly habits" and condemned the weekend drinking that left many mule spinners hung over on Mondays, retarding all mill operations. Mule spinners proved that "the more skillful the workman, the more self-willed and intractable he is apt to become."[41]

Automation of the mule revealed the power of invention as a tool of labor management. Calling mule spinners "one of their greatest evils," mill owners asked their machinists to make "a self-operated machine, which can be run by a boy, and will make [us] independent of the unreliable class of workmen we [are] compelled to employ."[42] The machinists set to work.

Ira Gay developed a prototype self-actor in 1828 at the Nashua Machine Shop, but almost a decade passed before William Mason perfected a working production model. The self-acting mule was a triumph of automation. It duplicated the subtle, rhythmic movements of the mule spinner perfectly and was justly acclaimed as an "iron man":

> *Apparently instinct with life and feeling, it performs its allotted course as implicitly as a mere water wheel, but the exquisite provisions for timing—what may be called the opportuneness of its movements—give it an air of volition and prevision.*[43]

Organized resistance by mule spinners slowed adoption of the self-actor until it became clear to all that the mechanical marvel was so complicated and troublesome that it needed a highly skilled attendant. The mule spinners' hegemony remained unbroken for several more decades.

Meanwhile, efforts to improve the throstle spinning frames continued. The goal, as always, was higher operating speeds combined with minimum labor requirements. But operating speeds on the spinning frames were limited by the "U"-shaped flyers, which tended to distort and wobble as their rotational speed increased. Two alternatives to the flyer were soon proposed: ring spinning, patented by John Thorpe in 1828, and cap spinning, patented by Charles Danforth in 1830. Both techniques were distortion-free at high speed, allowing dramatic increases in productivity per spindle, per man-hour, and per square foot of floor space.

A typical mule room, 1835. The mule spinner moves the carriage by cranking the large wheels at center. (Ure, Cotton Manufacture)

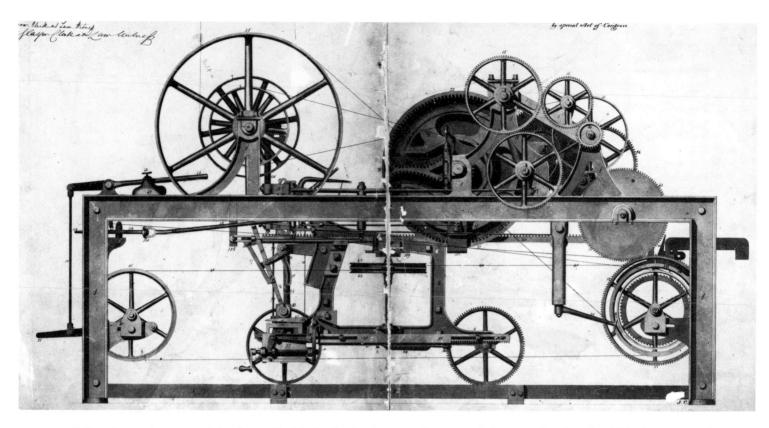

ABOVE: Self-acting mule patented by James Smith in England, 1834, and in America, 1838. BELOW: Some component parts of Smith's mule. The unusual gear at the center guides a small sprocket around the convoluted path which determines the reciprocating motion of the carriage. (National Archives)

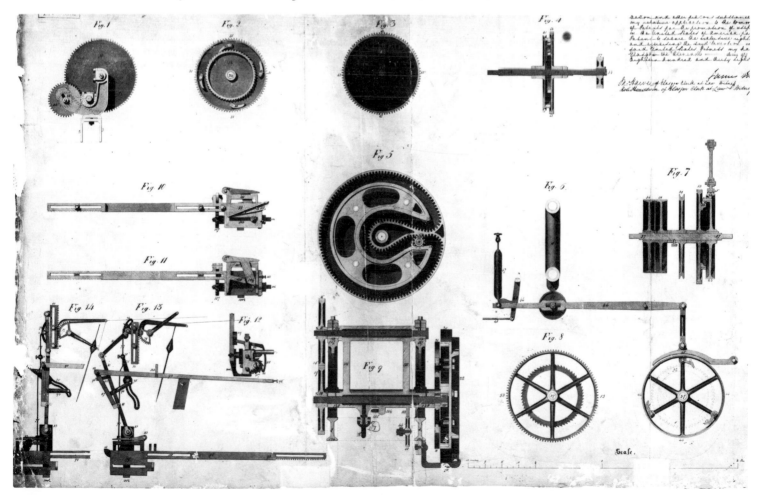

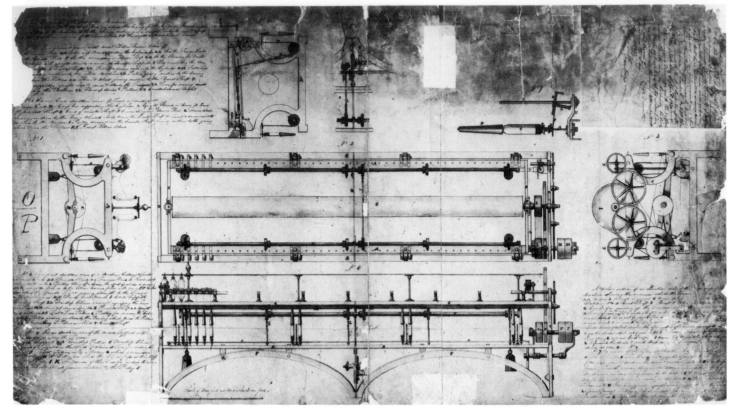

ABOVE: Charles Danforth's cap spinning frame patent, 1830. A top view is shown in the center of this oversize patent, with a front view below it and end views on each side. BELOW LEFT: Detail of the cap spinning mechanism, from Danforth's patent. A conical cap "D" is used instead of a flyer to guide yarn to the bobbin "C." BELOW RIGHT: Detail of John Thorpe's ring spinning patent, 1828. Thorpe replaced the flyer with a "c"-shaped ring traveling at high speed around a grooved circular raceway mounted on a plate which travels up and down the spinning bobbin. Spinning at over 8,000 rpm, this highly efficient design could double yarn production without any increase in power. Mechanical difficulties delayed its acceptance until after it was perfected at the Fales & Jenks machine shop in 1845. The Danforth cap, though slower, went into production almost immediately and proved very popular. (National Archives)

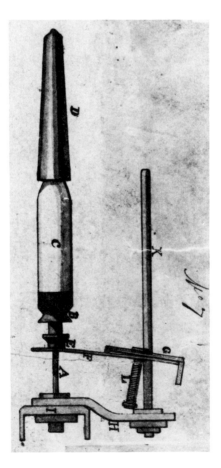

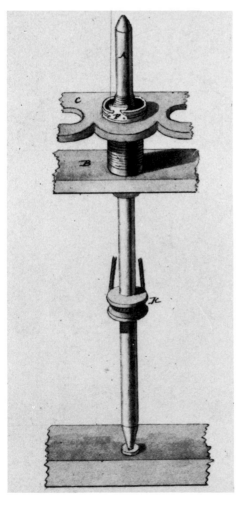

PATTERN WEAVING

LEFT: The fancy power loom, patented by William Crompton in 1837. Crompton was already experienced in English pattern weaving when he immigrated to the United States in 1836. His fancy power loom gave new variety to mechanical weaving by simultaneously expanding the possibilities for automatic harness selection and simplifying changeover between patterns. In Crompton's design the pattern is encoded in the arrangement of disks on rods linked together to form a timing chain, with each rod representing one "pick," or pass of the shuttle. As each rod passes over the indexing cylinder, at upper right, the disks on it activate levers that raise the appropriate harnesses. Patterns were easily changed by moving the disks or substituting a fresh chain. (National Archives). BELOW LEFT: "Improved Upright Lever Fancy Broad Loom," by George Crompton, son of the English inventor above. George learned machine skills at his father's shop, and later at the Colt pistol factory. He took over the business in 1849 and patented dozens of improvements on his father's design during the next two decades. The position of moveable disks on the rods of the timing chain (upper right) is still used to control the sequence of harness selection. An automatic drop shuttle box, designed by Lucius Knowles, has been added for selection of filling yarns. The Knowles drop box, carrying three shuttles, is mounted on the beater and activated by cams and levers that raise and lower the box to bring the desired shuttle into position to be hit by the "picker stick" and propelled through the shed. The U.S. Commission on Patents noted that "upon the Crompton loom, or looms based on it, are woven every yard of fancy cloth in the world." (Crompton Loom Works catalog; M V T M)

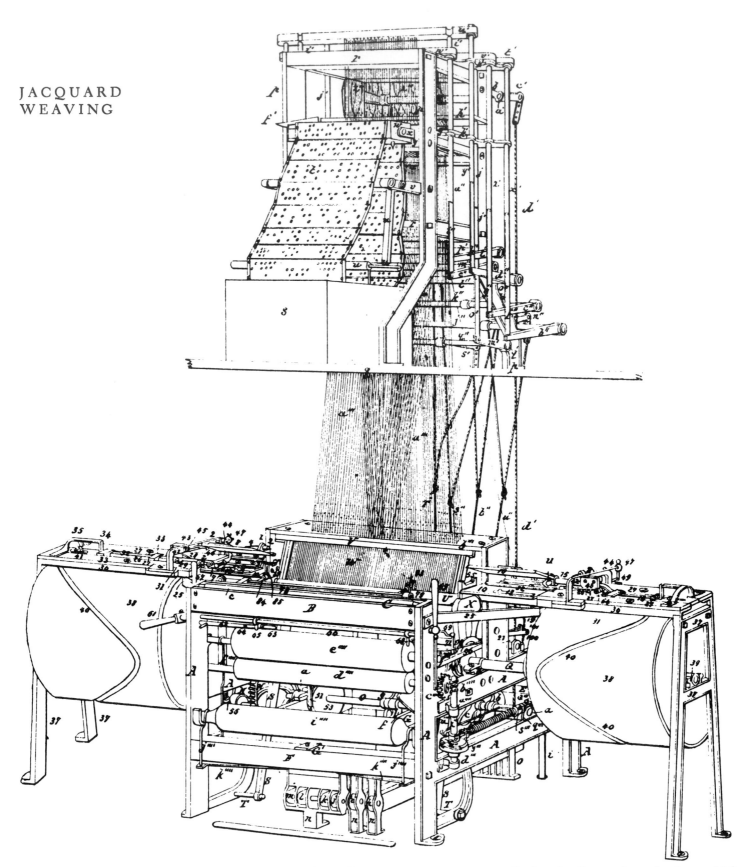

Patent drawing of Erastus Bigelow's carpet loom, 1842. This intricate machine, the mainstay of the Lowell Manufacturing Company's carpet mills and the basis for Bigelow's fame ("A name on the door rates a Bigelow on the floor"), utilizes a warp selecting mechanism (top) invented by Jacquard of France in 1804. The pattern is encoded in holes punched into cards read sequentially by the Jacquard mechanism, which raises each selected warp strand individually. The Jacquard head marks the first significant use of binary automation and is a direct ancestor of the modern digital computer. (National Archives)

DIVERSIFICATION

Calico printing machines, ca. 1836. Textile print-ing, an inexpensive and popular alternative to pat-tern weaving, was perfected in England and intro-duced at several American mills, including the Merrimack Manufacturing Company, in 1823 and 1824. Successful printing required precision ma-chining and highly skilled operators and engravers. Many American print works recruited experienced craftsmen in England and arranged for their pas-sage across the Atlantic. Kirk Boott even built spe-cial housing for his English printers at Lowell. Skilled and indispensable, the printers were re-ported to be as independent and dissolute as mule spinners, and for the same reasons. (Baines, Cotton Manufacture)

Upright rotary knitting machine by Tomp-kins, patented 1855. Semiautomatic devices for knitting had been evolving since the sixteenth century, but further development of the intricate mechanism had to wait for the refined machining techniques of the 1840s. Clark Tompkins, of Troy, N.Y., was only one of dozens of inventors who pat-ented knitting machines during the 1850s. (Asher & Adams, Pictorial Album)

POWER AND ENGINEERING

Industrial expansion required a corresponding increase in available power. At first, this need was met by locating new mills on larger rivers. But once the mill was built, expansion could be achieved only by more efficient use of the chosen mill privilege. Both Rhode Island and Waltham style mills were challenged by limited waterpower: the former, by the inadequacies of the streams themselves; the latter, by the rental of a fixed number of mill powers drawn off the main canal.

Mill owners took great interest in improved waterwheel designs as the easiest means to increase power. Although simple in concept, waterwheels follow complex hydrodynamic principles not well understood during the early years of industrialization. Often, millwrights could not even measure the efficiency of the wheels they built. In practice, the breast wheel design in which water enters the wheel above the axis was eventually accepted as the best alternative: its theoretical superiority was relatively easy to grasp, and its construction lay within the carpenters' and masons' capabilities. Most mills switched to breast wheel designs early in the century.

Breast wheels could never harness more than sixty percent of the theoretical power in the canal, but some increase in efficiency was gained by building the wheels on a gigantic scale: thirty feet in diameter at Lowell and over forty feet at some other locations. The wheels had the further disadvantage of being almost useless whenever the river rose above normal and forced backwater up in the tailrace against the wheel blades.

Improved waterwheel designs awaited progress in mathematics and hydraulic analysis. Benoit Fourneyron's water turbine, patented in France in 1832, signaled the critical breakthrough. Fourneyron added precisely curved vanes inside both fixed and moving sections of the turbine to guide the water along the spiral path that released maximum power. Efficiency increased to over seventy-five percent. Turbines had another crucial advantage; they were less vulnerable to tailrace flooding. Since water entered the turbine from above through an air-tight tube, the penstock, the power of a given design depended only on the rate of flow and the head, or difference in height between the canal and the tailrace. If high floodwater raised the level of the tailrace, head would decrease and the turbine would lose power, but only the most extreme flooding could stop it. Moreover, fully enclosed turbines could be installed well above the tailrace so that waste water was pulled away from the blades by suction, allowing easy access for inspection.

By the 1840s, Lowell needed more power for further expansion. An extensive program of research and experimentation in hydraulics and turbine design began under the direction of the Locks and Canals chief engineer, James Francis. His assistant, Uriah A. Boyden, worked to perfect the turbine. Tantalized by a bounty of four hundred dollars for each percentage point of efficiency gained over seventy-eight percent, Boyden raised turbine performance to eighty-eight percent. Francis expanded on Boyden's work and made great improvements in the design of efficient canals and flumes to feed the turbines soon installed at Lowell. During the 1850s, turbines were installed in

An axial view of the Fourneyron turbine, 1832. In this outward flow design, water enters along the axis and is guided by fixed inner vanes into the rotating outer wheel. (*Knight*, Mechanical Dictionary; M V T M)

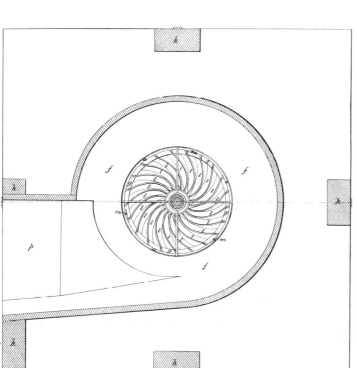
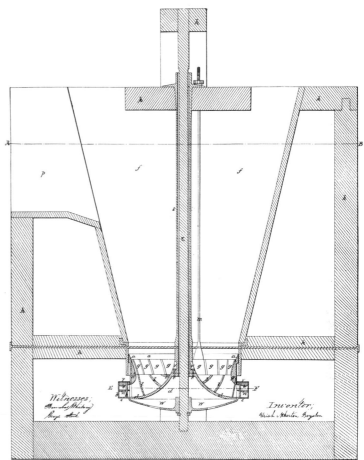

mills throughout New England. Conversion to turbine drive allowed mill owners to add machinery to mills whose size had previously been limited by the mill privilege.

Yet the turbine alone could not solve Lowell's problems. Investors wanted to increase the total power of the site so that more mill sites could be sold. In 1846, James Francis began work on a grand plan to bring more power to the thirsty mills. He raised the dam to create a millpond that extended twelve miles upstream to Nashua, New Hampshire, and built a new waterway, the Northern Canal, linking it to the earlier canals to increase and regulate power throughout the system. Forty new mill powers became available, for a total of 139.

Lowell had one last option for increasing its waterpower—reservoir control. Zachariah Allen, a Rhode Island manufacturer, had pioneered the reservoir idea in 1823, on finding he had built his Allendale mill at an inconsequential privilege. He enlisted mill owners upstream in a reservoir company that built an elaborate system of dams and gates to store power in a series of ponds for controlled release. Lowell carried Allen's precedent to its most arrogant conclusion by discreetly buying control of the headwaters of the Merrimack River—Lake Winnipesaukee, and Great and Little Squam lakes, in the White Mountains. The river had become one giant millstream. After

Axial and side views of Uriah Boyden's turbine. Although drawn for an 1853 patent, the main features of his 1844 design are clear: an outward flow turbine wheel similar to Fourneyron's and a penstock shaped to force water into an efficient spiral path towards it. Output was 75 horsepower. The efficiency of his 190 horsepower prize-winning turbine (1846) was increased further by unusually precise machining of all its parts, as James Francis, Boyden's superior at Locks and Canals, noted: "The workmanship was of the finest description, and of a delicacy and accuracy altogether unprecedented in constructions of this class." Boyden called this turbine a "hydraulic motor" and distinguished it from other water wheels by emphasizing that only the turbine allows water to act on all parts of the wheel simultaneously. Many other conflicting definitions are available. (Boston Public Library)

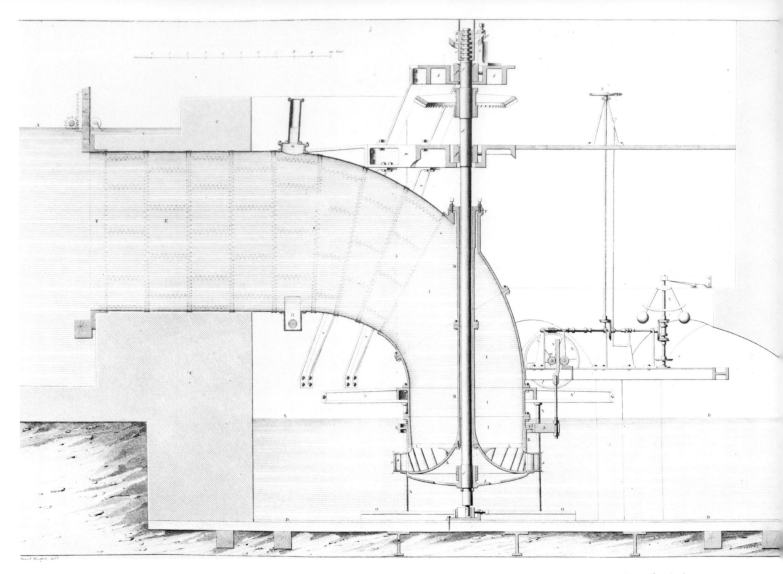

Cross section of the turbine built by James Francis for the Tremont Mills at Lowell. Francis tested this Boyden outward flow design extensively, comparing it to inward flow designs of his own at other test installations. Each had its merits. The Francis turbine was more efficient for low and medium falls, as at Lowell. This plate, from Francis's landmark treatise, Lowell Hydraulic Experiments (1855), shows the tapering penstock channeling water from the headrace of the canal at the upper left to the turbine wheel at the bottom center. The static inner guide vanes of the wheel are attached to a column surrounding the axle of the dish-shaped rotor outside and below it. A governor on the right regulates wheel speed through gates that control water flow through the wheel.

rowing up the Merrimack in 1839, Henry David Thoreau described the transformation that had already begun:

> *See how this river was directed from the first to the service of manufactures. Issuing from the iron region of Franconia, . . . with Squam and Winnipiseogee, and Newfound and Massabesic Lakes for its mill ponds, it falls over a succession of natural dams, where it has been offering its privileges in vain for ages, until at last the Yankee race came to improve them. . . . When at length it has escaped from under the last of the factories, it has a level and unmolested passage to the sea, a mere waste water, as it were, bearing little with it but its fame.*[44]

While steady improvements in hydraulic technology assured the prominence of waterpowered mills during this period, the steam engine began to assert itself as a viable competitor. Although British steam engines were known and admired in America before the 1820s, local development of the technology was slow. Mill owners had little interest in crude, inefficient steam engines as long as river power seemed abundant.

Philadelphia became the first center for American steam engine development. Oliver Evans, author of the *Young Millwright's Guide*, was one of the inventors who made workable engines there. The non-condensing, high-pressure "Columbian" engine he developed in 1804 made stationary steam power commercially practical. Three New England mills—two in Providence and one in Middletown, Connecticut—were using Evans engines before 1814.

Rhode Island area manufacturers soon felt the limitations of their water-power. The steam engine opened new possibilities for competition with the integrated factories north of them. Samuel Slater responded to the northern challenge by building the Providence Steam Cotton Mill in 1827. He installed an improved Evans design. Two years later, Zachariah Allen of Providence remarked: "So necessary to the wants of life at the present day are the products of machinery, that the Steam Engine has become almost as important as the plough."[45]

But the steam engine, more than any other machine of its time, required advanced machinery and metallurgy to be truly efficient. Steam technology

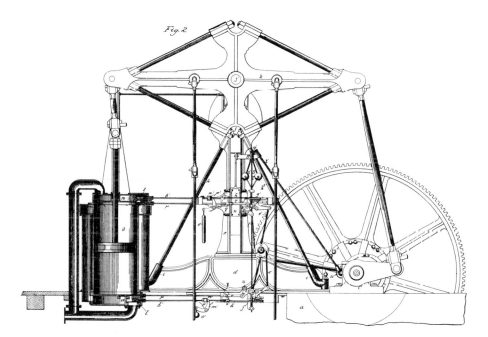

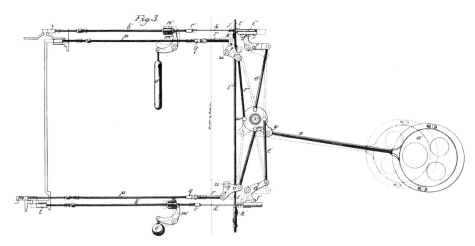

ABOVE LEFT: *Steam engine patent by George H. Corliss of Providence, R.I., 1849. This patent incorporates the automatic variable cut-off valves which were the basis for Corliss's success.* BELOW LEFT: *The automatic linkage mechanism for the Corliss variable cut-off valves, from his patent above. An eccentric yoke on the main drive shaft (right) causes a disk at the center to rotate back and forth. Linkage rods attached to the perimeter of the disk activate the valves. (Boston Public Library)*

reached a critical point during the next decade, when shipments of anthracite coal to the Northeast began and more refined engines became available. Between 1832 and 1838, twenty-six steam mills were built in Rhode Island. Fall River and a handful of other tidewater industrial centers also started steam mills during this period.

The brilliant work of George H. Corliss made Providence, Rhode Island, a center for steam engine manufacture during the 1850s. When Corliss came to Providence in 1845, the city had already established its reputation for quality machine work; Zachariah Allen had patented an automatic governor, and the Babcock and Thurston firm had two decades of engine building experience. Steam engine capacity in the city exceeded one thousand horsepower. Corliss built on this expertise, refined the designs of his time, and made Providence an undisputed leader in steam technology. The most important of his many contributions to engine design was an automatic variable cut-off mechanism patented in 1849, which regulated engine speed by varying the time during which steam entered the cylinder. Tremendous economies resulted. Although the Corliss cut-off was clearly based on work of earlier inventors, especially Zachariah Allen, Corliss was the first to incorporate the mechanism into a finely crafted, efficient, dependable engine providing a constant source of rotary power under varying load.

More frequently, steam engines were used as a supplement for waterpower from sluggish streams during dry seasons. Auxiliary steam power allowed older mills to install more machines and encouraged construction of large new mills at privileges that had sufficient power only during part of the year. The Waltham mill was an early user of auxiliary steam, and by 1845 Lowell, too, depended on it for continuous year-round operation.

The full value of improvements in machinery and power systems could not be realized until comparable advances were made in the power transmission systems linking them together. The gear drive arrangement inherited from England had serious limitations for American millwrights. Decades behind their English counterparts, American machinists were not yet able to make gears precise enough to run smoothly, quietly, and efficiently. Shafting was also a continuing problem, for the wrought iron shafts replacing their wooden predecessors were always heavy and rarely uniform in strength or cross section. Furthermore, these limitations in gear and shaft construction were all magnified by any increase in rotational speed. Thus, the only way to run a breast gear and shaft system of the 1820s effectively was to run it slowly, a conflict with the general trend of the times towards ever faster machine speeds.

Paul Moody demonstrated an alternative to heavy gearing when he built the Appleton mills at Lowell in 1826. Leather belts carried power from the wheel to intermediate countershafts on each floor and from the countershafts to the machines. But Moody's experiment was premature. He had only one part of the solution.

Experimenting at his mill at Allendale, Rhode Island, in the 1830s, Zachariah Allen came up with another ingredient—the understanding that lightweight shafting turning at high speed could carry the same power as the heavy shafts turning at slow speeds. Belts, too, carry power in proportion to

George H. Corliss, 1817–1888. (Van Slyck, Manufacturers)

A countershaft with self-aligning bearings. Shafts, pulleys, and bearings had to be carefully machined to turn perfectly at speeds that, by 1860, often exceeded 300 rpm. (Knight, Mechanical Dictionary; M V T M)

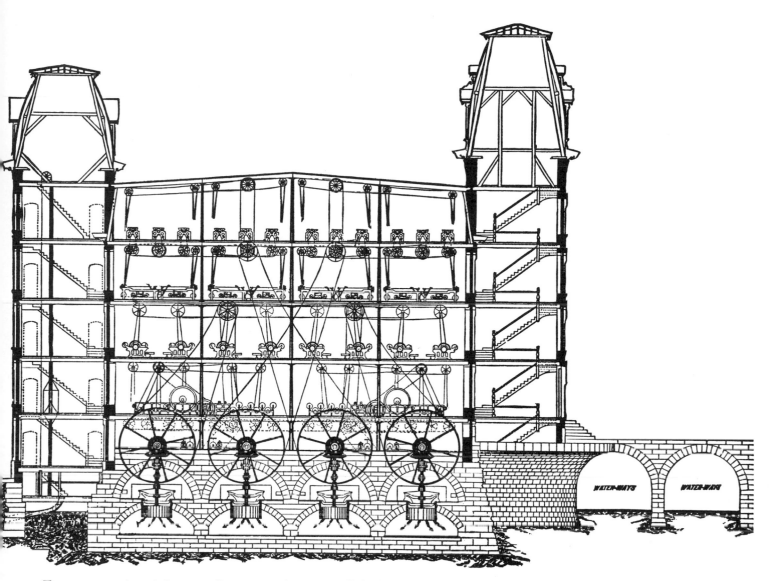

Transverse section of the Manville Company's No. 3 mill, built in 1874 in Manville, R.I. This drawing, from the 1875 catalog of the Leffel Company, which built the turbines shown at the bottom of the mill, represents state-of-the-art construction for its period and demonstrates the potential of advances in engineering occurring in the preceding decades. Each turbine has its own flume, tailrace, and 20-foot diameter 10-ton flywheel. Dressing machines are on the second floor, cards on the third, mules on the fourth, and either looms or frames on the fifth, below the almost-flat roof. The stair tower on the left contains an elevator. Enclosing nine acres of floor space, the mill was built to use the full 1,600 horsepower of the Blackstone River on the 18½-foot fall at this point, a scale which the new power systems made possible. An 800 horsepower steam engine supplemented the turbines during the four-to-seven-month period of low water. (M V T M) The list of materials included:

rough stone	8,160 cords
granite ashlar	9,110 cubic feet
bricks	5,605,800
cast iron	348,928 pounds
wrought iron	23,000 pounds
glass	34,994 panes
pine timber	860,000 board feet
spruce flooring	1,267,000 board feet
nails	65,500 pounds

their speed. In theory, a mill could be run on rubber bands and toothpicks—if they moved fast enough. Furthermore, lightweight shafting relieved the mill of several tons of unnecessary metal. Allen cited examples of mills whose floors had collapsed under the weight of their shafts.

Metal workers added a third ingredient to the solution by perfecting the

The Hamilton Mills, Lowell, Mass. The projecting central section was added in 1846 to connect the two mills built 1825–1826. (Lowell Historical Society)

cold-rolling process in the 1840s, facilitating production of perfect lengths of strong, light shaft. Improved lathes made the necessary bearings, pulleys, and flywheels possible. Finally, the turbine—by nature a high-speed device—gave an added impetus to bring all the components of the high-speed belt drive system together. By the 1840s the changeover had begun. Mills started during the following decades were designed from the beginning for belt drive with shafts running up to, and sometimes exceeding, three hundred revolutions per minute. They were built for speed. Belt drive became a hallmark of American mill design.

Improved power systems allowed mills with limited power to expand. One of the easiest ways to do so was to connect adjacent factories with additions that provided the extra floor space needed. As additions closed the gaps between mill units, the spaciousness of the early mill cities was lost. It was no longer possible to look past the factories to the river beyond. The mills created an almost solid wall between the city and the river.

The Rhode Island System

Starting scores of small mills modeled on the Rhode Island prototype, manufacturers in southern New England expanded their activities despite limitations on capital and waterpower. Although aware of the successful Waltham-style factories further north, they knew that neither imitation nor direct competition was possible. They therefore adapted their mills to fit specialized niches too small or too changeable for their hulking northern competitors. Their machines, especially the spinning mule, allowed diversification of products. Investment was cautious, creating a pattern of organic growth, with each small advance financed by previous success. Some of these enterprises grew to equal the northern corporations, but small businesses were more typical. Family partnerships controlled most Rhode Island style mills, each small group of owners adding its own idiosyncratic touch to its company.

Manufacturers continued to carve new communities out of the wilderness, making their company towns the outposts of rural civilization, as one pamphleteer described in 1849:

> In the most rocky and desolate situations, avoided by all human beings since the settling of the Pilgrims as the image of loneliness and barrenness, amid rocks and stumps and blasted trees, there is a waterfall. Taking its stand here, the genius of our age calls into almost instantaneous life a bustling village. Here factories are erected in this barren waste, and suddenly a large population is gathered. For this population everything necessary to the social state is to be created. The past contributes nothing.[46]

The isolated factory and its inevitable village required long-term investment, which mill owners protected with paternalistic control. Not only was the manufacturer the sole owner of the mill village, he was also its most permanent resident. "The operatives and overseers are only sojourners," the pamphleteer continued. "Not a man employed in the village expects to live and die [there]. . . . The capitalists are the parents of the village; they have called it into being, and they are responsible for its character, as truly as the parent for the character of his children."[47]

Respectable, well-maintained villages made good business sense: neatness, propriety, and tasteful arrangement attracted the most intelligent and dependable workers. The arrangement minimized mill town social strife, maximized productivity, and allowed small manufacturers to match the righteous propaganda of the boardinghouse mills north of them. Yet few villages were ideal; conditions varied widely, reflecting the mill owner's personality, the relative success of his business, and the type of workers he engaged. If the mill was sold to a new owner, the village that came with it was often refurbished to suit his taste.

The family labor system preferred in southern New England spawned a permanent class of factory workers moving at will from one mill town to another. Though their employment at a given mill was often temporary, their dependence on the factory system was not. Workers had few alternatives. The work was demanding, poorly paid, and dangerous, but they could not always do better. A life spent in a mill had its drawbacks, as Thomas Man, an eccentric Rhode Island poet, described in his curious epic, *Picture of a Factory Village*:

> There's nothing strange in his features,
> Looks like other Fact'ry creatures.
> Our life's in danger, exposed to constant harm,
> The wheels tear the hand, picker takes off an arm.
> A handsome girl is caught in a cursed drum,
> Dash'd from things of sense, into the world to come.
> Who would spend their time in such a place?
> Worse than Bastile—Inquisition of our race.[48]

Wages were generally lower than in northern mills. Male workers averaged $4.50 per week in 1830. Women earned two dollars, and children, sixty-seven

Globe Village, Mass., ca. 1822, eight years after the mill (center) was begun. The site was just upstream from South-bridge, on the Blackstone River. (Jacob Edwards Memorial Library, Southbridge, Mass.)

Harrisville, N.H. This midcentury view shows the modest scale and informal organization of the community built by the Harris family around their mill (lower right). The Harris family homes (upper center) overlook the village. A church, boardinghouse, and storehouses flank the mill pond (left). Although isolated in the hills of southern New Hampshire, Harrisville was a classic Rhode Island style village. (Historic American Engineering Record)

North Adams, Mass., in 1841, when it was just a village in a valley. (Boston Athenaeum)

cents. Although these modest earnings were spent at the low prices of the times—beef cost eight cents a pound, and three cents bought a glass of beer—mill wages rarely equalled the cost of living. Wages were often paid in credit, redeemable at the company store.

Mill stores served company interests by minimizing cash flow and making the indebted workers more dependent on the factory. Wide abuse of the practice justified its infamy. Work contracts required employees to make all purchases at the mill store. One Rhode Island mill posted a typical warning:

> *Notice. Those employed at these mills and works will take notice, that a store is kept for their accommodation, where they can purchase the best goods at fair prices and it is expected that all will draw their goods from said store. Those who do not are informed that there are plenty of others who would be glad to take their place at less wages.*[49]

Residence in company housing was mandatory and was usually accepted without resistance. While mill towns offered no alternatives, the housing they constructed was as good as unskilled workers could find elsewhere. Rents ranged from thirty-five to sixty-seven cents a week in 1826 and were still a bargain at fifty dollars a year in 1850.

Some mill owners deliberately spaced their housing for the most rustic and pleasing effect so that "a halo of neatness and salubrity pervades the village." In a rare first-hand account, dated 1847, T. Throstle, with some simplicity, described the ideal arrangement:

> *Sometimes it is a substantial stone-mill, seated on a level spot, just at the head of a beautiful valley, with pleasant dwellings, not clumped together, but scattered about it, each in the midst of a little clump of fruit trees, and high rocky hills, almost covered with trees, in the background, and a broad pond of smooth water stretching away between the opening hills.*[50]

Other mill towns grouped housing in classical rows near the mill. Few examples of either arrangement were perfect. Throstle observed an equally typical mill at Ponangansett, Rhode Island:

> *The dwelling-houses of the village form the least pleasing part of these scenes. They are crowded together close to the road on both sides of the bridge. They have no door-yards enclosed, their front doors open strait into the street, and back of the houses there is an open space common to them all, flanked by the pig-styes and cow-sheds. . . . The whole group has a slovenly appearance, and seems unfavorable to habits of tidiness or feelings of home. This bare, exposed appearance of the houses is characteristic of the factory villages generally. . . .*[51]

Throughout this period of rapid growth, Zachariah Allen represented the best qualities of the Rhode Island system. His extensive journals and publications give an unusually intimate view of an active, dedicated manufacturer. Allen converted the "solitary place" he bought for his first mill at Allendale in 1822 into "an industrious little village" with a stone chapel and a Sunday school, where "efforts were made to improve the men and the females there,

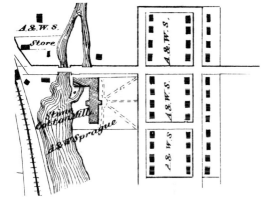

Arctic, R.I., as enlarged by the A. & W. Sprague Company after 1850. Three rows of workers' housing are to the right of the factory. Overseers' houses and the store are across the river from it. The A. & W. Sprague firm spanned three generations, beginning with William Sprague II, who built a mill at Cranston, R.I., in 1808. His sons Amasa and William III took over at his death in 1836 and continued the expansion he had begun. Amasa was murdered on New Year's Eve, seven years later, possibly as vengeance for the prohibition of liquor in his villages. William then ran the company alone, expanding control to nine mill villages before his death in 1856, when his son William IV and his nephew Amasa II took command. When the firm crashed into bankruptcy in the Panic of 1873, its losses reached $20 million. (Beers, Atlas of Rhode Island)

TOP: Sprague cloth label showing Arctic, R.I. Another version of this label shows monitor roofs on both mills across the river. (M V T M). CENTER: The Eldon Steam Mills, a cloth label. BOTTOM: Cloth label for a steam mill in Pawtucket, R.I., named in honor of Samuel Slater. (Both, Rhode Island Historical Society)

by courses of evening lectures and by the donation of instruction books." He called his travels from his home in Providence to Allendale "lonely pilgrimages to this Mecca of Worldly Toils."[52]

When Allen found he and other nearby manufacturers were losing money during the dry season, he organized the first reservoir company (1823), noting in passing that dry season unemployment reduced workers to "poverty and distress" that forced mill owners to extend them credit at the company store "in order to retain them for service . . . The heads of the families were thus brought into debt by their employers, which hopelessly depressed them, and then the manufacturers found it unavoidably requisite to cancel the debts due for the supplies of the poor families. In this way the profits of the manufacturers were diminished."[53]

During the 1830s, Allen organized the Manufacturers Mutual Fire Insurance Company—the first to use on-site inspection of insured factories—and experimented with steam engines and belt drive systems, all of which had profound effects on mill design. By 1853, he was ready for further expansion of his holdings. He bought an old mill at Georgiaville, Rhode Island, and designed a handsome new Greek Revival mill to go beside it. Having spent two hundred thousand dollars on the new mill by 1855, he remarked in his diary: "The magnitude of the works which I have executed there begin now to excite my astonishment at my own temerity in having adventured upon so bold an undertaking." He consoled himself with this reasoning:

In many of the acts of mankind, I feel impressed with the belief that individuals are urged on by instinctive feelings to fulfill a destiny originally designed by the Creator for extending the means of subsistence to increasing numbers of human beings. Without being actuated by a desire to accumulate money, but merely from a propensity to active business in engineering, I have doubtless been instrumental in furnishing employment to three or four hundred of my fellow human beings in the vicinity of the Woonasquatucket River for a Thousand years to come.[54]

Zachariah Allen, inventor, scientist, philosopher, and manufacturer, 1795–1882. (Greene, Providence Plantations)

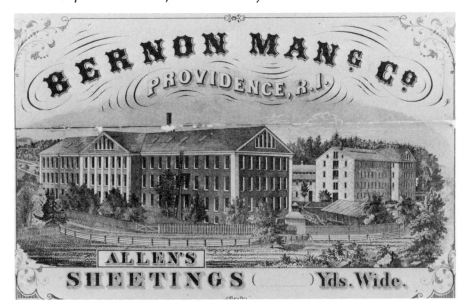

Mills of the Bernon Manufacturing Company at Woonsocket, R.I., cloth label. At right, the 1827 mill. At left, the Greek Revival mill of 1833, one of the most substantial and elegant in Rhode Island at this time. (Rhode Island Historical Society)

THE BLACKSTONE VALLEY

Blackstone Valley cotton mills, ca. 1844.

Mill town development reflected the natural dispersion of waterpower sites: each watershed bred a distinct mill town pattern. The most pronounced development occurred along the Blackstone River. The Blackstone Canal opened the area for rapid industrialization in 1828. By 1844, ninety-four cotton factories lined the banks of the river as it flowed fifty miles from Worcester, Massachusetts, to Pawtucket, Rhode Island. It became "the best harnessed river in the United States." Pawtucket, where the river met tide-water, and Central Falls, just upstream, offered a tightly spaced group of privileges. Although the Pawtucket community predated the textile industry, it eventually gave itself almost completely to it, as did Central Falls. Together, though remaining politically separate, the two communities formed a continuous urban-industrial environment packed with mills.

The waterpower configuration at Woonsocket, eighteen miles upstream, had superficial similarities to Lowell, though in miniature; but its evolution was vastly different—and typically Rhode Island. In both cases, a canal crossed a bend in a river below an important waterfall. At Woonsocket, the Blackstone River dropped thirty-nine feet within a mile, the main fall being

A romantic view of mills along the Blackstone River. (Rhode Island Historical Society)

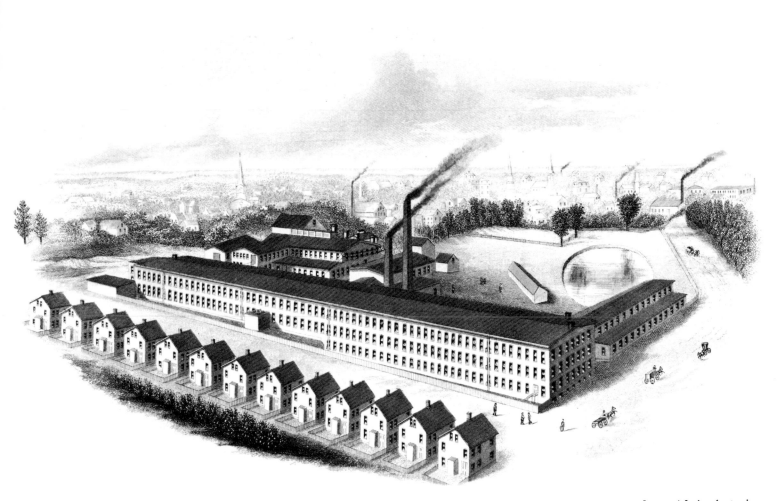

ABOVE: The Fales and Jenks Machine Shop, Pawtucket, R.I. This shop made spinning frames (see page 43) and worked to perfect Thorpe's ring spinning mechanism. (Van Slyck, Manufacturers) BELOW: Pawtucket, R.I., in 1836. Tidewater navigation ends at Pawtucket Falls, just right of center. Factories line the banks of the river near the falls. Pawtucket, with its factories, was a close ally of nearby Providence, where banking and mercantile interests, machinists and steam engine builders, manufacturers and politicians were concentrated. The two cities were the foci of the Rhode Island system. (White, Samuel Slater)

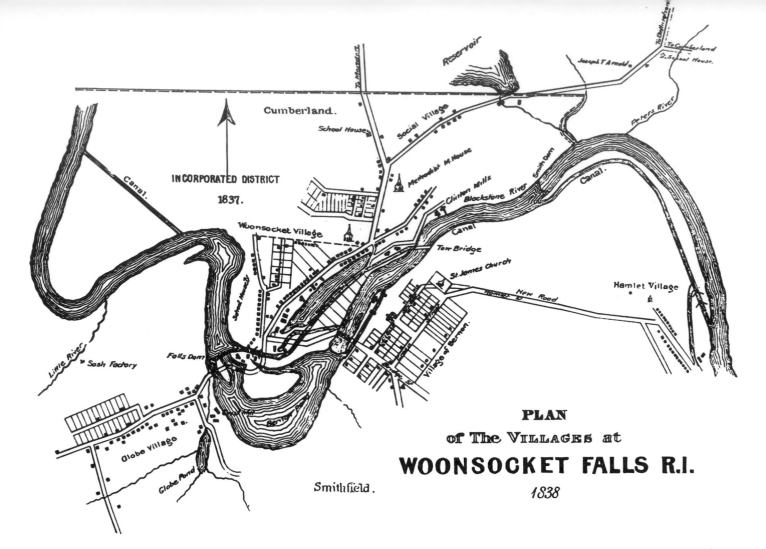

PLAN
of The Villages at
WOONSOCKET FALLS R.I.
1838

Map of Woonsocket Falls, R.I., 1838, showing five of the six villages. Jenksville lies just outside the map on Social Street, to the northeast. In this map the Blackstone River flows from top left to bottom right. Each curve of the river is traversed by a section of the Blackstone Canal. (History of Cumberland)

followed by two secondary ones. The Blackstone Canal cut across two opposite peninsulas in the undulating river, offering ample power for several factories around the upper falls and a smaller ration for the downstream section. Several other sites were available on the Mill and Peters rivers, nearby tributaries to the Blackstone. Despite the number of waterpower opportunities within walking distance of each other, the total power available was barely one-quarter that at Lowell. Yet Woonsocket's power, though limited and irregular, was easy for small companies to harness. Several independent companies staked their claims at the most important falls, and six distinct villages grew around them.

Woonsocket Falls Village was the pioneer. It grew up along the upstream canal, expanding from one factory and sixteen houses in 1820 to become a "large and thriving village" a decade later, boasting eight factories, sixty houses, eleven stores, a bank, and a post office. The mills here were powered by a trench running from the uppermost lock parallel to the canal. Mills were spaced along the island in between the trench and the canal, as at several of the larger mill cities. Since the trench ran under the main street, the village had the unusual situation of a row of mills opposite a row of shops.

While Woonsocket Falls Village was growing, the Social Manufacturing Company built Social Village, almost within shouting distance, but just far enough away to be separate. This village quickly grew to include twelve double cottages, fourteen four-family houses, two large tenement blocks, and a boardinghouse—all company-owned. The Globe, Bernon, Hamlet, and Jenksville communities soon joined these two pioneers. While each village grew, Woonsocket Falls retained its lead, the others becoming its satellites. Eventually, the six villages merged to create a city with no unifying plan.

The industrialization of the Blackstone was the pride of Rhode Island. Yet the factories themselves had serious shortcomings. James Montgomery, a mill agent for the York Manufacturing Company, described the area for British readers in 1844: "The whole of the cotton factories throughout this district, from Blackstone to Pawtucket, are of an inferior grade; much of the machinery is old and dirty, while the work is deficient in both quantity and quality."[55] Montgomery found only two mills worth calling "modern": one at Woonsocket, the other at Lonsdale. The Blackstone valley pattern was repeated, on a smaller level, on dozens of modest New England rivers: most notably the Woonasquatuckett (fourteen mill towns in sixteen miles), the Pawtuxet, and the Pawcatuck in Rhode Island; and the Quinebaug, Shetucket, and Hockanum in Connecticut.

ABOVE: *Clinton Mill and its housing; Woonsocket, R.I., ca. 1860. Social Village, in the background, is close by, but still separate from Clinton. When the railroad was built, the station was put across from the mill, making Clinton and Depot Square the hub of the town.* BELOW: *Social Mills, ca. 1860. (Both, Geldard, Cotton Manufacture)*

Boston Associates

A small elite of aristocratic Federalists dominated large-scale manufacturing between 1820 and 1860. This group, known as the Boston Associates, formed itself around the principal Waltham investors. During the years of Lowell's growth, it expanded to include approximately fifteen of Boston's most influential capitalists representing the city's most prominent families, among them Jackson, Appleton, Lawrence, Cabot, Lowell, Dwight, Amory, and Lyman.

The Boston Associates were the vanguard of New England capitalism. Manufacturing was only one of several means to their goal of maximum profit. They ruled from the stock exchange, their home turf, controlling 40 percent of Boston's banking, 77 percent of its fire insurance, 41 percent of its marine insurance, and nearly one-third of Massachusetts rail mileage. Several of the Associates gained political power to match, prompting Theodore Parker to write in 1845:

> *This class is the controlling one in politics. . . . It can manufacture governors, senators, judges, to suit its purposes, as easily as it can manufacture cloth. This class owns the machinery of society.*[56]

The Associates expanded their domain outward from Lowell to include ten of New England's most important waterpower sites, controlling one-fifth of America's cotton industry. Although unable to monopolize the industry, they were stronger than any combination of competitors. They began few communities of their own, preferring to take control of pioneering companies at valuable sites by stock manipulations during periods of financial distress. Though not uniformly profitable, their investments were always cunning.

The Associates selected Nashua, New Hampshire, as their first target for expansion outside of Lowell. Nashua presided over two excellent mill privileges on the Nashua River near its confluence with the Merrimack twelve miles north of Lowell. Here, Daniel Abbott, a local lawyer, had already begun construction of a speculative industrial complex. Organized as the Nashua Manufacturing Company, Abbott built a three-mile canal to power mills at the upper privilege and sold the lower privilege to the Indian Head Company for a woolen mill. By 1825 the machine shop and one mill at each privilege were complete. Abbott intended to copy Lowell, with its boardinghouses and promotional real estate system, and made some effort to plan the streets and housing around which the community would eventually grow. But inadequate construction and slipshod engineering made Nashua one of the least successful textile enterprises in northern New England.

Within four years of its incorporation, the Indian Head Company hung on the brink of financial disaster. The Boston Associates bought control at bargain prices, reorganized the business, renamed it in honor of P. T. Jackson, and then resold it two years later in 1831 for a substantial profit. Unfortunately, new investors in the Jackson Company didn't know that higher dams at Lowell would soon back water up against their lowest wheels. Manufac-

The Jackson Company, Nashua, N.H., ca. 1846. The site was originally owned by the Indian Head Company, then reorganized and named after P. T. Jackson. Both companies made woolens. (Fox, History of Dunstable)

TOP LEFT: *Patrick Tracy Jackson, 1780–1847, agent at Waltham and promoter of Lowell and Nashua.* (Illustrated History of Lowell, M V T M)

TOP CENTER: *Nathan Appleton, 1779–1861. "Accident, and not effort, has made me a rich man."* (Winthrop, Memoir of Nathan Appleton)

TOP RIGHT: *Amos Lawrence, 1786–1852, financier and philanthropist.* (Daguerreotype, Boston Athenaeum)

LEFT: *Abbott Lawrence, 1792–1855, manufacturer and statesman, candidate for vice-president, and ambassador to England. "How great is the responsibility of a rich man!"*

turing at Nashua would continue, but it never showed special promise. The Boston Associates moved on to more lucrative ventures.

The business depression that prostrated Nashua in 1829 was equally disastrous for an ambitious power project at Saco, Maine. Development around the forty-two foot waterfall near tidewater had begun four years before under the aegis of the Saco Manufacturing Company. The small merchants and professionals who controlled the company lacked experience and capital to carry out their grandiose plans. Poor engineering plagued construction of their first mill, which rose seven stories above a 210- by 47-foot foundation, the largest factory ever attempted in its time. The mill stood incomplete during the depression and burned to the ground a year later. A few months after the fire, the Boston Associates bought the 1700 horsepower privilege, with associated canals and real estate, at auction for sixty thousand dollars.

In 1831, the Associates formed the York Manufacturing Company to exploit these assets and began plans to develop Saco into another Lowell. Dur-

Mill view at Great Falls, N.H., ca. 1845. James Montgomery reported effusively: "This is one of the pleasantest and most beautiful manufacturing villages I have ever seen. . . . Along the outside of the Main Street are the boarding houses or dwelling houses for the Mill workers; these are neat brick buildings, three stories in height, and each building contains four tenements: there are seven of these boarding houses, set at equal distance from each other, which gives to the whole an appearance of neatness and uniformity. The Main Street, the Canal, and the Mills, are running in parallel lines with a large open area between them, and have a most delightful effect upon the mind of a stranger when he first enters the village. The whole plan of the village displays good taste, and its general appearance is delightful and beautiful in the highest degree." Note the similarity of foreground figures to the view of Dutton St., Lowell, page 28. (Boston Athenaeum)

ing the period of rapid expansion that followed, they used their immense capital to get power and construction concessions from desperate local promoters, reaping substantial profits along the way.

Similar stock manipulations extended Boston interests into New Hampshire at Great Falls and Dover. Of all the New Hampshire holdings, Manchester was the prize. Here the Merrimack River dropped fifty feet through "hideous rapids" at Amoskeag Falls—providing power for more than one hundred mills. Along the desolate east bank, the Amoskeag Manufacturing Company had started a grand system of power canals modeled on Lowell. Early investors included Samuel Slater and other Rhode Islanders. Careful plans were drawn for expansion of the site into a complete industrial city. But the sheer magnitude of the undertaking required high capitalization, and it provided the opportunity for the Boston Associates to purchase controlling interest in the company by 1836. Under their direction, Amoskeag eventually developed into the largest and most prestigious textile complex in New England.

Meanwhile, a company town called Cabotville was awakening just above

the confluence of the Chicopee and Connecticut rivers. George White included this description of the site in his Slater memoir:

> *Streets are cut in every direction and dwellings and shops are going up as if by some magic influence. . . . The water power at this site is immense; and as yet, scarcely begun to be occupied. There is a neatness, too, and good taste in the location of the streets and the arrangement of the buildings, which reflects great credit upon those who have superintended the arrangement. The cotton factories are extensive, and in appearance resembling those at Lowell.*[57]

The resemblance to Lowell was hardly surprising, considering that its local promoter was Edmund Dwight (Timothy's cousin), an in-law of Henry Cabot and Thomas Perkins, his Boston collaborators. Three companies—the Dwight, the Cabot, and the Perkins—presided over this village of fourteen mills. Cabotville was a minor gem of Boston style. The village eventually became part of Chicopee, Massachusetts.

The York Company mills, Saco, Me. Tidewater navigation reaches the factory site, facilitating transportation of raw materials and products. Frontispiece for James Montgomery's Practical Detail of the Cotton Manufacture, 1840. Montgomery had been the York Company agent.

Northern view of Cabotville, Mass., in 1838, when the community had about 2,000 inhabitants. (Barber, Massachusetts)

NEW CITIES: LAWRENCE AND HOLYOKE

During the prosperous years between 1843 and 1847, stock in Boston-owned mills paid dazzling dividends and traded at high premiums. Investors eager to share the profits crowded the stock market, offering their capital to fuel another wave of expansion. Most of these investors knew nothing about manufacturing. They wagered blindly on the industry's leaders.

In 1845, Abbott Lawrence shepherded a group of potential investors to Bodwell's Falls, twelve miles below Lowell on the Merrimack. He was there to charm them into his new venture: the Essex Company. After hearing Lawrence's plan for an imperial manufacturing city tentatively named "Merrimack" (but later named for the Lawrence family), the guests perambulated the grounds, then repaired to a local inn and drank repeated toasts to his wisdom and boldness. The new city, they agreed, would be the queen of mill towns.

Isometric view of the Bay State Mills, Lawrence, Mass., with housing at rear, as planned in 1846. By 1855, the factories and three of the four housing blocks were complete. Each block is divided into 8 sections, each containing 14 bedrooms and housing 36 mill worker boarders. Sewage from boardinghouse privies is piped into the canal at the far right. (M V T M)

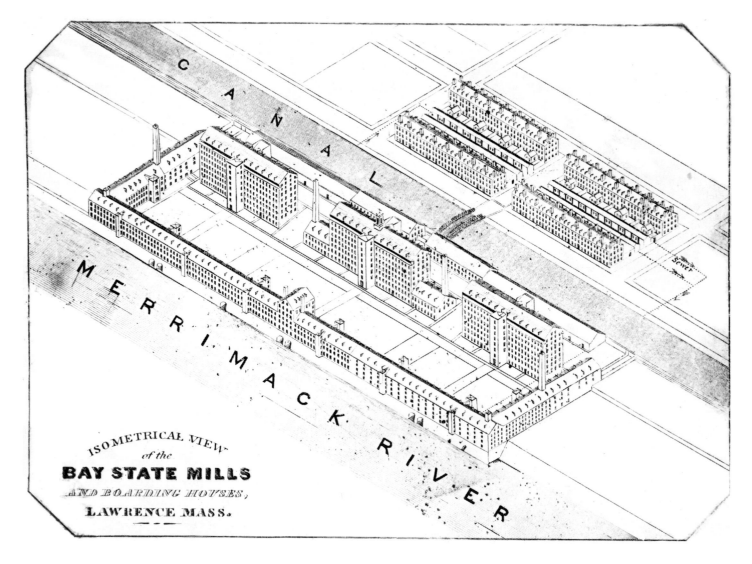

Here the situation was unique: power and opportunity were combined in a totally virgin location. No one had ever tried to harness the river here because there were no partial solutions. The eleven thousand horsepower potential of the site could be exploited only by constructing the largest dam yet attempted on the Merrimack, a 1,629-foot granite arc twenty-six feet high. A million dollar capitalization equipped the Essex Company to begin the daring scheme, but many times that amount would eventually be needed to use the location fully. The venture assumed that additional investment would pour into Lawrence as it had Lowell.

The Essex Company built a skeleton city between 1845 and 1849. Charles Bigelow, the superintendent and on-site engineer, directed the Irish workers

Pastoral view of Lawrence, Mass., ca. 1855, looking west from near the reservoir.

Detail of the same view. The huge Lawrence Machine Shop is in the foreground, left of center. The housing for its mechanics is two blocks northeast (right) of it, within easy walking distance. Mills lining the canal behind the Machine Shop are, from left to right, the Pemberton, the three Bay State Mills, and the Atlantic Cotton Mills. The Pacific Mills are out of sight behind the Atlantic buildings. Long, low rows of mill housing are across the canal from the factories. The tower at center marks City Hall. (Both, M V T M)

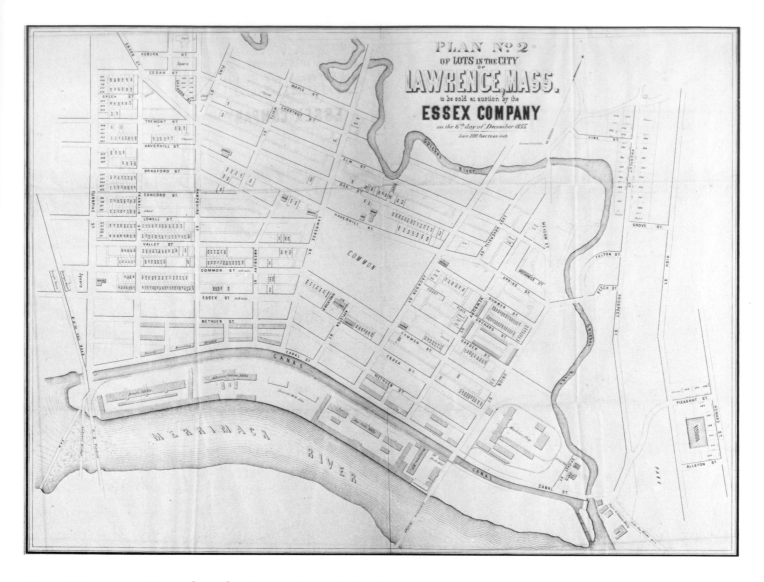

Map of Lawrence, Mass., 1855, showing lots to be auctioned by the Essex Company. The long, narrow mill island between the canal and the river allows the most economical placement of the factories upon it —from left to right, the Pacific Mills, the Atlantic Mills, a vacant site later occupied by the Lower Pacific Mill, the Bay State Mills (later reorganized as the Washington Mills), the Pemberton Mill, and the tiny Duck Mill. The Machine Shop lies between the canal and the Spicket River (right). The reservoir, from which the preceding views are drawn, is at the extreme right. (MVTM)

who built the dam, a huge power canal, and factories for Essex's two manufacturing subsidiaries, the Atlantic Cotton Mills and the Bay State Mills. Near the end of the canal rose the mammoth Lawrence Machine Shop, intended to earn equally large profits by building and equipping new mills.

Bigelow's work followed a detailed plan for a complete city designed by Charles Storrow, a waterpower engineer and Essex Company treasurer. Substantial company housing was provided close to the gently curving power canal. The rest of the company land was blocked off into residential and commercial districts and sold in parcels to adventurers who wanted to join the city. The company laid out streets and parks and promoted churches, schools, municipal buildings, and a library. A grand boulevard, named Essex Street after its patron, stretched parallel to the canals to serve the business district. Strict zoning regulated the buildings along it.

But market conditions reversed soon after Lawrence began. A severe depression replaced the years of prosperity that had spawned the city. Squeezed between high prices for raw cotton, low product demand, and excess production capacity, New England mills paid dearly for their overexpansion. By 1850, coarse sheeting, the staple product of the northern mills, was selling at

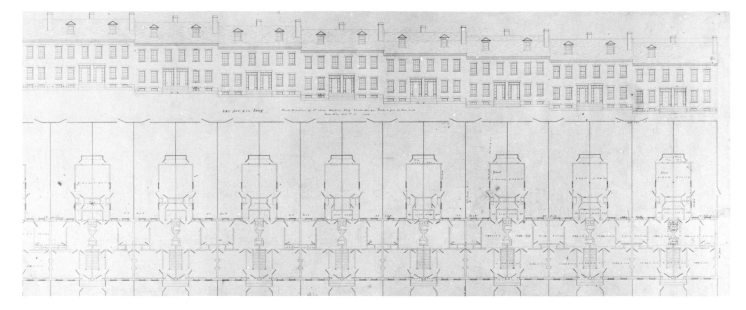

seven percent *below* mass-production cost. At the end of the year, *Scientific American* reported,

> The once busy wheel, which gave motion to thousands of spindles and hundreds of shuttles, stands gloomy and motionless, like a worn-out warsteed. . . . From Rhode Island, that busy cotton cloth-making hive, we learn that about seventy factories have stopped; from Lowell and the eastern manufacturing villages, we hear the same ominous reports.[58]

Lawrence was born at the worst possible time. Predicated on expansionist economics, the city had little choice but to continue. The Essex Company promoted two new mills, the Pacific (1852) and the Pemberton (1854), to bring business to the idle machine shop, but the stock wouldn't sell. The Boston Associates in general, and Abbott Lawrence in particular, were forced to increase their stake in Lawrence and underwrite its growth. Abbott Lawrence's personal investments in the ill-fated city exceeded one million dollars.

The monetary crisis of 1857 burst the Lawrence bubble. Unable to find new credit, the Pemberton and Bay State Mills and the Machine Shop went bankrupt at a 4.35 million dollar loss. The Essex and the Pacific companies lost another 1.5 million dollars. Lawrence became a six-million dollar disaster.

Holyoke, the sister city of Lawrence, fared no better. Here, a few miles north of Cabotville, the Connecticut River had tempted speculators to harness New England's grandest waterpower as it crashed sixty-five feet down Hadley Falls and subsequent rapids. Even at low water, more than fifty thousand horsepower awaited. As at Lawrence, full use of the river required the vast capital and daring speculation that only the Boston Associates could provide.

Led by Edmund Dwight of Cabotville, the Boston Associates took over the Hadley Falls Company, a local venture that had made partial use of its

Front view and ground plan for Machine Shop housing at Lawrence, Mass. Skilled and indispensable, the machinists rated more spacious housing than the mill workers who ran the machines. (M V T M)

ABOVE: The dam at Hadley Falls, Mass.,
as rebuilt after the fiasco of 1848. The dam
is 35 feet high, 2,000 feet long, and con-
trols an 8,000-square-mile watershed. Generating an average of 20,000 horsepower
year round, the dam could harness over
35,000 horsepower during high water. The
sloping front section was added in 1868 to
reduce erosion of the river bed. (Holyoke
Water Power Co.)

RIGHT: Map of Holyoke, Mass., as planned
by the Hadley Falls Company, ca. 1847.
Shading indicates the canals. Water is used
first by factories beside the straight upper
canal (center) and emptied into a common tailrace canal running parallel to it.
This lower canal leads the water back towards the river, then curves around between
the Machine Shop and mechanics' housing
before continuing on to feed a second string
of factories (bottom) between it and the
river bank below the rapids. Land is reserved for two boardinghouse blocks opposite each factory site. (Green, Holyoke)

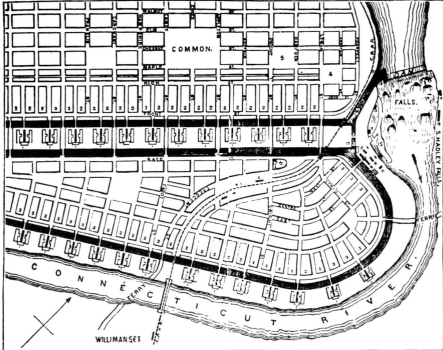

privilege. They reorganized the company and capitalized it at $2.5 million. As the construction began in 1847, the Chicopee *Telegraph* prophesied, "We may safely say that no enterprise has yet been undertaken in the United States combining so many advantages and so many elements of future greatness."[59]

Irish laborers started construction of the two-thousand-foot dam and carved a two-level canal system into the land enclosed by the river bend. A grid of city streets was laid out, with east-west streets named for the company directors and north-south streets named for Massachusetts counties. The dam was completed in November of 1848. Company officials, invited guests, and townspeople gathered to watch it fill up. Their applause for this newest Yankee triumph over nature changed to terror as one leak after another appeared. The river rose behind the flimsy wooden structure, nearing its boiler-plate lip. Suddenly, it broke through, carrying everything before it away in a "magnificent and frightful" torrent of flotsam.

With undiminished optimism based on predepression prosperity, the Hadley Falls Company began a new stone dam, which held firm. By 1850 the first two factories—the turbine-powered Lyman Mills—were finished, and Holyoke became an incorporated city. It was an inauspicious year to begin. Twenty-four of the twenty-five mill sites lay vacant. The Hadley Company had no market for its real estate or waterpower, nor work for its machine shop. Holyoke had barely 3,700 residents, including 1,000 company employees and 120 paupers. The first of several cholera epidemics had already swept the city.

The Boston Associates launched a vigorous campaign to recruit new capital, simultaneously expanding their own interests with another cotton mill. Their efforts brought in two paper mills, the forerunners of an industry that would eventually dominate the city. But disaster struck when the Hadley Falls Company's main source of credit went bankrupt in 1857. The city proved unable to support its creator. The bankrupt company and its three million dollar assets brought only $325,000 at auction the next year.

The Lawrence and Holyoke disasters cost the Boston Associates and their followers over ten million dollars. Clearly, something had gone terribly wrong. Private correspondence between the promoters at Holyoke analyzed the debacle:

> There was an original error of judgment on the part of the leaders of this enterprise, and also on the part of those who took the stock, as to want of, or the call for, such a mighty power. . . . I presume that a large part of the subscribers, did in a large measure, base that belief upon that of their leaders, in whose combined prudence and energy they placed great confidence. . . . And all were mistaken . . . so far as we had any ideas of our own that there was or would be a use for the vast water power, early enough to reimburse the outlay.[60]

Commenting on the losses at the Pacific Mill, "which was got up by Mr. Abbott Lawrence as a sort of glorious achievement of Manufacturing Magnificence," Zachariah Allen observed: "Dearly did he pay for this vainglorious indulgence of his pride."[61]

Carpet manufacturer Erastus Bigelow blamed the whole joint-stock corporation system for the recent disasters. Bigelow believed that industrial growth should proceed along a natural course in which "every new undertaking should surpass its predecessors in the simplicity and economy of its arrangements, and the efficiency of its action." He admired the success and stability of privately owned factories in southern New England and Great Britain that followed this pattern. "Lawrence, the latest and most complete experiment in corporation enterprise, should have been its greatest success and its crowning triumph," he argued. "How far from this it actually is, I need not say."[62]

Bigelow characterized the corporate system as inherently expansionist. Overdependent on outside capital, the textile industry could no longer manage its affairs in its own best interest. Factories had become pawns in much larger capitalistic schemes. The corporation system magnified the changing mood of the stock market and suffered from excessive feedback, both positive and negative:

> It precludes the only growth that is desirable—a natural and continuous one. Under it, all efforts for extension, for diversification and improvement, are inevitably periodical, and, for that reason, comparatively ineffective. It

Erastus A. Bigelow, 1814–1879, carpet manufacturer and inventor. The jacquard-woven upholstery of his armrest represents his product. (Lowell Historical Society)

induces periods of excessive activity, followed, necessarily, by periods of undue rest.[63]

Paroxysms of corporate expansion were further hindered by exuberant profit-taking, absentee management, inexperienced direction, shortages of skilled labor, inadequate market analysis, and a consequent overconcentration on a single low-profit product. From this "artificial and incongruous" position, the huge new corporations started operation with handicaps unseen in more modest ventures. Bigelow saw these disadvantages to be "not accidental or temporary: they spring from the system and must ever attend it."[64]

The Bigelow pamphlet noted that "capitalists who have invested under the stimulus of high profits are impatient for results, and urge [the manufacturer] to hasty action or ill considered plans."[65] The Holyoke Dam was an early example. The prophetic truth of Bigelow's observation became appallingly clear on the tenth of January, 1860, when the Pemberton Mill at Lawrence collapsed with terrific suddenness, trapping nine hundred workers, most of them women, in less than sixty seconds. Rescue efforts had barely

Cartoon from Vanity Fair, *entitled "The Building of the Pemberton Mills."*

HARPER'S WEEKLY.

A JOURNAL OF CIVILIZATION.

VOL. IV.—No. 160.]   NEW YORK, SATURDAY, JANUARY 21, 1860.   [PRICE FIVE CENTS.

Entered according to Act of Congress, in the Year 1860, by Harper & Brothers, in the Clerk's Office of the District Court for the Southern District of New York.

RUINS OF THE PEMBERTON MILLS, AT LAWRENCE, MASSACHUSETTS, THE MORNING AFTER THE FALL.—[FROM A PHOTOGRAPH BY WHIPPLE, OF BOSTON.]

begun when fire broke out in the wreckage. Eighty-eight deaths and 275 injuries were finally counted.

Subsequent investigations revealed that cast iron pillars of mediocre quality within the mill had caused the collapse. Although extensive testimony was taken from all witnesses, contractors, and Pemberton authorities, no irrefutable evidence of corporate negligence was produced. Some contemporary accounts of the collapse, however, report that sample pillars that had failed preliminary testing were installed anyway, and never replaced. Other evidence suggested that the mill had even more extensive defects when completed in 1854—that its floors were too weak for machines, its workrooms lacked fire sprinklers, and even the waterwheel was improperly installed. The mill, then, had needed expensive alterations. Some were attempted, others ignored.

After the disasters at Holyoke and Lawrence, public opinion turned against the Boston Associates. Their era of textile influence was over. Members of the group and their descendants were still to play prominent roles, however, in other industries. General Electric, American Telephone & Telegraph, and Western Electric are part of their legacy. These early capitalists left behind a mammoth system for textile manufacturing tragically ill-suited to the industrial realities of the period. Yet their bankrupt cities did not dissolve into the dust from which they had come. They continued to grow, with their long-lived factories and machines, and occasionally they prospered.

Labor

THE FACTORY CONTROVERSY

Faced with accelerating industrial expansion, New Englanders began a vigorous public debate on the role and responsibility of the factory. Few realized that industrial imperatives alone would determine the outcome.

Rhode Island mills, with their working families and child labor, showed the earliest signs of labor degradation. Initially, rapid turnover of mill girls camouflaged the long-term effects of factory life further north. But intense industrial competition soon made speedups and increased work loads inevitable there, too. Real wages dropped, and working conditions grew worse. By 1828, when the Waltham-style industry's first tentative strike ruffled the Cocheco Mills in Dover, New Hampshire, the change had begun. Abortive strikes during the next decade marked its spread through the mill cities.

Accusations of declining conditions became public in 1839 as a series of articles in the Boston *Times* claimed that mill workers worked "incessantly," without improving themselves, to one end: "When they can toil no longer, [they] go home to die." A local doctor reported venereal disease among the mill girls. Other observers said the Lowell brothels lured mill girls into the profession. *The Lowell Offering* and other industrial apologists answered these charges, insisting that mill girls were as independent, virtuous, and healthy as always. Dr. Elisha Bartlett, Lowell's first mayor, described their salutorious life:

OPPOSITE: *The wreckage of the Pemberton Mills, Harper's Weekly, 21 January 1860. The accompanying text, titled "The Slaughter at Lawrence," read:*

"*Society is unanimous in its verdict on the terrible disaster at Lawrence; every one denounces the builder and the proprietors of the Pemberton Mills. It may be, of course, that the information on which this opinion is based is erroneous. There may be exaggeration in the stories which are circulated with regard to the insecurity of its owners. If so, the parties in interest will naturally clear their skirts as speedily as possible. Meanwhile it is asserted, without substantial contradiction, that the Pemberton Mills were regarded from the first as an unsafe and unstable edifice; that, some years since, extraordinary measures were required to keep the walls together; and that experienced builders had long prophesied their downfall. If the evidence bears out these assertions a responsibility at which all good men shudder weighs on the proprietors of these mills; they are, in fact, before God and man, guilty of the deaths of some two hundred innocent creatures.*"

> . . . *this state is better calculated for manufacturing than farming. This causes it to be more like England, because where manufacturing flourishes Tyranny, Oppression, and Slavery will follow. . . . As to the manner of living there is not a King on earth that can live better. We have everything to eat that a reasonable man can wish for. We have beef or pork three times a day, potatoes, cheese, butter, tea and coffee and sometimes milk. . . .*—A letter written in 1827 from South Leicester, Massachusetts to England.

They are regular in all their habits. They are early up in the morning, and early to bed at night. Their fare is plain, substantial and good, and their labor is sufficiently active and sufficiently light to avoid the evils arising from the two extremes of indolence and over-exertion. They are but little exposed to the sudden vicissitudes and to the excessive heats or colds of the seasons, and they are very generally free from anxious and depressing cares.[66]

Both sides were partly right. The apologists looked back at an idyllic age now almost over. The investigative press saw a future that had just begun.

But the conservative defense soon became untenable. Operative resistance to speedups and wage cuts spawned more frequent strikes and more explicit condemnations of factory life. Mill workers signed petitions like this one, addressed to the Massachusetts legislature in 1845:

We, the undersigned peaceable, industrious, hardworking men and women of Lowell, . . . in view of our condition—the evils already come upon us, by toiling from thirteen to fourteen hours per day, confined in unhealthy apartments, exposed to the poisonous contagion of air, vegetable, animal,

An idealized view of the Boott Mills and the genteel citizens of Lowell, from Gleason's Pictorial and Drawing Room Companion, 1852. (Boston Athenaeum)

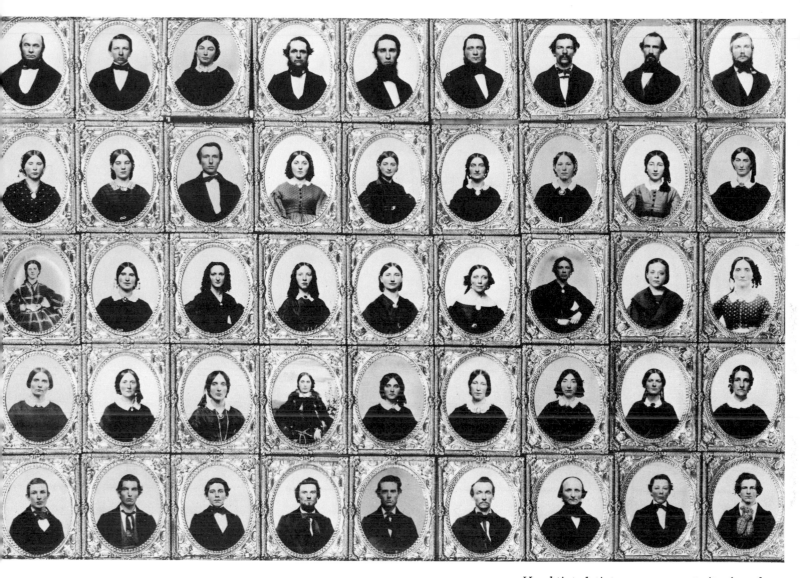

and mineral properties, debarred from proper Physical exercise, time for Mental discipline, and Mastication cruelly limited; and thereby hastening us on through pain, disease, and privation, down to a premature grave; . . . seek a redress of those evils, daily strengthening, and imposed upon us by [the corporations].[67]

Scandalous mill town housing came to light. The Lowell *Courier* found a house in the town center sheltering 120 persons of twenty-five different families. Elsewhere in Lowell, twenty-two persons of four families were found living in a single cellar. Two years later a sanitation report rated mill town conditions below those in state prisons.

Writing at Walden in 1842, Thoreau had early expressed the evolving sensibility of his time:

Hand-tinted tintype group portrait of card room employees at Mill No. 5, Amoskeag Manufacturing Company, Manchester, N.H., ca. 1855. (Manchester Historic Association)

"Their life in the factories was made pleasant to them. In those days there was no need of advocating the doctrine of the proper relation between employer and employed. Help was too valuable to be ill-treated."—*Harriet Robinson, remembering her youth at Lowell*

I cannot believe that our factory system is the best mode by which men may get clothing. The condition of the operatives is becoming everyday more like that of the English; and it cannot be wondered at since . . . the principal object is, not that mankind may be well and honestly clad, but unquestionably, that the corporations may be enriched.[68]

Revelations of fact and expressions of opinion such as this discredited the factory system by the 1850s. Few now agreed with Nathan Appleton that the industry had "added greatly to the mass of human happiness."

THE TEN HOUR STRUGGLE

In 1823, workers at the Cocheco Company of Dover, New Hampshire, signed the following agreement before employment:

We, the subscribers . . . agree to work for such wages per week, and prices by the Job, as the company may see fit to pay, and be subject to the fines, as well as entitled to the premiums paid by the company.[69]

Most mills demanded similar "free contracts," rationalizing their carte blanche control by presuming each worker to accept the work voluntarily.

Work schedule, Holyoke, Mass., 1853. (Green, Holyoke)

Industrialists saw Lowell as the culmination of this "perfect imperium in imperio"—a realm in which "absolute despotism" and "absolute democracy" coexisted. "Free subjects" could, if dissatisfied, depart at will—their places to be taken by more submissive recruits.

This may have been true during Lowell's early years. But Lowell's first strike in 1834 signaled that "perfect democracy" was already slipping away. When the Lowell management announced a fifteen percent wage cut, between eight hundred and two thousand mill girls left the factory, proclaiming solidarity against "the oppressive hand of avarice [that] would enslave [them]" and resolving, "We will not go back into the mills to work until our wages are continued as they have been."[70] Yet, after only a weekend, almost all of the participants gave way, returning to work at reduced wages.

Wage cuts at Dover and Chicopee soon followed, provoking similar turnouts, with equally humiliating results. Though better organized at each succeeding strike, the mill girls invariably returned to work. Either unwilling or unable to return home, these girls in their submission marked the beginning of an established factory class in the northern New England mills. Speedups and wage cuts continued. Work loads increased as mass production reached its stride. Facing long working hours, previously tolerable at a more leisurely pace, workers agitated for a ten-hour day.

Though prosperity returned in the early 1840s, workers who had had wage cuts were not benefited. Another wave of strikes swept the mills. Growing aware of the politics of their struggle and noting that Britain had begun to enact labor legislation, workers despaired of management philanthropy and turned to the state legislatures for protection. Labor petitions flooded the Massachusetts legislature, each longer than the one before, culminating in a regional petition in 1845: more than two thousand workers demanded the ten-hour day "in the absence of a special agreement," as if legislation could guarantee their freedom of contract.

In response, the Massachusetts legislature appointed a "Committee on Manufactures," America's first governmental investigation of industry. After enjoying a red carpet tour of Lowell, the committee, which was happily composed of management sympathizers, "returned fully satisfied that the order, decorum, and general appearance of things in and about the mills could not be improved."[71]

Astonished labor associations accused the committee of "cringing servility to corporate monopolies" and regrouped for another attack the next year with a standardized petition. Ten thousand Massachusetts workers signed the resolution "to prohibit all incorporated companies from employing one set of hands more than ten hours a day." The forty-five hundred names from Lowell filled a 130-foot scroll.

A second legislative committee rejected the petition, arguing that industrial regulation should not apply only to corporations nor abridge the workers' freedom of contract. If operatives wanted to work more than ten hours a day, the committee argued, they should be free to do so.

A ten hour law that passed the New Hampshire legislature in 1847 contained a free contract exemption for the mill owners' benefit. The *Indepen-*

The first two feet of a ten-foot petition from Fall River mill workers to the Massachusetts legislature, 1845, asking for "a law constituting Ten Hours a days work in all corporations." Only men's names appear on the scroll. (Massachusetts State Archive)

"Bell Time," a woodcut from a drawing by Winslow Homer for Harper's Weekly, 1868. The accompanying text read: "The scene sketched is at Lawrence, Massachusetts . . . but the drawing will apply to dozens of New England factory towns: the same faces, the same costumes, the same characters may be seen at 'bell-time' on the streets of every great manufacturing town in New England and the Middle States. . . . [It is drawn] with great power and effect, and his picture will provide a study to every intelligent reader." (Boston Athenaeum)

dent Democrat warned: "The ten hour law will not reduce the hours of labor. . . . Its authors did not intend any such result."[72] True to form, mill owners circulated new contracts restoring previous working hours, blacklisting those who refused to sign. Personal freedom had acquired a perverse twist for workers dependent on factory wages. Entrenched in the mills and protected by the legislatures, corporate power squashed all threats to its sovereignty.

The depression years following 1848 left labor without bargaining power. Mill town streets were "literally swarming with worthy females and laborers seeking employment." This labor surplus, a reversal of the prevailing shortage in earlier decades, put workers in competition with each other for mill jobs. Those unable to move to other towns and other industries had to accept whatever the mill owners offered. When labor agitation reappeared with the return of prosperity in 1852, it had shifted to a more political domain. Although women, children, and immigrants—the bulk of the work force—were all unable to vote, politicians could now advance their careers by opposing the discredited corporation system and promoting the interests of workers no longer daring to speak for themselves.

Corporation mills appeased their opponents by cutting the working day to eleven hours in 1853. Rhode Island passed a ten hour bill the same year. It was compulsory for children but optional for adults, and workers again signed the mill owners' contracts and returned to a twelve-hour schedule. Widespread evasions and abuse made even the child labor laws effectively optional.

IMMIGRATION

The northern mills, with their degenerating factory conditions and high labor turnover, were rapidly exhausting New England's labor supply. America was expanding rapidly, the general standard of living was rising, and unskilled labor had a widening range of alternatives to textile work. From the 1840s onward, the mills relied more and more on labor contractors, reaching deep into the hinterlands to meet their insatiable needs:

> A long, low black wagon, termed a "slaver," makes trips to the north of the State cruising around Vermont and New Hampshire with a commander who is paid $1 a head for all [the girls] he brings to the market and more in proportion to the distance—if they bring them from a distance, they cannot easily get back.[73]

Despite these efforts, more and more Yankee daughters left the mills. The first of many generations of immigrants took their places. Each group considered its move a step upward.

Irish immigrants had worked in the industry since the early days of Lowell when Kirk Boott met a group of laborers who had walked from Boston to the Merrimack. Their contract was sealed at the local tavern. A typical wage was seventy-five cents a day and three jiggers of whiskey. Excluded from company housing, Irish families gathered on unclaimed land nearby and established enclaves known variously as "The Acre," "The Patch," or "New Dublin." These improvised communities were generally crowded and sordid. In Lowell's Irish quarter, one-half of a small house sheltered seventy-two persons! Primitive sanitation bred epidemic disease with alarming frequency, hitting Irish camps hardest. By 1835, Lowell's Irish numbered about six hundred, including almost 250 who worked inside the factory at menial tasks.

The Irish had established their beachhead in the mills by 1846, when the potato famine brought thousands more to New England. Mill closings and slowdowns following the depression of 1848 put native workers on the streets. When prosperity returned, the Irish took their places. Virulent Yankee prejudice greeted these interlopers as a "sea of ignorance, swollen by waves of misery and vice." Labor organizations condemned "foreign laborers whose habits of cheap living enable them to work at very low wages." Workers at Manchester blamed management for "the recent importation of Irishmen into this place for the purpose of driving out our Yankee laborers."[74]

Yet the immigrant did not force the Yankee from the mills. Intolerable conditions did, and new trades provided other alternatives. The immigrant filled the vacancies, tending the new generation of high-speed machines,

A cartoon entitled "Paddy's ladder to wealth in a free country," 1857. Construction work was the Irishman's first opportunity for mill town employment. (Library of Congress)

which demanded tractability more than skill. The industry welcomed the proletariat it had opposed decades before. Accustomed to poor conditions in the "old country," desperate immigrants had no high expectations for the manufacturer to meet. Once accustomed to the factory, they stayed, for they could do no better. Their choices were limited, and the factory wage was a significant improvement over the economic status they had left behind.

Two weavers holding their shuttles, tintype, ca. 1865. (M V T M)

Immigrant families filled the corporation boardinghouses and presented Waltham-style mill cities with the new challenge of children. For the first time, these communities began to breed their own workers. The mill city became a blank slate that management could write on at will. Inviting Horace Mann to design an educational system for Lawrence, Charles Storrow asked:

Where else can you find as here the elements of society ready to be molded into a good or an evil state: nothing to pull down, all to build up: a whole town composed of young people to influence and train as you would a school.[75]

Mann compared the productivity of mill girls and illiterate immigrants and concluded that education had "a market value. . . . It may be turned to pecuniary advantage." The Essex Company donated land for eleven schools where teachers were advised to "assiduously teach their pupils to avoid idleness, truancy, falsehood, deceit, thieving, obscenity, profanity, and every other wicked and disgraceful practice."[76]

Mill city schools trained youth for factory life, as Slater's Sabbath schools had done. Inevitably, Waltham-style mills followed Slater's logic further and began employing immigrant children in the factory. From the 1860s onward, child labor was common throughout the New England industry.

MECHANIZATION

The factory controversy and ten hour legislation were only diversionary skirmishes, ineffective efforts to create a working arrangement for opposite and hostile parties: the central issue was the identity of the worker in an industrial society. Preindustrial America had perceived the machine as a liberator, freeing humankind from drudgery. As the machine evolved towards high-speed, continuous production, the Northeast learned it was just as naturally a tyrant. The machine's positive, life-promoting attributes were invariably accompanied by its destructive and coercive effects. Gradually the machine displaced all other sources of value, including the worker, and became the most progressive element in the new economy. Mill, town, and labor all served the machine. The mill town provided the social matrix in which the industrial worker would evolve: dependent, one-dimensional, and dehumanized. This deterministic, utilitarian world made room for little but factory life. As long as labor was transient, the mill town's socializing power was tempered. With the growth of a permanent and immobile factory class, however, the power of the machine to mold individuals and societies became inescapable.

While Americans appreciated early the "dexterity" and "magic" of machines, they slowly recognized the aggressive quality of technology—the "metallic necessity, the unbudging fatality . . . [and] the autocratic cunning" of machinery, as Melville wrote in 1855.[77] The machine made labor "the ceaseless, servile waiter of an untiring despot of iron and brass; a tyrant that has no heart to feel, no soul to pity."[78] Like many mill girls, Lucy

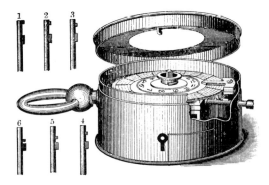

Watchman's time clock, used to guarantee that the night watch was ever vigilant. (*Knight's Mechanical Dictionary;* M V T M)

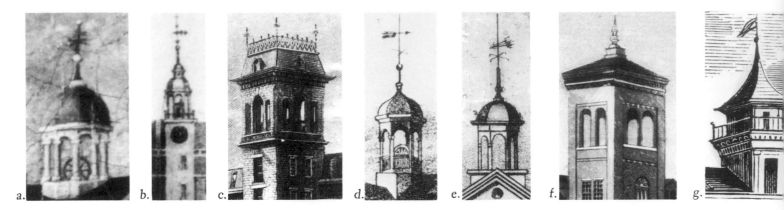

Bell towers.

a. *Boston Manufacturing Company, Waltham, Mass., 1814.*

b. *Eagle Mills, North Uxbridge, Mass., 1829.*

c. *Merchants Manufacturing Company, Fall River, Mass.*

d. *Lowell Machine Shop, Lowell, Mass., 1823.*

e. *Hamilton Mills, Lowell, Mass., 1846.*

f. *Slater Cotton Company, Pawtucket, R.I., 1869.*

g. *Eldon Steam Mills, Pawtucket, R.I.*

h. *Social Mills, Woonsocket, R.I., 1841.*

i. *York Manufacturing Company, Saco, Me., 1823.*

j. *Great Falls Manufacturing Company, Great Falls, N.H.*

k. *A. & W. Sprague Mill, Baltic, Conn.*

l. *Hockanum Mill, Rockville, Conn., 1854.*

m. *Mechanics Mills, Fall River, Mass., 1868.*

Larcom found herself driven by her machine: "The half-live creature . . . was aware of my incapacity to manage it, and had a fiendish spite against me. It was humiliating."[79]

In any mass production industry, maximum efficiency, and hence profit, is achieved by constant operation at top speed. Automation and speedups forced workers to adjust to the pace of the machine and reduced their actions

A narrow-fabric weaver winding bobbins beside her loom. This delicate woodcut by Winslow Homer is an illustration from stanza 5 of The Song of the Sower, by William Cullen Bryant.

*Fling wide the grain for those who throw
The clanking shuttle to and fro,
In the long row of humming rooms,
And into ponderous masses wind
The web that, from a thousand looms,
Comes forth to clothe mankind.*
(MVTM)

to repetitive essentials. Factory work threatened to change human beings into mechanical components of the industrial system. Traditional guidelines for human value and personal accountability did not apply in this world of piece rates and time clocks. "The laborer does not belong to himself," warned a letter to the New York *Tribune* in 1850. "[He] has no right to be, and exists but upon sufferance. He is emphatically a wage Slave."[80] Symbolizing mechanical tyranny, the factory bell regulated mill town life. Bell time gained even more perverse meaning when crafty mill owners began slowing their clocks down to artificially prolong the working day and get more value from their workers.

The industrial idyll at Lowell, where mill girls could read on the job and daydream beside the loom, was possible only in an immature industry. Such benign treatment of workers was an untenable anachronism by 1855, when a Fall River mill owner expressed a more modern contempt for labor:

> As for myself, I regard my work people just as I regard my machinery. So long as they can do my work for what I choose to pay them, I keep them, getting out of them all I can. What they do or how they fare outside my walls, I don't know, nor do I consider it my business to know. They must look out for themselves as I do for myself. When my machines get old and useless, I reject them and get new, and these people are part of my machinery.[81]

Design for a one dollar bill planned for issue by the Manufacturers Bank of Lowell, but never circulated, 1860. (Lowell Historical Society)

IV

Mature Industry

1860-1920

Fall River, Mass., 1877. (Courtesy of Goodspeed's Book Shop, Inc., Boston)

Watershed

As the nation girded itself for the Civil War, northern industry had divided allegiances. Largely dependent on slave-grown southern cotton, it had a vested interest in the outcome. Factory workers and their partisans shifted their attacks from the mill owners to their southern counterparts and allies, the slave owners, and supported Abolition more vigorously than they had the ten hour movement before it.

Textile magnates, on the other hand, sided with the South—the source of their raw materials and a segment of their market, creating what Charles Sumner called in 1848, "an unholy union or rather conspiracy between the cotton planters and flesh-mongers of Louisiana and Mississippi, and the cotton spinners and traffickers of New England—the lords of the lash and the lords of the loom."[82] Nathan Appleton, Abbott Lawrence, and their associates supported slave interests in Congress and treated plantation owners with self-serving deference.

The war forced cotton manufacturers to speculate on the future of cotton growers across the Mason-Dixon line. Neither knew how high the price of cotton would soar nor how long the war would last. Many mills gambled on a

Fire engine built by the Amoskeag Manufacturing Company. The firm built 550 of these engines between 1859 and 1876 for an international market that included Russia, Chile, Japan, and China. A contract for 25,000 Springfield muskets also helped Amoskeag survive the Civil War years, as did the manufacture of 500 McKay sewing machines. Other Manchester firms made locomotives and American flags during the same period. (Boston Athenaeum)

BUILT BY THE
AMOSKEAG MANUFACTURING CO. MANCHESTER, N.H.

ABOVE: *A Union officer, ca. 1863. Civil War uniforms were among the first significant mass-produced garments, marking the official beginning of the ready-to-wear market, which achieved ever-increasing prominence during the final decades of the century.* (*Boston Athenaeum*) BELOW: *Two versions of a "morning negligee" from the fashion page of Harper's Monthly, April 1861. Evolving styles increased per capita cloth consumption and opened new and changing markets for sophisticated fabrics.*

short war and soon found themselves without cotton, forced to curtail operations or shut down entirely. The Lowell corporations demonstrated a disastrous "lack of sagacity and forethought" by selling cotton inventories—prewar price, twelve cents a pound—at thirty cents a pound after two years of fighting. Their "stupendous blunder" became clear as cotton prices climbed to seventy cents in 1864 and passed one dollar the next year. The result was catastrophic: "Nine of the great corporations of Lowell, under a mistaken belief that they could not run their mills to profit during the War, unanimously, in cold blood, dismissed ten thousand operatives, penniless, into the streets!"[83] As a result, five thousand citizens, one-sixth of the prewar population, emigrated from Lowell. Laid-off workers deserted other mill towns. Many never returned.

The Bates, Hill, and Androscoggin Mills in Maine at Lewiston and the Pacific Mills at Lawrence, Massachusetts, gambled on a long war and laid up large cotton inventories before hostilities began. High profits from domestic production and war contracts rewarded their speculation; all four mills expanded their plants. During the war decade, Lewiston's population grew by eighty percent.

With King Cotton straightjacketed, the woolen industry profited from army clothing and blanket contracts and finally established a stable niche of its own in the market. Textile machine shops also prospered during the war by converting to arms manufacture. The war left New England mills in a rearranged hierarchy. Those few mills that profited had a substantial head start on their competitors when prosperity returned. Wartime performance conditioned expansion during the boom years following Appomattox.

Steam Cities

Formulae for postwar success included an important new factor: the steam engine, which had finally come of age. Although steam power and waterpower had coexisted in the industry since the 1820s and had competed equally since the 1840s, only after the Civil War did steam mills take a significant share of the market.

Waterpower, though God-given, had never been free; elaborate hydraulic systems were costly to build and maintain. Furthermore, waterpower was neither dependable nor steady. Droughts, high water, and freezes, meant that water mills ran only intermittently. The use of waterpower dictated fixed industrial locations, usually inland away from raw materials, labor, and market, and added extra transportation costs to production. The main advantages of waterpower were its independence from fuel and the slow depreciation of permanent installations.

Once perfected, the steam engine became a more reliable, versatile, and mobile power source than the water turbine. Knowing neither time of day nor season, steam power could be installed at moderate cost and kept in constant operation. Print and dye works requiring process heat could reuse the waste steam, reducing costs further.

Although steam mills still needed water for boilers and for processing, their

modest requirements largely freed them from the arbitrary river geography governing water mill locations. While waterpower had led to a dispersion of isolated factories, steam mill economy favored concentration at a few coastal locations where transportation costs were minimized, labor was plentiful, and local investment capital was available. As the *Niles Weekly Register* put it: "It is cheaper to use steam power in the midst of a dense population, than to use water power, which often makes it necessary not only to build a factory, but a town also."[84] New England's port cities, especially Fall River and New Bedford, offered optimal conditions and hosted the region's most aggressive steam mill development.

The Corliss Centennial Engine, 1876. This engine, which stood at the center of Machinery Hall at the Philadelphia exposition and powered 14 acres of machines surrounding it, was the triumph of Corliss's work. Many awestruck observers found it a symbol for America's conquest of mechanical power. An emissary from the French government reported: "The lines were so grand and so beautiful, and the whole machine was so harmoniously constructed, that it had the beauty, and almost the grace, of the human form."

FALL RIVER

Early mills at Fall River, then known as Troy, lined the Quequechan River in its short, precipitous drop from Watuppa Lake to the sea. The river's eight falls combined to make this the best tidewater privilege in southern New England. It was perfect for industrialization—big enough for profit and expansion, yet small enough to be developed by local capital without interference from Boston. Here three local merchant-industrialists—Richard Borden, Bradford Durfee, and Oliver Chace—established their manufacturing dynasties, concentrating particularly on print cloth while also developing iron making and shipping.

By 1845, six cotton mills, two calico mills, and an ironworks had harnessed all of the river's available power. Profits from the water mills were taken to finance a second generation of factories run entirely by steam, located along the seashore and beside Watuppa Lake. Aggressive antebellum management followed a policy of "provident care of small beginnings, unpretentious and

Birds-eye view of Fall River, Mass., in 1877, following its period of most rapid growth. The central section of this view is shown enlarged on page 102. Early water-powered factories cover the steep descent of the Quequechan River, ending at the Print Works (bottom center). The second generation of steam mills lines the banks of Watuppa Lake (top center) and Laurel Lake (far right). This view dramatizes the conjunction of waterpower, steam power, tidewater navigation, and entrepreneurial vigor which made Fall River dominant in textiles at this time. (Goodspeed's Book Shop, Boston)

silent, but unremitting energy, and a singularly wise and tenacious grasp of opportunity."[85]

Fall River profited during the Civil War and was well prepared to take advantage of the prosperity that followed. It had capital, skilled labor, and courageous management. Its coastal location favored steam power and gave print cloth manufacturers a small but significant edge over competitors along the rivers to the north. Eight new companies brought their mills into production between 1863 and 1868, more than doubling the city's capacity to over one-half million spindles, and indeed Fall River replaced Lowell as the leading city of American textiles.

Boom years following 1870 fueled the city's most dramatic expansion. Between 1871 and 1872, fifteen new corporations built twenty-two mills while their predecessors extended their own operations. By 1876, Fall River's forty-three factories had an installed capacity of well over one million spindles, feeding yarn to more than 30,000 looms. Fall River grew faster than any other textile city of its time. One out of every four new spindles added to New England between 1850 and 1875 was placed in Fall River. The city controlled one-sixth of all New England cotton capacity, and one-half of all print cloth production. Fall River rightly called itself "Spindle City"—preeminent in America, second only to Manchester, England, in the world.

Fall River's astonishing growth reflected a single-minded purpose. Seven-eighths of the urban labor force worked in textiles. It was a one-industry city,

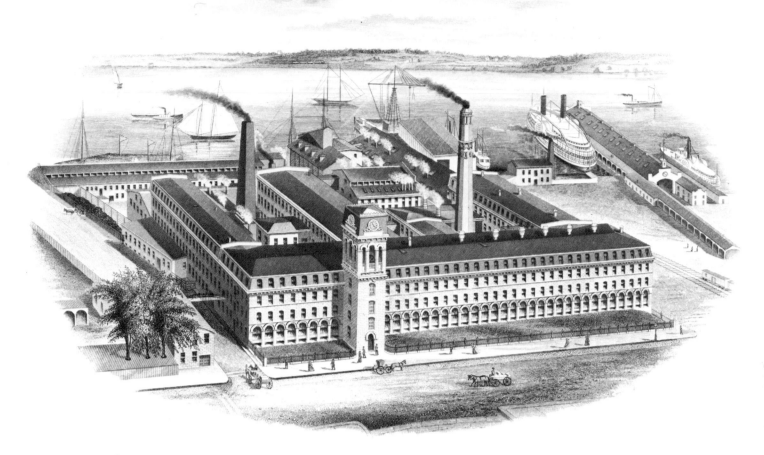

concentrating almost exclusively on print cloth. For three generations the Borden family dynasty ruled. Unquestioned leaders of industry in this one-dimensional city, they dominated scores of smaller investors and manufacturers through an elaborate system of interlocking directorships of the city's most important corporations and institutions.

The Bordens had a strong hereditary claim to Fall River industrialization, having originally owned the entire Quequechan River. Richard Borden established the family's dominion in textiles in the 1820s. Reaping vast profits, he ended Fall River's isolation by promoting steamships to Providence and New York and railroads to Boston. His younger brother, Jefferson, and his uncle,

American Print Works, Fall River, Mass. Built by Holder Borden in 1835 and rebuilt following a fire in 1867, the Print Works was the mainstay of Fall River's preeminence in printed cloth. Employing over 1000 workers, it could print 20 million yards of calico per year, handling the output of 6 large weaving mills. The tidewater location was ideal for bringing coal to its steam engines and for shipping out the finished product. (Van Slyck, Manufacturers)

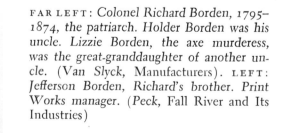

FAR LEFT: Colonel Richard Borden, 1795–1874, the patriarch. Holder Borden was his uncle. Lizzie Borden, the axe murderess, was the great-granddaughter of another uncle. (Van Slyck, Manufacturers). LEFT: Jefferson Borden, Richard's brother. Print Works manager. (Peck, Fall River and Its Industries)

LEFT: *Colonel Thomas James Borden, 1832–1902. He built the Richard Borden Mill in 1871 as a tribute to his father, succeeded his uncle Jefferson as agent of the Print Works, and, like Colonel Richard, controlled numerous other family concerns.* CENTER: *Richard Baxter Borden, 1834–1906, son of Colonel Richard, and president, director, and treasurer of mills, banks, and insurance companies. (Both, Representative Men of Southeastern Massachusetts)* RIGHT: *Matthew C. D. Borden, 1842–1912, third son of Colonel Richard. Educated at Andover and Yale, Matthew was a connoisseur of fine books, paintings, yachts, and horses. While he spent most of his time in New York, his influence at Fall River was ensured by succession, in 1887, to control of the Print Works, which he had already reorganized into the American Print Company. He wrote: "I believe in success, and the greater the better. I believe in the accumulation of wealth, without any limit, except, always, that fixed by clean and honorable methods, but I believe, also, that unusual success brings with it inseparably extraordinary responsibility." (Holt, Bristol County)*

Holder Borden, soon joined him, expanding and consolidating family control over the all-important Print Works. Jefferson managed the Print Works for thirty-eight years, while serving as president of five textile corporations, the iron works, the Borden mining company, and a bank. Richard, known as Colonel Richard after the War of 1812, founded five of the city's largest mills and directed two more. He was also director of two banks, the iron works, the reservoir company, the furnace company, and the gas company, while maintaining extensive interests in steamboats, railroads, and mines. Colonel Borden represented manufacturing interests at the federal level during terms in both Senate and House and was also a member of the Electoral College, casting his vote for Lincoln. His sons carried the dynasty on past the turn of the century.

The city of Fall River grew along with the textile industry and mirrored its one-sided intent. Mill expansion in the early 1870s increased the textile labor force to over fourteen thousand and added twenty thousand people to the city population. Most of the new citizens were foreign-born immigrants. Virtually all families in the burgeoning city depended on the mills.

In 1875, the city had more than twelve thousand units of company

Border City Mills, Fall River, Mass. The company employed 900 workers, some of whom lived in 20 corporation housing blocks, 9 of which are visible at left. The roof was flattened in 1874. (Peck, Fall River)

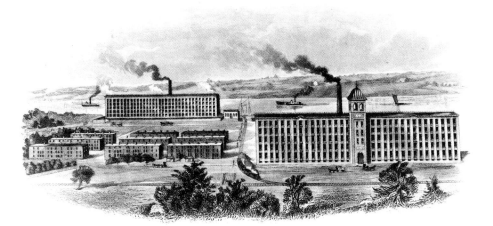

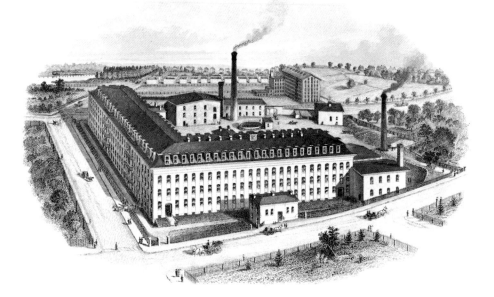

Davol Mills, Fall River, Mass. The Robeson Mill and the Borden Blocks (housing for the Richard Borden Mill) are in the background beside Watuppa Pond, left rear. (Van Slyck, Manufacturers)

Spinning room, Cornell Mill, Fall River, Mass., 1912. (Photograph by Lewis Hine; Library of Congress)

Ring spinners in a Fall River cotton mill, from a hand-colored postcard, ca. 1911. (Fall River Historical Society)

housing—not the well-spaced boardinghouses of early Lowell or the cottages of rural Rhode Island, but rows and rows of multifamily frame tenements. Privately owned tenements supplemented this company housing. Fall River management deplored the Lowell boardinghouse system as "the morbid excrescence, the fungus growth, of a large accumulation of people in the cities." Their alternative, the rented tenement, demonstrated their lack of interest in corporate paternalism. Board of Trade propaganda attributed this to respect for individual freedom and manhood, leaving workers "perfectly free to live as they please, to organize as they deem best, and, finally, to work in one mill or another, or not at all, as they may choose."[86] The industry's laissez-faire approach to their dependent city did, however, have a compelling explanation: it was cheaper, easier, and more profitable. Mill tenements plumbed new depths.

NEW BEDFORD

Industrialization at New Bedford followed a different schedule. The city lived and breathed for whaling, which had not yet peaked in 1847, when the first steam mill, the Wamsutta, started production. After the discovery of petroleum in 1859, whaling began an accelerating decline into obsolescence. New Bedford merchants sought new investment opportunities and decided to follow Fall River's example. Wamsutta had been earning respectable profits for twenty-four years before the second company, the Potomska Mills, joined it. Even though Potomska was an immediate success, ten more years elapsed

Cloth label for Wamsutta Mills. (M V T M)

Portuguese mill workers of New Bedford, Mass.,. photographed and captioned by Lewis Hine in 1912:

"Manuel Sousa and family. On right end is brother-in-law; next him is his father who works on the river. Manuel (appears to be 12 years old) wearing sweater and his arms folded, he has been a cleaner in the Holmes Cotton Mill for two years. John, Manuel's brother (next to him in photo) works in City Cotton Mill. . . . All very illiterate. John and Manuel are the only ones who can speak English and they only a little." (Both, Library of Congress)

"Manuel Soarels . . . works in Bennel Mill. Sweeps in #4 spinning room, has been there one year."

before New Bedford turned more of its resources from whaling to manufacturing. Twenty-four textile companies incorporated during the three decades following 1880. All their mills were built for steam power.

By 1911, New Bedford had surpassed Fall River in spinning capacity and was still growing. Feeding on profits from World War I, the mills expanded until 1920, when production peaked. By then, seventy factories crowded the port. More than forty thousand New Bedford mill workers were tending 3.5 million spindles and 55,000 looms.

While Fall River concentrated on print cloth, New Bedford specialized in sheeting. Both emphasized quality to further differentiate their products from the coarse goods made by their northern competitors. The humid coastal location facilitated fine cotton work by minimizing static electricity and maximizing the fragile cotton fiber's elasticity and break strength. Hence, labor costs were reduced and production increased. The mills equipped themselves for quality work, relying first on mule spinning, then later on perfected high-speed ring spinning.

Of the two cities, New Bedford earned the higher reputation for quality work. Wamsutta led the way, having recognized early that its reputation added value to its product. Percale sheets, a Wamsutta creation and trademark, became synonymous with highest quality and fineness. New Bedford also outdid Fall River in indifference to the urban environment. Neither city had any plans for urban organization, and both bred tenement housing remarkable only for its unrelieved bleakness, institutionalizing declining conditions demonstrated earlier along the Merrimack. Fall River had grown up with, and around, one industry and had at least achieved a grim mill town uniformity. New Bedford, on the contrary, had had a respectable identity of its own as a whaling port before textiles replaced the romance of the sea with the rigor of the mill. Smokestacks now commanded the skyline as ships' masts no longer could. Rapid, unplanned industrial expansion exploded chaotically.

The Immigrant Cycle

Mill closings and army drafts during the Civil War depleted New England's industrial work force, and when prosperity returned after Appomattox, many northern mills faced severe labor shortages. Mill owners believed immigration would solve their problems: workers were recruited from Quebec and the British Isles through advertisements, and labor contractors promised steady work at high wages.

Irish immigrants had already established themselves in the mills. British, French-Canadians, and Germans made up the second wave of a continuing cycle of immigration that brought one nationality after another to the factory. For immigrants arriving without savings, skills, or an understanding of English, American opportunity meant starting at the bottom of the economic ladder—the New York sweatshop or the New England mill. More than any other factor, this flood of immigration determined the character of mill communities between the Civil War and the first world war.

Each successive national group made its way to the factory town to occupy the lowest ranks of the work force, replacing earlier immigrant workers who had already advanced to more skilled positions. Each nationality participated, in turn, in an immigrant cycle leading from helpless destitution toward economic and social stability, from powerlessness to influence, and from alien status toward Americanization.

French-Canadians were the first and most important group to occupy post-Civil War mill towns. The provincial farms of Quebec, divided and redivided by each generation, could no longer support the rural population. As the news of mill town opportunity south of the border spread rapidly through the province, an unprecedented migration began. One-third of Quebec had moved to New England by the turn of the century, and most of these people went straight to the mills.

Mill owners found the *habitants* of Quebec ideally suited to unskilled textile work. Provincial traditions and fervent Catholicism combined to make them uncommonly tractable. A typical contemporary report listed the qualifications of the French-Canadian for mill work:

> *He is quick to learn, active and deft in his movements. . . . Docility is one of his most marked traits. He is not over-energetic or ambitious. His main concern is to make a living for himself and his family, and, if that seems to have been attained, he is little troubled by restless eagerness to be doing something higher than that at which he is at present engaged. Above all, he is reluctant; as compared to the Irish, to join labor unions and is loath to strike.*[87]

French-Canadians indeed preferred mill work over all other occupations and showed particular tolerance for the most menial positions. By 1885, almost half of all doffers (one of the lowest-level mill jobs) in Massachusetts were French. Observers also noted another desirable attribute of the French-Canadians: they bred large families and did not hesitate to send their women and children into the mills. Parents were willing accomplices for the mill owner, whose abysmally low wages made child labor a necessity for family survival.

The French-Canadians were the first immigrants to be segregated by language as well as nationality. The Irish dialect had been ridiculed, but it was at least comprehensible. French, on the other hand, increased the isolation of the *habitants* and forced them to rely more than ever on their own enclaves for support, security, and social identity.

Once established in a particular town, the French enclave drew new immigrants to it. From this base, the newcomers explored nearby mill towns for opportunities, creating an expanding pattern of settlement. The southward migration was initially directed towards the mills of New Hampshire, Maine, and Massachusetts. During the 1870s, it extended even further south into Rhode Island and Fall River. The next decade brought the *habitants* into Connecticut.

French communities grew up in several mill cities: Lewiston, Lowell, Fall

Lewis W. Hine (1874–1940), one of the most committed, inspired, and prolific of all documentary photographers, created an invaluable record of immigrant life in and around New England mills just before the first World War as part of his work for the National Child Labor Committee. Hired as an investigator and cameraman, he photographed in dozens of mill towns, concentrating on those where child labor was prevalent: villages dominated by French Canadians and cities which primarily attracted European immigrants. Each of the thousands of photographs he took is carefully captioned with personal data on the children and observations about their lives. Hine believed child labor was immoral, as well as inefficient, and he was deeply concerned about the permanent damage he found it did to mind and body. The following captions are quoted as written by Hine. (All, Library of Congress)

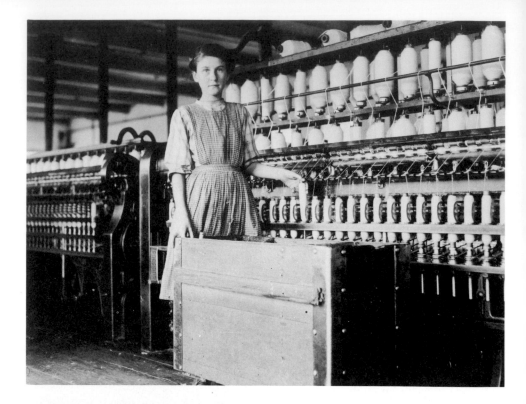

ABOVE: "Winchenden, Mass. Sept. 1911. Adrienne Pagnette, an adolescent French illiterate, speaks almost no English. Is probably 14 or 15. Doffs on top floor spinning room Glenallen Mill."

LEFT: "Winchenden, Mass. Sept. 1911. Family of Adrienne Pagnette: The three standing in front row are Adrienne, Anna, and Francis. . . . Anna said she was 12 years old and helped older sister in Mill. Been at it all summer. She stands next Adrienne. Francis has regular job doffing, says he is 15.... Family consists of 17 members, 8 or 10 of them in the mill; almost every one of them illiterate. Stooping, reaching and pushing heavy boxes is bad for young adolescent girls."

RIGHT: "Lawrence, Mass., September, 1911. (left to right) Thomas Lesesque, Wilfred Valliere. Both work at Wood Mill."

RIGHT: "Overcrowded home of workers in cotton mill, Olneyville, Providence (R.I.). Eight persons live in these three small rooms, three of them are boarders, inner bedrooms are 9 x 8 feet, the largest room, 12 x 12 feet. Polish people. Property owned by the mill. Rent $4.50 a month."

LEFT: "Chicopee, Mass. November 1911. Tony Soccha. . . . A bobbin boy in #7 room: been working there a year."

RIGHT: "6 pm, May 25, 1909. Coming out of Amoskeag Manufacturing Co., Manchester, N.H."

River, and Holyoke each had its "Little Canada." Fall River's French-Canadian population leaped from five hundred to eleven thousand in the decade following 1870. Only the two smallest mill cities—Biddeford, Maine, and Woonsocket, Rhode Island—however, were more than forty percent French. The migration focused mainly on the small textile villages in southern New England. By 1880, at least one-third of all French-Canadian immigrants had settled in towns with populations under seventy-five hundred, forming a majority in several of them. At Manville, Rhode Island, and Grosvenordale, Connecticut, more than seven out of ten citizens were French-Canadian.

In these rural mill towns, the *habitants* could recreate provincial Quebec culture and insulate themselves from what seemed "the cold hospitality of native New Englanders." Here the immigrant was surrounded by compatriots. Neighbors, fellow workers, and parish priest were all French. Language was no longer a handicap, as the English-speaking minority was forced to learn French to get by.

Construction of an ornate Gothic church of their own was the first and highest priority for nascent French-Canadian enclaves. Once installed, the priest, the Mass, and the parochial school all served as guardians of French tradition, institutionalizing resistance to assimilation into the American melting pot. To carry the crusade for linguistic identity beyond the church walls there were French newspapers and mutual aid societies. The Société St. Jean Baptiste was particularly influential in this process, exercising a social and philanthropic role in most French-Canadian communities. Its motto, "Our Religion, Our Language, Our Customs," declared its conservative intentions.

The church and the mill symbolized the split allegiances of the village that was located between them, their respective bells alternately summoning the citizens to work or to pray. While providing a vital link with the homeland, the church was no match for the mill, which claimed most of the parishioners' time and energy. Here the immigrant was in daily contact with other religions and persons of other nationalities, sharing with them the all-American experience of factory work.

IMMIGRANT CITIES

While French-Canadians established their mill town niche, the third great wave of immigration was under way, funneling a mixture of Swedes, Italians, Portuguese, Poles, Armenians, Russians, Greeks, Turks, and other eastern Europeans into Ellis Island. Like the French before them, thousands of these immigrants approached the American dream by working in New England mills. Yet none of them shared the *habitant's* love of small-town isolation. The focus of immigration now shifted decisively to the mill cities.

Whether by accident or intention, each nationality selected certain cities for preferential settlement. The Poles concentrated at Holyoke. The nation's largest Greek community sprang up at Lowell. The Portuguese and Cape Verdians preferred Fall River and New Bedford, which they knew well from

. . . foreign is every day replacing native skilled labour. . . . Indeed, the great number of foreign workmen employed in all the branches of American Industries is very remarkable. . . . Nearly all the hands at present in American cotton, woolen, and worsted mills, and in the foundries and rolling-mills of the country, are of recent foreign extraction.—A government sponsored report on the "condition of the Industrial Classes in the United States," 1869.

An immigrant ship arriving at New York, ca. 1887. (Culver Pictures)

the whaling era. With localized industrial expansion making Fall River, Lawrence, Manchester, and Lowell especially attractive to immigrants, these four soon exceeded all other American cities in percentage of foreign-born residents.

Lawrence became the queen of immigrant cities. At its peak, fifty-one nationalities speaking forty-five different languages were counted within a mile of the mills. By 1910, ninety percent of Lawrence's citizens were first- or second-generation Americans, few of them speaking English. Aided by prosperity in the woolen industry, the city had recovered from its first disastrous decade. In the 1870s, it even achieved a measure of acclaim for its enlightened concern for labor.

But massive European immigration between 1890 and 1912 combined with declining industrial conditions to produce an unusually desperate environment. Housing went from bad to worse as multistory wooden tenements were thrown up to accommodate the surge of immigrants. Tenements rose higher each decade, crowding so close together that a housewife could hang her pots and pans on the outside wall of the adjoining tenement. Apartments offered few amenities, and even windows were a luxury. Increased rents following the sale of company housing at the turn of the century forced most families to take in boarders and fill every room with beds. Even the kitchen—the social center of the apartment and the only source of heat—served double duty as a bedroom. Privacy was nonexistent. As immigrants were packed tighter and tighter into the slums of central Lawrence, population density soared to over one hundred persons per acre. At the center of the immigrant area, density reached six hundred per acre—equaling the most populated blocks of Harlem.

Nor did Lawrence have a monopoly on overcrowded housing; Holyoke was not far behind, boasting the largest and worst tenements of any manufactur-

> *Work!*—W O R K!!—W O R K!!! *must be the order of the day with all who emigrate to better their fortunes. To honest and prudent industry every thing will be conceded, to indolence and imprudent movements*—N O T H I N G B U T D I S A P - P O I N T M E N T. *The roughest of first appearances must not be minded, but a vigorous and resolute hand put forth, and all discouraging appearances will melt as the mists of the morning before the rising sun.* —quoted from John Regan's "The Emigrant's Guide to the Western States of America," ca. 1852

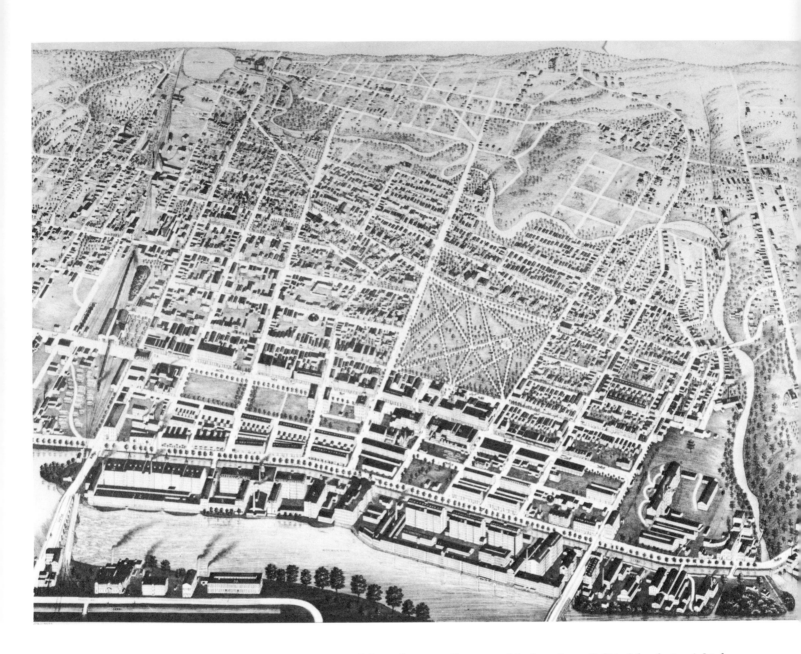

Lawrence, Mass., in 1876, when more than one-half its citizens were foreign-born, most of them Irish. By 1910, only one Lawrence resident in ten was born in America. (M V T M)

ing city in Massachusetts. One superblock at Lowell fitted for forty-eight four-room apartments housed three hundred persons. Only half the rooms in this block had windows. Central Falls, Rhode Island, had a brief moment of glory as the second most densely populated city in the world!

Health inspectors reported a "fearful mortality" stalking the immigrant districts of mill cities, deemed "hotbeds of disease." Crowded, unventilated apartments bred tuberculosis. A "poisonous miasma" surrounded the privies between tenements, combining with polluted river and canal water to add typhoid and cholera to the list of mill city scourges. Waves of disease swept down the Merrimack, as one city after another drank water contaminated by mill workers upstream and passed their recontaminated wastes down the river. Disease followed the immigrant cycle, striking destitute newcomers with special virulence.

Infant mortality reached devastating heights. At one point, forty-four percent of all deaths at Lawrence and over half of all deaths at Lowell struck infants. Holyoke had the highest infant death rate in the nation, sharing its record for overall mortality only with Fall River. Rumors spread that mothers were choosing infanticide, and using the canals for disposal.

Labor conditions offered no respite from these urban horrors. Wages ranging from $3.60 to $7.00 a week in the 1890s could not meet increased costs of living: real earnings had in fact declined. The most recent immigrants, always at the bottom of the pay scale, could barely make ends meet. Workers put in a sixty-hour week and shouldered increasing work loads as machine speeds increased. A "tired hopelessness" and "an underfed, prematurely old look" were reported spreading among them.

The close, humid, lint-filled air within the mills propagated pneumonia, tuberculosis, and other respiratory diseases. By the turn of the century, nearly seventy percent of all deaths among textile workers at Lawrence were caused by respiratory disease. One spinner in three died before completing ten years of factory work. Half of these victims were under twenty-five years of age.

Yet none of this wretchedness stopped the cycle of immigrant advancement. Each group found, in time, a measure of security in employment and association, in the church and in the family. Since increasingly desperate conditions hit the newcomer hardest, the preceding groups could still agree with the Lawrence *Journal* that "the March of Progress is ever upward and onward." And however minute this progress became, it appeared more significant, by contrast, as slum housing and unskilled wages—the newcomers' lot—slipped ever lower.

Water Powered Classics

MANCHESTER, NEW HAMPSHIRE

Serious attempts to tame the tremendous waterpower at Amoskeag Falls began in the 1820s under the aegis of the Amoskeag Manufacturing Company. Controlled by Rhode Islanders for its first decade, Amoskeag set the pattern for future growth by raising a dam and digging two parallel canals to feed the long rows of mill sites marked out on the east bank of the Merrimack. This early scheme included the outlines of a planned manufacturing city on the hillside flanking the upper canal.

Only after the Boston Associates took over in 1836 was there enough capital to develop the site properly. Kirk Boott, who had built Lowell, was called in to consult. Expansion modeled on Lowell continued. Rows of stepped boardinghouses went up. Elm Street, the main commercial artery, was planted with trees. Strict zoning kept the buildings along it within narrow aesthetic limits.

Manchester might have continued on the same crisis-ridden path as the other Boston Associate cities had not the appointment of William Amory as

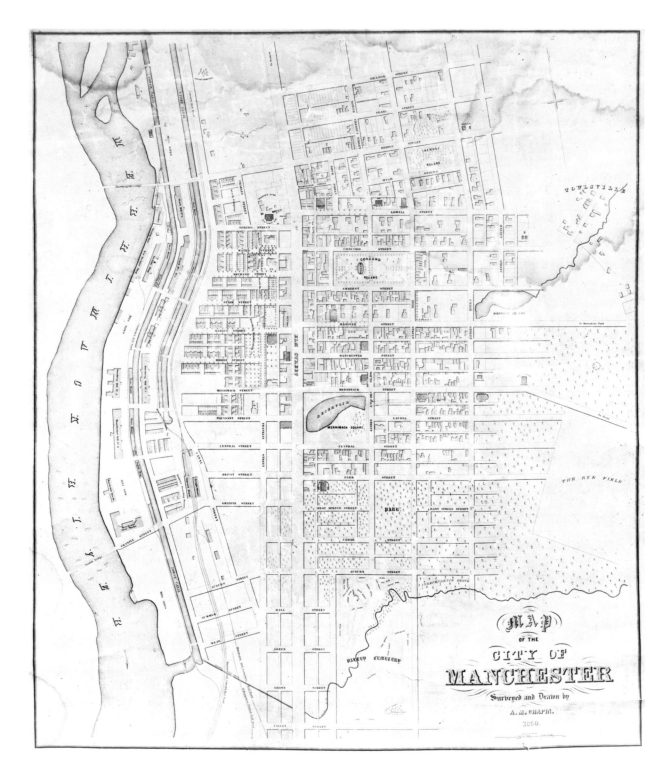

Map of the city of Manchester, N.H., 1850, by Chapin. Two gently curving parallel power canals feed the Amoskeag mills on the narrow islands bordering the Merrimack River (left). The total length of the mill zone is over one mile, allowing room for enough factories to use its full 16,000 horsepower potential. Mill housing is across from the mills. (Manchester Historical Association)

Amoskeag treasurer changed the city's destiny within a year of the Boston takeover. Amory, a highly educated and prudent businessman not overly given to greed, made the crucial decision to abandon the get-rich-quick promotional pattern typical of Boston ventures in favor of steady, conservative growth of the parent company. Amoskeag retained control of real estate and waterpower while expanding its own machine shop and cotton mills. The few independent companies that shared the Amoskeag complex were later reabsorbed into the parent firm. Manchester became, in effect, New England's only one-company city.

Amory astutely guided the Amoskeag company through a thirty-nine-year period of alternating booms and depressions that ruined many competitors but brought steady growth to Manchester. Recapitalized at three million dollars in 1849, the company became New England's largest. It remained preeminent throughout Amory's tenure, earning average dividends of eleven percent while growing to include nine mills (125,000 spindles and 3,500 looms) employing eighteen hundred women and half as many men. When Amory left the company in 1876, Amoskeag was in an excellent position for further growth. During the thirty years that followed, the company expanded more than fivefold, becoming a diversified manufacturing behemoth.

Absentee ownership and direction always characterized Amoskeag company policy. Neither the treasurer nor the principal stockholders spent much time

The Amoskeag Manufacturing Company, ca. 1870. Both the upper and lower mill islands are developed, but the earliest mills have not yet been connected together. (Van Slyck, Manufacturers)

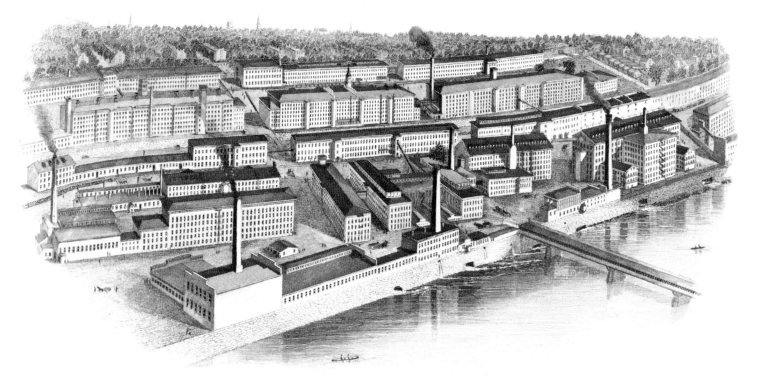

in Manchester; nor had they any personal interest in the future of the city beyond the profit it could earn. On-site management was delegated to the resident agent, who had dictatorial control over all details of industrial and urban growth. Ezekiel Straw and his family filled this office for three generations following 1858, giving the company a valuable uniformity of oversight. Since almost all construction was executed by the Amoskeag machine shop under the agent's supervision, the complex had a remarkable consistency of architectural style and urban concept. Everything about it said *Amoskeag,* and said it the same way.

What little power remained in the public domain was severely compromised. From afar, Amory commended his puppets in city hall for the "enlightened self-interest" that led them to accept "our mutual dependence and identity of interest as the only basis of growth and prosperity to either."[88] Ebbing and flowing to the pace of only one giant company made the city unique; it shaped its growth and conditioned its eventual death.

Though the mills and the dependent city were built solely for profit, Amoskeag did make the community attractive and pleasant by mill city standards. The company recognized its dual responsibilities as the life force of a company town and the principal employer in an immigrant city. Amoskeag provided land for churches, schools, and civic buildings, and donated parks, bridges, and a library to the city. Mill housing, though repetitive, was well designed, soundly built, and conscientiously maintained. Labor contractors solicited immigration by promising steady work at good wages that would quickly repay the cost of passage. The company came closer than most to fulfilling the promise. As long as the mills were running, each immigrant group found its chances for survival and eventual prosperity in Manchester as good as in any other mill city, and probably better. The company was able to attract and hold a superior class of workers.

A surge of expansion and consolidation after the turn of the century increased company employment to sixteen thousand; employee turnover raised the total number of company dependents during this period yet higher. Responding to stiffening competition, Amoskeag increased machine speeds and work loads. Reacting to the massive strike at Lawrence in 1912, however, it also increased wages and promoted a remarkable display of conspicuous paternalism. Amoskeag informed prospective employees:

> It is true that the large company to which [the workers] sell their labor treats them as its own children. . . . That is the reason why the Amoskeag company has never had any trouble with its employees. It treats them not as machines, but as human beings, as brothers who have a right not only to wages, but also to the pleasures of life. . . .[89]

One company plan offered plots of residential land to employees with more than five years of service, sweetening the deal with low down payments and easy terms on interest-free mortgages. Amoskeag streamlined its real estate holdings in the process. Employees could also buy Amoskeag stock on a delayed payment plan, which ultimately benefited the company. Both programs increased the worker's vested interest in the success of the firm.

ABOVE: Workmen unloading cotton at the Stark Mill, Manchester, N.H. LEFT: Amoskeag counting house. (Both, Manchester Historic Association)

Amoskeag mill yard, ca. 1878.

Weaving room in Amoskeag's Coolidge Mill, 1912. (All photos, Manchester Historic Association)

Two thousand horsepower Corliss steam engine in No. 7 mill, Central Division, at Amoskeag. An earlier iron flywheel on this engine exploded in 1891, tearing out the roof and walls of the engine house. The wooden flywheel replacing it was 30 feet in diameter and 9 feet wide. The engine powered four mills.

The 265-foot smokestack built in 1883 after the company began supplementing its waterpower with steam.

As the largest textile company of its time, Amoskeag was a popular subject for postal card and stereopticon photographers.
ABOVE: Panoramic view of the mill zone from the west bank of the Merrimack.
RIGHT: The power canal, from Granite St.
BELOW: Simulated moonlight view from the dam, looking downstream towards the mills. (All, Manchester Historic Association)

Manchester, N. H.
Canal and Amoskeag Mills.

Mills from Amoskeag Bridge, Manchester, N. H.

Stereopticon views of Amoskeag.

Carding, Langdon Mills.

Warping, Mechanics Mills.

Weaving, Mechanics Mills.

The main channel for Amoskeag paternalism was the Textile Club, which promoted social and recreational events, correspondence courses, and classes in textile and domestic skills. A ball park was rebuilt into Textile Field, where capacity crowds watched company-sponsored athletics. Children played in the company playground and cultivated gardens nearby, both in the shadow of the mills where they would soon start working. At the same time, the company expanded its welfare program to include a mill doctor, a dental clinic, and a visiting nurse service. Modest pensions rewarded a few aged workers after exceptionally long service to the company.

Amoskeag's exemplary, though self-serving, paternalism program camouflaged steady erosion of its competitive position during the years surrounding World War I. Intermittent prosperity meant frequent short time and occasional shutdowns in the mills. Even regular wage increases could not meet the rising cost of living. Without steady employment or viable wages, Manchester workers became increasingly dependent on Amoskeag, whose paternalism only tempered their difficulties. The termination of all company welfare programs following the strike of 1922 marked the official beginning of a corporate decline already well advanced.

THE QUINEBAUG AND SHETUCKET VALLEYS

Windham County, in northeastern Connecticut, had always been comparatively backward, isolated from the seaports to the south and the urban centers to the east and west. Its worthless glacial soil, never attracting serious farming, left it vulnerable to "premature depopulation and decrepitude."

The area did, however, have one significant asset: a variety of potent waterpower sites along the Quinebaug and Shetucket rivers and their tributaries. Early Rhode Island industrialists recognized the value of these privileges, setting up young Smith Wilkinson, Samuel Slater's nephew and former doffer, at Pomfret Factory (later Putnam) in 1806. Slater's outpost at Webster later commanded the Quinebaug's main upstream tributary, the French. His brother John, and later his sons, guarded the lower river at Jewett City. Subsequent development along the Quinebaug was so strongly biased to the east that one venerable mill agent insisted, "There is not a mill village on the Quinebaug that does not owe its existence to Rhode Island manufacturers or Rhode Island capital."[90]

The Quinebaug Valley's classic era began soon after the Civil War, as established mills developed their privileges to the limit. Little mills on inconsequential streams made modest additions. Miniature cities grew around closely grouped privileges at Putnam, Danielson, Jewett City, and Willamantic, though a few of the most important and challenging power sites still remained untapped. By this time, major investment in isolated waterpowered mills was already in anachronism, as steam-powered success at Fall River demonstrated. Nonetheless, Rhode Island capitalists started a handful of huge water turbine factories during this period, surrounding them with extensive new mill villages. These daring ventures were the ultimate in water-

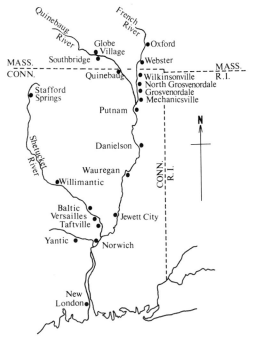

Significant mill towns in the Quinebaug River watershed.

powered industry as they knew it, and the last of their kind.

The two sister villages at Grosvenordale represented all that classic mill towns could be. Each had an earlier existence: the downstream privilege as Masonville; the upstream, as Fisherville (known locally as "Mount Hunger"). The parent company, founded by Amasa Mason, grew out of the first and colonized the second. Dr. William Grosvenor, Mason's son-in-law, took over the business in 1848 and engineered the expansion. Consolidation was complete by 1868, when Grosvenor renamed the company and both villages after himself.

Work began immediately at the upper privilege. The dam and canals were rebuilt to power a new mill of ambitious scale. Grosvenor retained one of Rhode Island's best mill architects—F. D. Sheldon—and spared no expense to make this the perfect factory. It was later praised as "a model of architectural proportion, beauty, and adaptation of design. . . . filled with machinery which for general style and convenient arrangement has no superior in New England."[91]

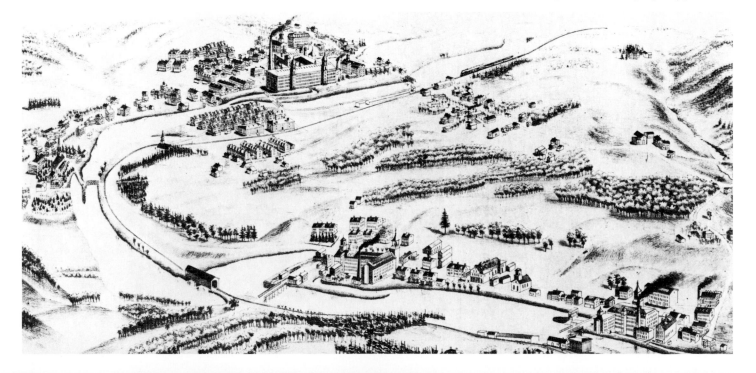

North Grosvenordale mills No. 2 (center) and No. 1 (right), in 1876. The boarding-house on the hilltop behind them served transient workers. (Van Slyck, Manufacturers)

Dr. William Grosvenor. Although born in Putnam (1810), Grosvenor built his mansions in Providence and Newport, R.I. Grosvenor's son continued the absentee management after his father's death. At all times, on-site responsibility was delegated to the agent. (Greene, Providence Plantations)

Two monumental towers soared above the mill, relieving its hulking mass with a Lombard Romanesque flourish—and stating company philosophy with unmistakably phallic ostentation. Paternalism would rule in North Grosvenordale. The towers overlooked three zones of formally arranged housing. The spartan wooden tenements and housing blocks were no match for the grandiose brick mill. Surrounded by wilderness, the town crowded close to its liege in medieval fashion. Leaving little space between houses, the plan was suffocating. Fresh paint, picket fences, and flowers provided by the company were only cosmetic touches on what was a rigidly pragmatic village. From his porticoed mansion beside the canal above the mill, the resident agent ruled over a miniature kingdom whose social hierarchy was fixed in brick, mortar, granite, and timber. Virtually everything within his view belonged to the company.

French-Canadians poured into North Grosvenordale to work in the new mill. The paternalistic town suited them well. Their children worked beside them. Within a decade, three out of four residents of the village were French. The English-speaking minority dominated skilled and managerial jobs. Swedes and "Greeks"—actually Turks, Rumanians, Yugoslavians, and Albanians—followed. By the turn of the century, ninety percent of the villagers were first- or second-generation immigrants. While the company often segregated each group in work crews within the mill, the workers themselves established de facto segregation in their housing, preferring to live with neighbors of their own nationality.

Villagers led routine, humdrum lives, shuttling between the mills and houses with regular detours to the church and company store. Church groups and mutual aid associations structured the village's limited social life while reinforcing linguistic divisions. Sports and outings afforded occasional recreation.

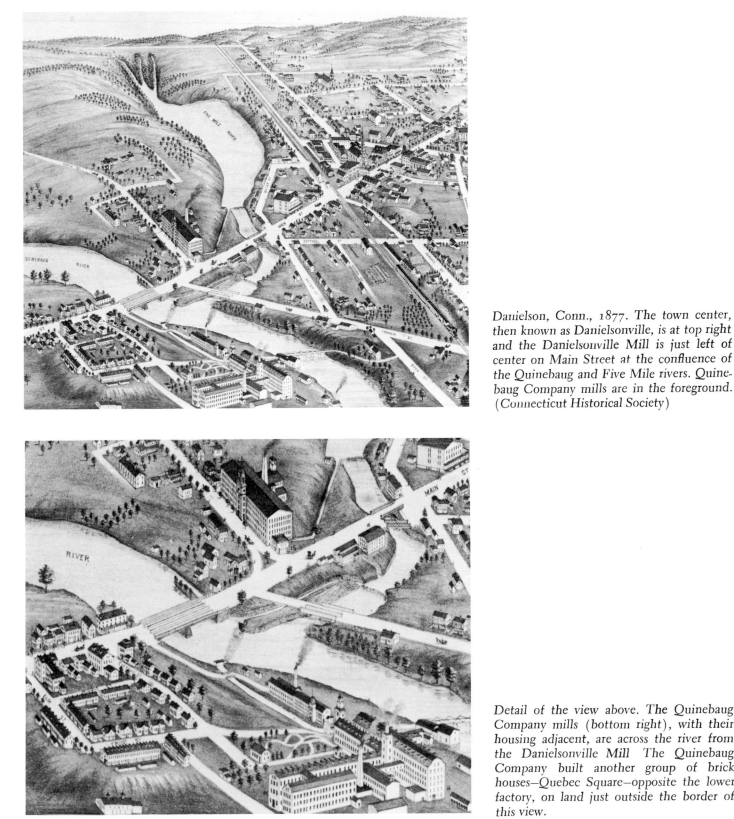

Danielson, Conn., 1877. The town center, then known as Danielsonville, is at top right and the Danielsonville Mill is just left of center on Main Street at the confluence of the Quinebaug and Five Mile rivers. Quinebaug Company mills are in the foreground. (Connecticut Historical Society)

Detail of the view above. The Quinebaug Company mills (bottom right), with their housing adjacent, are across the river from the Danielsonville Mill The Quinebaug Company built another group of brick houses—Quebec Square—opposite the lower factory, on land just outside the border of this view.

As it matured, the village grew more American. Mill work came to transcend national origin and incubated common values. Civic pride coalesced around communal needs—the village fire engine—and shared challenges—World War I. Baseball, the great American equalizer, ritualized competition between immigrant groups, whose isolation slowly gave way to community.

Variations on the North Grosvenordale theme developed downstream. Across the river from Danielson, capitalists from Rhode Island converted a tiny factory settlement—pioneered by the Tiffany family, of subsequent jewelry fame—into another classic industrial village ruled by the Quinebaug Company. Substantial brick housing units here grouped into squares expressed a refined sense of social organization. Each family could till a plot in the communal garden. Many kept cows and pigs to supplement their diet.

One of the Quinebaug Company's promoters, Amos D. Lockwood, developed the privilege further downstream at Wauregan—an Indian name meaning "pleasant valley." Lockwood, an experienced mill engineer trained at Slatersville, laid the groundwork for a model community nestled in the bowl-shaped valley beside a model mill. When he left to become chief engineer for the Bates Company at Lewiston, village authority passed to the resident agent, James S. Atwood. The Atwood family eventually assumed ownership of the company, their mansion commanding the valley below. Everything within sight was theirs.

Atwood joined forces with Rhode Island and Massachussetts industrialists to build the Ponemah Mill on the Shetucket River just outside Norwich. Edward Taft organized the company, whose stockholders included J. F.

Ponemah Mills, Taftville, Conn., 1876. The long rows of company housing opposite the mill are not shown in this view. The tremendous power of the Shetucket River in the background allowed the Ponemah Company to build a proportionately large mill—750 by 75 feet—in 1867, extended later to a length of one-third mile. (Van Slyck, Manufacturers)

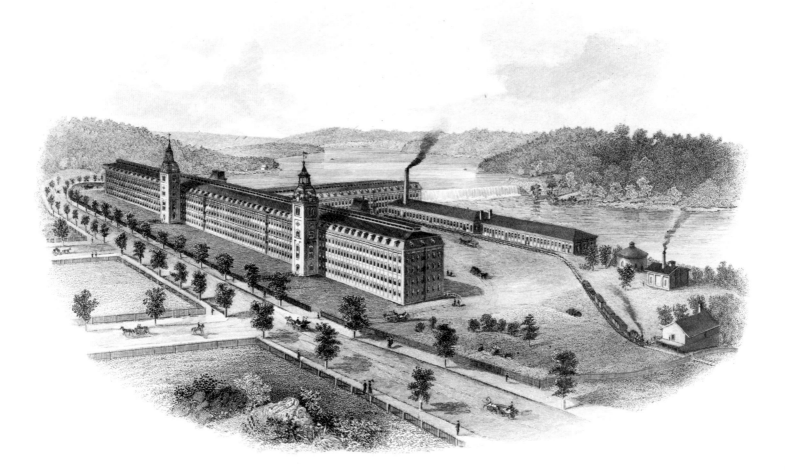

The Yantic Woolen Mills, Yantic, Conn. Yantic was a small fiefdom just outside Norwich. This bleak winter view is taken from the owner's mansion, ca. 1870. (Yantic Fire Department)

The millrace at Yantic, Conn., ca. 1900. (Art of Norwich, Leffingwell Inn)

Slater, J. C. Whitin, W. S. Sayles, and E. P. Mason—all preeminent in waterpowered manufacturing and machine building. Ponemah would be the culmination of all their experience. The virgin site was christened Taftville.

Ponemah was built concurrently with North Grosvenordale, both factories sharing the same architect. Village organization was identical in concept, differing mainly in adaptation to local terrain. Yet Taftville had distinct advantages over its sister village. Available waterpower here exceeded all other privileges in southern New England. Proximity to tidewater navigation at Norwich minimized village isolation and maximized commercial advantage. The potential of the site and the organization of the company made Taftville a hybrid of Rhode Island, Merrimack, and Fall River prototypes.

When completed in 1871, the Ponemah mill was the largest single building for cotton manufacture in the nation. The company built 170 wooden tenement houses on the hillside for some fifteen hundred operatives. Two brick blocks opposite the mill sheltered the company store, boardinghouse, post office, and social hall. A large company farm fed the village. As usual, the agent supervised village life from his mansion on a knoll above.

ROCKVILLE

The Hockanum River drops 283 feet over 13 separate falls as it passes through Rockville, Connecticut, creating what was "one of the finest and most easily available water powers in America." The river's unusually pure water was also ideally suited for the finest wool processing. These assets predetermined Rockville's future as a multiple-mill town for quality woolen manufacture, an industrial gem.

Rockville originated as a colony of an earlier settlement downstream, where John Warburton, an English émigré, had built Connecticut's first textile mill in 1795. With the special perverseness of mill town names, this early site was known, sequentially, as MacLean's Mills, Kelloggville, and Talcottville as it passed through the three families who succeeded Warburton. While puny waterpower made this an inconsequential site, one local journalist found the village notable for its "high moral and religious character," the "Puritanical whiteness" of mill, store, and dwellings, and its "window blinds of the regulation and time-honored green."

MacLean, Kellogg, and Talcott each started building mills in Rockville in the 1820s, when it was still "an exceedingly lonely place." Their first mills were soon joined by mills of other companies at the falls above and below. Since each fall was within earshot of the next, the string of mills formed the core of a modestly diversified town. Rockville never experienced the rigid one-company uniformity of its predecessor.

Yet one company and one family did eventually dominate the town. The main agent of this transformation was George Maxwell, who came to Rockville in 1847, started a general store, then wisely married Kellogg's daughter. He began consolidating his father-in-law's mills and the town's best independent mills into the Hockanum Company in 1860. The reorganization coin-

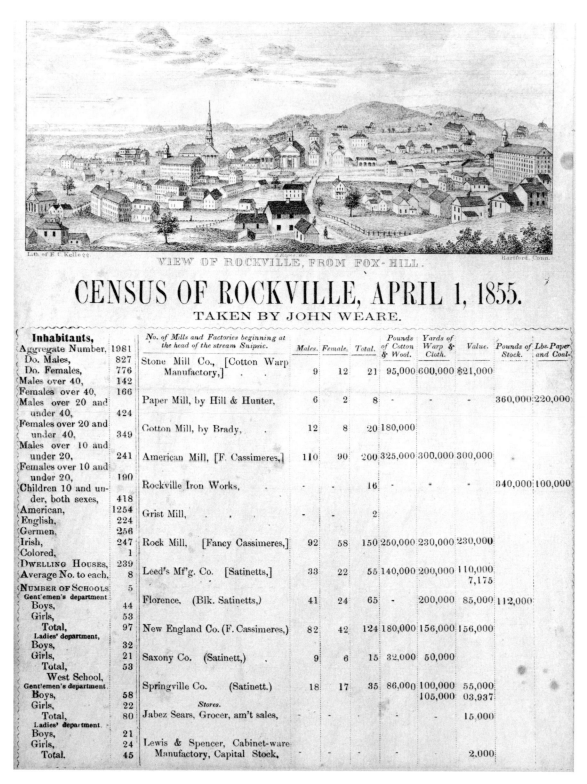

VIEW OF ROCKVILLE, FROM FOX-HILL.

CENSUS OF ROCKVILLE, APRIL 1, 1855.

TAKEN BY JOHN WEARE.

Inhabitants,		No. of Mills and Factories beginning at the head of the stream Snipsic.	Males.	Female.	Total.	Pounds of Cotton & Wool.	Yards of Warp & Cloth.	Value.	Pounds of Stock.	Lbs. Paper and Coal.
Aggregate Number,	1981									
Do. Males,	827	Stone Mill Co., [Cotton Warp Manufactory,]	9	12	21	95,000	600,000	$21,000		
Do. Females,	776									
Males over 40,	142									
Females over 40,	166	Paper Mill, by Hill & Hunter,	6	2	8	-	-	-	360,000	220,000
Males over 20 and under 40,	424									
Females over 20 and under 40,	349	Cotton Mill, by Brady,	12	8	20	180,000				
Males over 10 and under 20,	241	American Mill, [F. Cassimeres,]	110	90	200	325,000	300,000	300,000		
Females over 10 and under 20,	190									
Children 10 and under, both sexes,	418	Rockville Iron Works,	-	-	16	-	-	-	340,000	100,000
American,	1254	Grist Mill,	-	-	2					
English,	224									
Germen,	256									
Irish,	247	Rock Mill, [Fancy Cassimeres,]	92	58	150	250,000	230,000	230,000		
Colored,	1									
Dwelling Houses,	239	Leed's Mf'g. Co. [Satinetts,]	33	22	55	140,000	200,000	110,000 7,175		
Average No. to each,	8									
Number of Schools	5	Florence, (Blk. Satinetts,)	41	24	65	-	200,000	85,000	112,000	
Gent'emen's department										
Boys,	44									
Girls,	53									
Total,	97	New England Co. (F. Cassimeres,)	82	42	124	180,000	156,000	156,000		
Ladies' department,										
Boys,	32									
Girls,	21	Saxony Co. (Satinett,)	9	6	15	32,000	50,000			
Total,	53									
West School,		Springville Co. (Satinett.)	18	17	35	86,000	100,000 105,000	55,000 03,937		
Gent'emen's department										
Boys,	58									
Girls,	22	Stores.								
Total,	80	Jabez Sears, Grocer, am't sales,	-	-	-	-		15,000		
Ladies' department										
Boys,	21									
Girls,	24	Lewis & Spencer, Cabinet-ware Manufactory, Capital Stock,	-	-	-	-		2,000		
Total,	45									

View from Fox Hill, with Census of Rockville, Conn., 1855. Three mills, all with bell towers, are shown. Reading downstream from right to left: American Mill, Rock Mill, Leed's Mill. (Vernon Historical Society)

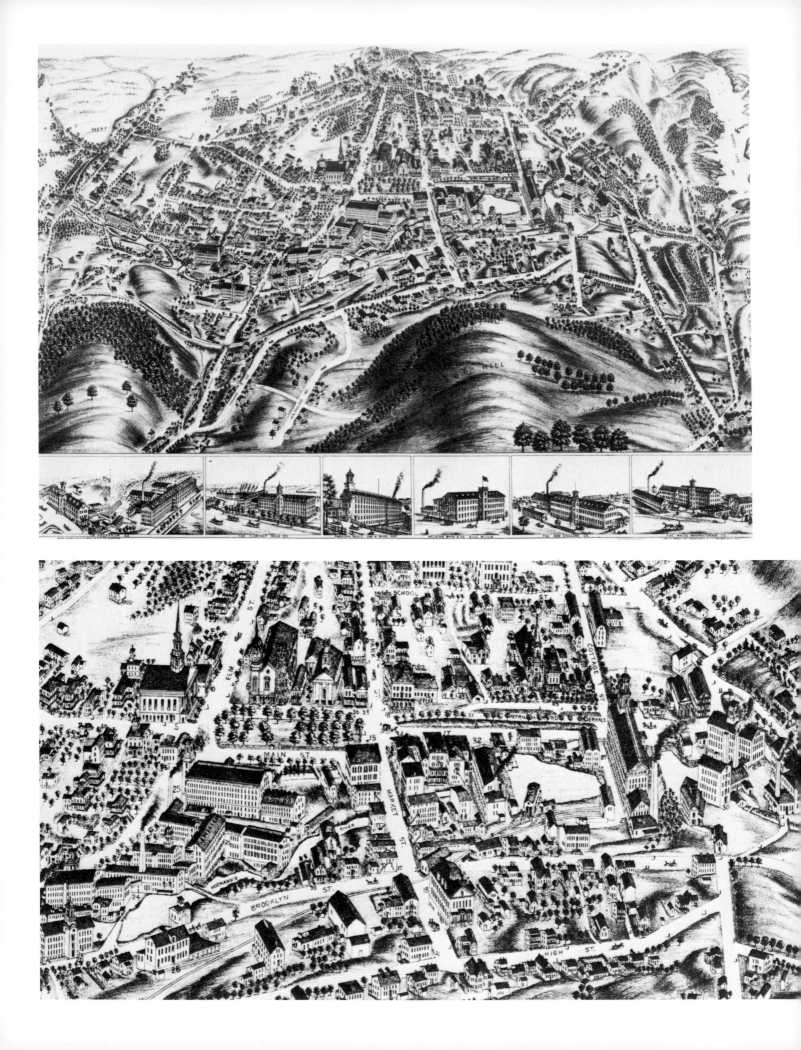

OPPOSITE: *Birds-eye view of Rockville, 1877, with an enlarged detail below it.* BELOW: *Rockville in 1895, with a corresponding detail below. Both enlargements cover the same area as the 1855 census illustration (previous page), but the viewpoint is shifted upward and to the left so that Fox Hill (where the earlier artist stood) appears in the bottom right corner. The sequence of mills in this area is indicated on the schematic on the next page. Such comparisons show the elegance and richness of detail achieved in the birds-eye style which flourished between 1850 and 1920. Perspective has been adjusted to reveal maximum information from an imaginary viewpoint. The lithograph itself was drawn from sketches made at ground level.* (MVTM; *Connecticut Historical Society*)

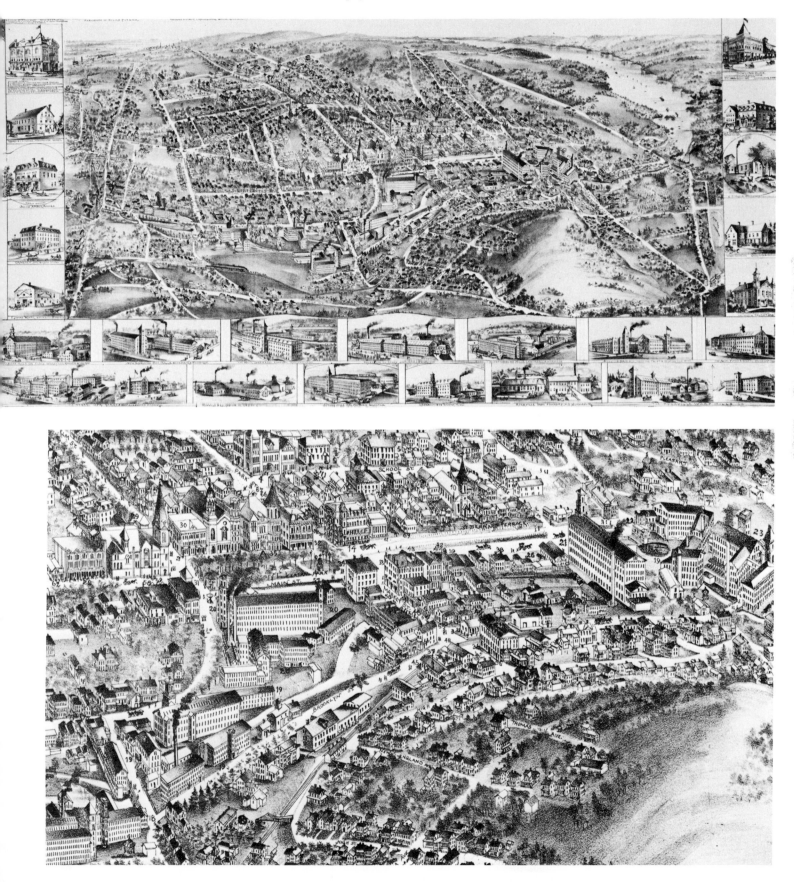

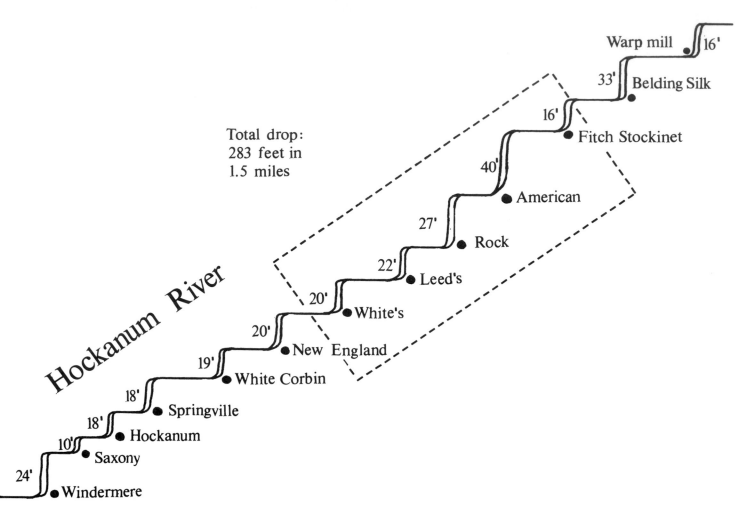

The sequence of Rockville mills in 1884. The detailed views on the three preceding pages cover the outlined area.

cided with improvements in machinery and market conditions for wool. Under Maxwell's direction, the Hockanum Mills seized their opportunity and gained a nationwide reputation for finest quality woolens and worsteds. Presidents Harrison, McKinley, and Theodore Roosevelt wore inaugural suits of Hockanum Worsted.

The Maxwell family controlled seventy-five years of Rockville development before relinquishing their company to the M. T. Stevens Company. During the Maxwells' reign, the village grew into a "thriving, bustling, progressive" town. The New York *Daily Graphic* published this description in 1889:

> *The streets and walks are broad and well kept, and the dwellings, ranging from the neat and substantial cottages of the mill operative to the elegant and costly residence of the manufacturer, contribute materially to the air of thrift and general prosperity which pervades the town. Perhaps the most noticeable, as well as remarkable, thing about Rockville is the practical non-existence of poverty, rowdyism and other objectionable characteristics of the average mill town.[92]*

The Maxwells embellished the town with a fine library and hospital and supported civic institutions and philanthropies to protect their investment in quality. Their efforts made Rockville the pride of the woolen industry.

The Hockanum (right) and Saxony Mills at Rockville. Woodcut, 1874 (M V T M)

Study in Francis T. Maxwell's mansion, ca. 1900. Unseen doors at the left open onto a classic ornamental garden, while the glass doors at right open onto the foyer and the grand porticoed porch overlooking the center of Rockville. (Rockville Elks Club)

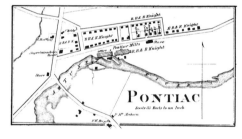

TOP LEFT: Benjamin B. Knight, 1813–1893, the financier. CENTER LEFT: Robert Knight, 1826–1912, the executive. (Both, Fruit of the Loom; MVTM). TOP RIGHT: Cloth labels used on Fruit of the Loom fabrics. The Swaar apple at center was the first of the series. (Fruit of the Loom). CENTER RIGHT: Northeast view of the mills and bleachery at Pontiac, R.I., 1883. (Van Slyck, Manufacturers). BOTTOM LEFT: Pontiac, R.I., 1870. (Beers, Atlas). BOTTOM RIGHT: Dodgeville, Mass., in 1867, thirteen years after it was bought by B. B. & R. Knight. (Geldard, Cotton Manufacture)

B. B. & R. KNIGHT

Rhode Island, the birthplace of the cotton industry, also hosted that industry's greatest partnership: The B. B. & R. Knight Company. Within one generation, the two brothers, Benjamin and Robert, brought seventeen mill villages under their control. When Robert died in 1912, his obituary read: "the largest individual cotton manufacturer in the world." Their brand was Fruit of the Loom.

The Knight story is a rags-to-riches classic. The men were the sons of a farmer. Benjamin went into the grocery business near the Sprague Print Works. Robert, thirteen years younger, passed his youth in a cotton mill, spent a few years in his brother's shop, then became clerk of a company store at nearby Clarksville. Robert bought part-ownership in the mill when Clark, the owner, left to serve a term in the Senate. He bought out his senior partner five years later and brought in Benjamin. The brothers renamed the village Pontiac (1852), as if to signal their ambition for prowess and leadership.

Every few years, the brothers bought another mill village. Many of their mills were acquired at bankruptcy sales following the collapse of the Sprague family empire in 1873. B. B. & R. Knight never started villages of their own, preferring to expropriate and expand the initiatives of others. Major renovations and additions usually followed Knight control, along with company enlargement of the villages. Consequently, the firm grew in two directions at once—bigger and better mill villages, and more of them. Robert rode his white stallion from one to another, overseeing all company activities.

Knight employment exceeded six thousand by 1886, growing on and off until 1920. The expansion created a labor shortage French-Canadians could not fill; waves of Italian immigrants were brought into the Pawtuxet Valley. Company agents met immigrant boats at Ellis Island to ensure a steady supply of workers. When production finally peaked, the Knight mills wove seventeen thousand *miles* of cotton a year for the Fruit of the Loom label.

Cloth label of Baltic, Conn., ca. 1865. The Knights bought this mill after the Sprague bankruptcy in 1873. (Rhode Island Historical Society)

V

Senescence

1900-1975

Ten Amoskeag mechanical department workers in 1922, with cumulative textile experience exceeding 500 years. (Manchester Historic Association)

Challenge

MOBILITY

New England textiles enjoyed a century of unchallenged supremacy by virtue of having monopolized the nation's motive power, venture capital, and mechanical skill. Yet by the 1880s, technological change had canceled this monopoly, giving new mobility to all aspects of American society, including the textile industry itself. Steam power made this mobility possible, freeing the nation from dependence on fixed energy sources like waterfalls. Exemplifying speed and power, the steam railroad revolutionized transportation and nourished its dependent sibling, the stationary steam engine, by linking it to the coal mine. In both its forms, the steam engine freed the textile manufacturer from the river—to bind him to the rail.

Simultaneous expansion of the nation and its railroads changed the industrial landscape. New England, having little to recommend it except a commanding head start, was no longer the center of things. Becoming truly mobile for the first time, the textile industry was free to migrate to new locations where operating costs were lower.

Always a highly competitive, easy-entry industry, textile manufacture was especially sensitive to small changes in locational advantage: investment had followed shifting opportunity, bringing first Rhode Island, then the Merrimack River, then Fall River to prominence. Few manufacturers knew for sure what the destiny of a chosen region would be. Complacent northern mill owners believed New England's dominion would continue; but a new generation of southern industrialists disagreed, insisting that the optimum location

Delivery of a Draper model A loom with Northrop battery in South Carolina, 1896. A horse, a mule, and an ox are hitched to the cart, probably for comic effect. Between 1900 and 1914, over 234,000 of these looms were sold, 65 percent of them to southern mills. (Wannalancit Textile Co.)

for cotton manufacture was the South and boasting, "Here the cotton grows up to the doorsteps of the mills, and supply and demand clasp hands."[93]

As it turned out, the South was right. Equipped by northern machine shops, both steam- and water-powered cotton mills flourished in several southern states and eventually grew into an industry that rivaled, then surpassed, and finally suffocated its northern parent. During this slow, but inexorable migration, mill owners in both regions had to cope with the uncertainties of an evolving industrial climate. Sharing common needs, neither had an absolute advantage over the other. Yet, while none of the southern assets were decisive in themselves, the combination of small advantages made the region irresistible to new development, and the trend was established.

Raw material. Only short-staple cotton, an inferior grade, was growing at the southern mill's doorstep. Most New England mills in fact used cotton grown west of the Mississippi or imported from abroad, and they paid little more for it than the South did. But the coarse-goods mills above the Merrimack depended on the shorter fiber; these were the hardest hit by southern competition. In woolen and synthetic fibers, the South had no geographical advantage.

Power. The South could operate its steam engines more cheaply than the North because it was closer to Appalachian coal. Northern mills found this significant only in proportion to their own dependence on steam. Under ideal circumstances, waterpower was still cheaper, though always limited. Waterpowered mills could survive; but for expansion, steam was required. Eventually electrification made steam power optional, but the South had the advantage of lower electric rates, too. Northern water mills could, and did, minimize the southern advantage by generating electricity of their own, buying only a part of what they needed.

Skill. The Civil War and Reconstruction left the South with a surplus of poor white labor willing to trade red-dirt farming for low-paying factory work. This unskilled labor pool was most advantageous for the manufacture of low quality mass-production work. Decades passed, however, before the South had the skills needed to compete with northern fine-goods mills.

Location. Although closer to coal and cotton, the South was further from New York, the garment center and principal market. It also had a drier climate unsuited to fine cotton work and lacked pure, soft water for finishing. Technology eventually lessened these restrictions with three inventions: the telegraph, the humidifier, and the water softener.

Incentive. A clear advantage. The South *wanted* the textile industry, of which the North had grown tired. Southern legislation assured a benign industrial climate by minimizing taxes and avoiding labor reform. Southern communities tempted industry with cheap land, low assessments, and an eagerness to adapt to industrial life.

Age. New England's first century of textile experience brought it the wisdom—and the inertia—of age. Conversely, the southern industry was young, vigorous, and better able to respond to the rapidly changing times. The South built on what the North had learned, unhampered by tradition and uninhibited by any industrial status quo.

The automatic humidifier, patented by J. G. Garland of Biddeford, Maine, in 1881. This simple device, which combined compressed air (upper tube) with water (lower tube), allowed any mill, anywhere, to manufacture fine cotton goods under the humid conditions which favored such work. Thus one of New England's prime manufacturing advantages—a naturally humid climate— was eliminated. (Boston Public Library)

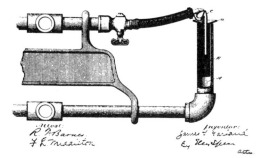

AUTOMATION

While working to perfect their textile machines, New England machinists provided the South with new opportunities to magnify its advantages. Two important mechanical breakthroughs brought first spinning, then weaving, closer to total automation.

High-speed ring spinning was finally perfected by Sawyer in 1871. This high-production technique was applied first to coarse yarns, then later to finer counts. The South depended on it from the start; it matched their needs and improved mechanically along with them.

Coarse production received a second boost from inventor J. H. Northrop at the Draper Company loom works at Hopedale, Massachusetts. In 1894, Northrop perfected an automatic bobbin changer, thereby eliminating one of the weaver's principal responsibilities. With its cylindrical "battery" of bobbins, the device, built on the same principle as the submachine gun, also had its appearance and effectiveness. It was an engineering marvel: "one of the most perfect implements ever devised to perform a series of intricate, yet restricted movements."[94] Continuous operation and the reduced need for skilled labor made this an absolutely revolutionary automaton.

Yet the first Draper looms equipped with Northrop batteries had their limitations for New England: they could not weave the patterned fabrics that made up sixty percent of the region's product. Furthermore, early models could use only strong, ring-spun yarns, which excluded mule-spun cotton and wool. Lastly, the loom was three times as expensive as the best nonautomatic competitor.

Southern mills bought most of the early Draper/Northrop looms, which met their needs perfectly. Established mills in the North were more cautious

The Northrop battery of a Draper model A loom with other parts of the loom erased. Fresh bobbins are held in the cylindrical battery. This illustration shows a fresh bobbin being inserted into the shuttle while an empty bobbin is ejected into the hopper below. (Both, Labor Saving Looms; Wannalancit Textile Co.)

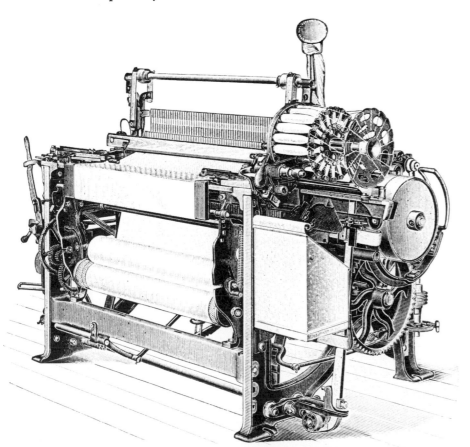

A Draper model B loom, with Northrop battery mounted on the right. This loom was designed for light goods and print cloth, and manufactured until 1898. Improved models were capable of increasingly complex weaving.

The final surge of textile industry expansion in New England required further increases in available power. Evolving technology provided important new options—the steam turbine and the electric motor—while raising the older steam engine and water turbine to the highest possible efficiency. During the first half century of American textile mills, virtually all motive power was waterpower. But by 1870 millstreams supplied less than half the New England industry's needs, and, by 1932, barely one-fifth. For many mills, the installation of electric generators at the wheel and electric motors at the machine was one of the last efforts at modernization before shutdown. RIGHT: Engine room, Pacific Mills, Lawrence, Mass., 1914. (MVTM). BOTTOM LEFT: Steam turbine boiler room at the North Division power plant, Amoskeag, 1915. Two rows of 32 boilers each produced 9,600 horsepower. BOTTOM RIGHT: Turbine wheel installation at the new Amoskeag electric generating station, 1915. (Both, Manchester Historic Association)

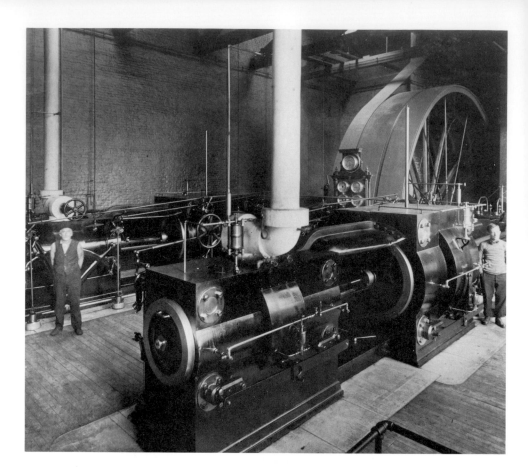

about replacing their old looms. Each mill dealt with the automation challenge on its own terms. Some ignored it. Some limited their conversion cost by modifying existing looms to accept a Northrop attachment. Others waited more than fifteen years for improved models adapted to their product.

Too many mill owners bet *against* the inexorable advance of technology—and lost. Automation was in fact inevitable. Management found false security in its long-lived but old-fashioned machines, which kept on producing long after they became obsolete. Mills that were profiting on aging looms were, in fact, running on their own depreciation. As new installations were increasingly concentrated outside New England, the region found itself surfeited with antique machines. In 1928, a typically conservative New Bedford mill had no looms or spindles less than twenty-five years old. Henry Ford bought some of their machines for his museum!

THE LABOR FACTOR

The steady pressure for labor reform legislation that began during the infancy of the textile industry finally brought results in the closing decades of the century. Massachusetts, the first to go beyond the ineffectual laws Rhode Island and New Hampshire had passed in the 1840s, set a ten-hour day as the maximum for women and children in 1874. The minimum age for child labor rose to thirteen in the 1880s. By the turn of the century, prohibitions on night work for women and children had eliminated the night shift completely in some areas.

Southern laborers had no such protection. They worked as long as the mill owner wanted and accepted the wages he offered. Although New England textile wages had risen slightly, they were still among the lowest in American industry, but southern wages were lower yet—often half or less than half of earnings in the North. Child labor was three times as common in the South. The strong North-South labor differential continued until National Recovery Administration legislation in 1933. In the meantime, poor white southerners gave industrialists in their homeland the advantage that immigrants had given earlier to New England: an abundance of cheap, unskilled, and tractable labor.

Unable to wring more hours from their workers, New England mills tried to compete by demanding higher production per hour. Machines were cranked up to their highest possible speeds. "Stretchout"—an increase in machines assigned to each worker—accompanied the "speedup." Management justified both techniques by the "grim necessity of the moment." Both were vilified by labor, now "worked like slaves" and "driven to death."

Frederick Taylor, the father of time and motion studies (and the discoverer of high-speed tool steel), laid the groundwork for speedups and stretchouts. His analysis of industrial work assumed an ignorant, irresponsible laborer; increased output had to be sought by means of rigid compartmentalization of jobs and strict behavioral control. An Amoskeag mill agent stated the central philosophy of Taylorism when he equated maximum production per worker

UPPER LEFT: Mr. Brainerd, overseer of cotton carding at Pacific Mills, Lawrence, Mass., 1914.

UPPER RIGHT: Mr. Eastwood, overseer of the grey worsted cloth room at Pacific Mills, 1914.

LOWER LEFT: Walter Parker, agent at Pacific Mills, 1913. (Essex Company photographs; M V T M)

LOWER RIGHT: Mill owner's house, Arkwright, R.I., 1936. (Photograph by Joseph McCarthy; Providence Public Library)

TOP: "Shots of the young workers going to Ayer Mill, 6:30 to 7 a.m. All work. Lawrence, Mass. Sept. 1911." (Lewis Hine)

ABOVE: Mill housing at Pawtucket, R.I., 1936. (Joseph McCarthy)

RIGHT: "Some of the Small Boys working in Amoskeag Manufacturing Company Manchester, New Hampshire. Photo taken at noon, May 25, 1909." (Photograph and caption by Lewis Hine; Library of Congress)

Two government agencies created during the Depression, the Works Progress Administration and the Farm Security Administration, sponsored photographers who recorded the decaying mill town environment of the 1930s. Joseph McCarthy photographed Rhode Island for the WPA in 1936, concentrating on architecture and including several town views. Of the several FSA photographers who visited New England's company towns, Jack Delano was the most prolific. Walker Evans, one of the most important and respected FSA photographers, recorded American Woolen installations several years later for Fortune magazine. BELOW: Woonsocket, R.I., 1940. (Jack Delano; Library of Congress). BOTTOM: Baltic, Conn., 1940. The Baltic mill is in the background, behind its housing. (Jack Delano) OPPOSITE TOP: Free Reading Room, Fiskeville, R.I., 1936. (Joseph McCarthy, Providence Public Library.) OPPOSITE BOTTOM: Mill buildings, Woodville, R.I., 1936. (Joseph McCarthy)

Sorting and cleaning silk, Cheney Mills, South Manchester, Conn., 1914. (Stereo card; Library of Congress)

Mill workers' cottages, Fiskeville, R.I. (Mc-Carthy photograph; Providence Public Library)

with "the highest degree of civilization." Mill workers knew better. They despised the time-study men, with their clipboards, stopwatches, and lab coats, for Taylorism only made their difficult situation worse, adding further dehumanization to their exhaustion.

Stiffening competition and excessive capacity forced mill owners to add "short time" (operation of the mill at partial capacity with a shortened work week) to the workers' trials. Wild fluctuations of industrial activity, and consequently intermittent employment, became common as manufacturers tried in vain to synchronize production with ever-changing market conditions. Between shutdowns, workers reduced to short time took less pay home.

Declining conditions and rising expectations brought the beginnings of unionization to New England after the turn of the century and triggered long, acrimonious strikes. The Fall River strike of 1904 was a sign of the changing times. When the city's mills cut wages and workers refused to accept the amount of money offered, a "lockout" began, which shut eighty-five of the city's mills for six months. Thirty thousand workers were unemployed. Thirteen thousand Fall River residents, mostly the mobile Englishmen, packed up in disgust and left town.

THE LAWRENCE STRIKE

In 1912, Lawrence was gripped by a strike that publicized the increasing desperation in the mill cities. Lawrence, which had first been nurtured by its arrogant namesake, had later become a stronghold for yet another mill town megalomaniac—William Wood, president of American Woolen Company.

Wood, the son of an Azores seaman with an anglicized name, rose through the ranks in the Wamsutta Mill of New Bedford, then served as treasurer of the Borden Mills at Fall River, and finally emerged as assistant manager of the Washington Mills at Lawrence. Owned by Frederick Ayer of Boston, the Washington Mills was one of the city's largest firms. Wood consolidated his position there further by marrying Ayer's daughter. When an unfavorable tariff caused a textile panic in the late 1890s, Wood advised his father-in-law to buy up bankrupt mills and consolidate them into American Woolen, a daring new conglomerate that became official in 1899. Wood served as treasurer, and succeeded to the presidency when Ayer died.

By 1905, Wood had the power and resources to build the world's largest cloth factory at Lawrence and name it for himself. More than one-third of a mile long, with thirty acres of floor space under one roof, it was an industrial giant with peak employment of almost ten thousand. The Wood Mill symbolized William Wood's dictatorial control over American Woolen, which in turn controlled almost half of Lawrence's textile capacity. Having consolidated his power, Wood now ruled from a mansion, dressed in elegant suits and spats, and turned to merciless exploitation of the working class from which he had come.

Together, the Wood Mill and the Washington Mill added sixteen thousand jobs to Lawrence within ten years, bringing in immigrants so desperate for work that:

Husky, able-bodied men would steal by the watchmen and get into the mill and then beg for a job where they could make any wages at all. There are

William Madison Wood (1858–1926). Although Wood's actions during the strike suggest consuming greed and total insensitivity to labor, in later years he was comparatively generous to American Woolen Workers. Yet when he built his model mill community—Shawsheen Village—just south of Andover, Mass., it was for management only. Blue-collar labor commuted to Shawsheen from Lawrence. His spirit was finally broken by intense IRS investigation and the tragic deaths of his son and daughter, causing him to leave American Woolen. Two years later, on a Florida beach, he put a pistol in his mouth and committed suicide. (Keogh, Lawrence; M V T M)

THE WOOD MILL, LAWRENCE, MASS., THE LARGEST WORSTED MILL IN THE WORLD. TOTAL LENGTH OVER 1000 FEET. TOTAL FLOOR SPACE 3,000,000 SQ. FT. COST $3,500,000. EMPLOYEES 7,000. WILLIAM M. WOOD, PRES.,

Wood Mill, Lawrence, Mass. Postal card, 1909. (M V T M)

able-bodied men today in the Lawrence Mills doing children's jobs, taking children's places, and receiving pitiful children's wages.[95]

Lawrence's destiny had become dangerously entangled with William Wood's.

The Lawrence strike began on January 12, 1912, after American Woolen announced that a wage cut would accompany reduction of the work week from fifty-six to fifty-four hours as required by law. Wildcat strikers rampaged through the Wood Mill, cutting belts and breaking machines. The strike quickly spread to the Washington Mill. By the next day, fourteen thousand Lawrence workers were on strike. The local chapter of the Industrial Workers of the World (IWW) called in Joe Ettor and Bill Haywood, the best "Wobbly" organizers. Two weeks later Ettor met with Wood in Boston. Ettor demanded a fifteen percent raise across the board. Wood refused.

Wood's uncompromising position sparked street violence and the fatal shooting of a young woman striker. Police arrested a suspect and jailed Ettor for inciting him. Simultaneously, Wood added to the confusion by urging one of his henchmen to plant dynamite around the city in an effort to discredit the strikers. Martial law closed in. The New York *Times* lead headline announced: "Real Labor War Now in Lawrence."

The strike grew to include twenty-three thousand workers, forcing Lawrence mills to shut down completely. Recognizing the linguistic fragmentation of the city, the IWW preached "solidarity" and formed strikers of many nationalities into a unified front to resist American Woolen efforts to break

Parade of 15,000 strikers at Lawrence, Mass., January, 1912. (Brown Brothers)

Workers' children at the Lawrence train station, 1912. Publicity resulting from the militia action strengthened the IWW bargaining position. (Brown Brothers)

them. Yet local support for the strike was not universal. The early immigrants, especially the French and Irish, did not want to risk security so arduously gained. While IWW banners proclaimed: "Arise!!! Slaves of the World!!!/No God! No Master!/One for all and all for one!" indignant Lawrence conservatives paraded: "For God and Country / The Stars and Stripes Forever / The Red Flag Never."[96]

Tension rose as the strike dragged on into February. Wood remained firm, declaring: "American Woolen owes Lawrence nothing!" Striking families matched his determination; they began to send their malnourished children to sympathizers in other cities. On the forty-third day of the strike, the militia stopped the emigration by attacking the crowd of parents and children at the railway station and throwing them into their paddy wagons. The Boston *Common* reported the police "clubbed, choked and knocked down women

On February 24 and 25, soldiers and policemen forcibly prevented parents from sending their children away from Lawrence to cities that offered food and shelter

Editorial cartoon condemning militia action at Lawrence. (Colliers, 24 February, 1912)

and children, the innocent wives and babies of the strikers."[97] The sheer brutality of the action galvanized nationwide support for the strikers. Support demonstrations were even held in European capitals. A Senate investigation opened the Pandoran box of Lawrence exploitation. Wood was forced to negotiate.

After sixty-three bitter winter days, American Woolen surrendered and agreed to strike demands for wage increases and time-and-a-quarter overtime. Eugene Debs called the Lawrence victory "one of the most decisive and far-reaching ever won by organized workers."[98] Wages for textile workers rose throughout New England. Labor organizations in other industries gained new strength. Organized labor had found solidarity and established itself as an effective adversary to big business, including textiles.

Then, in war prosperity, labor found respite that concealed the growing weakness of northern industry. With the postwar depression, massive strikes returned. Thirty-five thousand New England operatives joined the United Textile Workers strike in 1918. Lawrence began a five-month strike the following January.

Wage reductions throughout New England precipitated another chain reaction of strikes in 1922. Rhode Island workers struck first, fighting a 22½ percent wage cut in the B. B. & R. Knight mills. Operatives in several New Hampshire, Massachusetts, and Maine mills soon joined strikes of their own. Two weeks later, Amoskeag announced a twenty percent wage cut and a simultaneous increase in the work week from forty-eight to fifty-four hours. Amoskeag workers shut the whole complex down for nine months. When mills in Nashua, Lawrence, and Maine finally repealed their wage cuts, Amoskeag was forced to go along. The bitter, bloody strike in Rhode Island lasted the longest—thirty-four weeks—and started B. B. & R. Knight on a quick slide into bankruptcy.

Amoskeag Manufacturing Co. made this 95 × 50 foot flag in July 1914 as an exhibition of World War I patriotism. Each star was one yard in diameter. Photo by Harlan Marshall, Camera Section, Amoskeag Textile Club. (Manchester Historic Association)

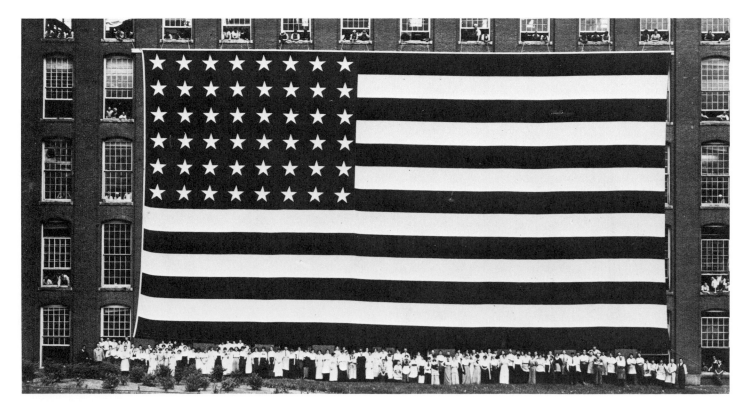

While labor unionized and became conspicuous as the New England mills' most unwanted adversary, the South was free to grow, unhindered by unions, strikes, or restrictive legislation. Low wages and long hours became the South's most attractive assets. Running on one shift, forty-eight hours a week, northern mills could not possibly compete with multiple-shift southern plants that could run continuously, and hence more profitably. "Give us fifty-four hours and we'll fight the world," wailed northern mill owners, begging for uniform, nationwide labor standards. But labor strife was only the last and most tragic addition to the load of problems that finally crushed New England manufacturing.

Response

INERTIA

As New England became an increasingly grim and disreputable environment for textiles, new investment wisely concentrated in the South, where the industry grew steadily larger. Each addition was more modern—and more capable—than the one before. The South expropriated northern monopolies one by one, conquering new markets with each passing decade. In 1880, four-fifths of America's textile industry was in the North. In the sixty years before the ratio was reversed, northern industry continued making spasmodic attempts to respond to the challenge. By mid-century the retreat had become a rout.

As it occurred, the shift in industrial activity left New England overburdened with excess, obsolete capacity. Giant mills far exceeded any economies

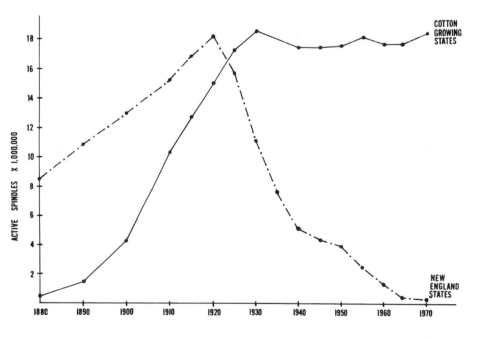

A comparison of spinning capacity in New England and the South, 1880–1970, based on Bureau of Census statistics.

of scale and were difficult to adapt to changing needs. The thousands of machines inside represented a colossal investment in the past and forced an inflexible commitment to the status quo.

The old-guard conservatism of New England management only made matters worse with the sinecures and ineptitude of family control. Second- and third-generation mill owners had little interest in their inherited factories. They had lost their nerve for initiative, allowing the southern competition to dictate the rules of the game. This proved disastrous. The deck was stacked so heavily in favor of the South that New England could win only through radical modernization of its facilities, techniques, and attitudes; but New England chose passive resistance.

The deceptively gradual shift of power confused northern management. Mill owners in fact had ample warning, had they acknowledged it. Danger signals had been evident since 1850, when *Scientific American* had cautioned:

It is our opinion that there have been too many of our factories engaged in making coarse goods. At the North this is self-evident, for coarse goods can be manufactured cheaper at the South, and with the great number of factories now in operation [in the southern states], how can it be expected that our northern manufacturers can long keep the field against them— they cannot do it.[99]

By the turn of the century, southern competition had indeed become a significant market factor. But there was never an abrupt, industry-wide challenge to the North. Instead, industrial vitality eroded away—unevenly but continuously—under increasingly effective and diversified southern competition. The least competitive mills—large and small—fell first. As *Scientific American* had predicted, these early victims were producing coarse goods. The most modern, quality-oriented mills, especially those at Fall River and New Bedford, enjoyed a few extra decades of immunity.

To complicate the trend, intermittent periods of prosperity accompanying both World Wars allowed remaining northern mills a succession of profitable Indian summers that camouflaged their weaknesses. These respites affected the industry unevenly: wool generally fared better than cotton, fancy goods better than plain, and finishing better than manufacturing. But they all had one thing in common: all were temporary. Between boom years, postwar slumps and the Depression made the industry "extremely competitive and depressingly unprofitable." Hard times took their toll.

The Fall River and New Bedford empires were slow to realize the danger of their position. Both crashed towards bankruptcy in the 1920s, immediately following their most prosperous years. Between 1922 and 1932, Fall River management liquidated seventy-three of the city's mills and three-quarters of its capacity. Sixty-three of these mills had been controlled by twenty-six corporations that disappeared completely. New Bedford suffered the "withering loss" of twenty-one thousand textile jobs. Yet enough mills hung on until World War II to keep Fall River the biggest New England textile center. Half of the urban labor force still worked in textiles and found a few final years of prosperity.

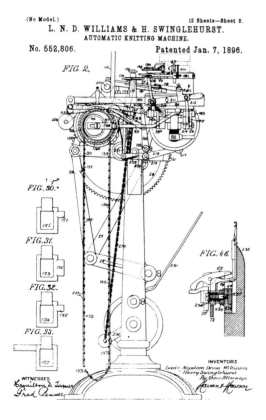

Knitting machine patent, 1896. The increasing demand for knits was almost exclusively supplied by southern mills. Slow to convert, weaving mills in the North suffered serious competition. (Boston Public Library)

(No Model.)   12 Sheets—Sheet 2.
L. N. D. WILLIAMS & H. SWINGLEHURST.
AUTOMATIC KNITTING MACHINE.
No. 552,806.   Patented Jan. 7, 1896.

Some mill villages proved amazingly resistant to the changing climate. The Grosvenordale Company, for example, survived until 1942, then passed the village on to another firm, which was able to wring another dozen years' operation from it. Wauregan Mills, one of the most tenacious, hung on until 1958, and Harrisville, New Hampshire, made it to 1974.

Synthetic fibers gaining acceptance after 1920 complicated the erosion still further. Here New England had an opportunity to regain industrial leadership: synthetics had no preferred location. Competing most powerfully in the quality market, synthetics challenged New England to provide a sophistication that the South was only beginning to exhibit. The North could have kept its hegemony in fine goods by dominating the new technology, but New England mills showed little enthusiasm for synthetics. The North also demonstrated a fatal inability to adapt to rapidly changing styles that characterized the market after World War I. Low labor costs in the South combined with more progressive management to give the industry there greater flexibility to switch from dying product lines into more popular fabrics.

The truth is that the textile industry in the North had entered a phase of creeping senility, enlivened only by occasional paroxysms of accommodation. Amoskeag, for instance, started a modest rayon division in 1926. After seven years of steady profits, the rayon division required expansion to remain competitive; but Amoskeag chose to liquidate it instead. New Bedford foolishly converted much of its capacity from fine goods to coarse yarn for automobile tire fabric, then quickly lost the business to the South.

CONSOLIDATION AND LIQUIDATION

Most companies responded to the increasingly hostile industrial climate, on the one hand, by streamlining their operations and, on the other, by mini-

Postal card of the 1936 flood, Lewiston, Me. The flood in 1936 and two hurricane-induced floods in 1934 and 1956 destroyed several New England mills and damaged many others. Because waterpowered mills were usually located on the river banks below the falls, they were extremely vulnerable to flooding. During the nineteenth century, damaged mills were usually rebuilt immediately after the freshet had subsided. But twentieth-century floods, though no bigger, were the last straw for companies already on the verge of bankruptcy. The mills at Mechanicsville, Conn., and Manville, R.I., for example, burned to the ground within days after the 1956 flood ravaged them. They were never rebuilt. (W. S. Libbey Co.)

mizing their losses. Liquidation was a popular technique for achieving both ends, allowing the company to convert its unwanted assets into working capital. Housing was sold off to workers and absentee landlords. Idle capacity and troublesome divisions were eliminated.

Liquidation can be used to prune and revitalize a company, nourishing its reduced assets with a proportionately larger working capital, or it can be used to kill it off. Whether partial or total, liquidation releases only part of the mill's value—its resale or scrap price. Production potential of the liquidated property is wasted unless a similar textile employer takes over the operation. Used machinery dealers scavenged off the dying textile industry in New England, exporting liquidated equipment to the South and to developing foreign nations. Jacob Ziskind, one of the boldest liquidators, took over the venerable Merrimack Manufacturing Company mills at Lowell and ran them around the clock for another ten years. The mill closed soon after his death and the machines were exported.

Those parts of the industry spared from liquidation became pawns in complex consolidation and reorganization schemes. American capitalism had often used the textile industry as its laboratory; the spate of mergers and vertical and horizontal integrations simply brought experimentation up to date. American Woolen was one of the pioneers, bringing sixty mills under its dominion by 1924.

Several mills in Maine, and especially Lewiston, got involved in a devious electric power monopoly scheme engineered by Walter Wyman of the Central Maine Power Company and Samuel Insull, public utilities baron of the Midwest. Wyman salvaged the conglomerate's holdings after Insull's empire collapsed in 1932, running the mills off and on for more than twenty more

Sawyer Woolen Mills, Dover, N.H. The community surrounding these two mills was originally known as Sawyerville. American Woolen bought the company, and many other small firms like it, to process the waste wool from their huge worsted mills at Lawrence. The Sawyer Mill was already partly shut down when Textron took over American Woolen in 1954. (Boston Athenaeum)

years. In Massachusetts, twelve mills in the Berkshires and the southeastern part of the state merged to form Berkshire Fine Spinning Associates. The J. P. Stevens and M. T. Stevens companies expanded from North Andover further into New England and then into the South. Deering-Milliken (synthetics) and Pepperell (Lady Pepperell towels) extended their influence outward from Biddeford, Maine.

By 1920, more than half of New England's textile workers were controlled by a few dozen of the region's largest companies. Recombinations, mergers, and consolidations only delayed the inevitable, breeding corporate giants with enough resources and common sense to move South.

TEXTRON

Consolidation, liquidation, and synthetics nourished the industry's most portentous offspring: Textron, the nation's first diversified conglomerate and still one of the biggest. Royal Little, the last of the mill town tycoons, built Textron. When he had finished, New England's textile industry had lost its last major battle.

Little started with limited cash but with excellent credentials. The impetuous daring of his West Coast youth was tempered by a Harvard education and channeled by his uncle, Arthur D. Little, the industrial chemist who held patents on artificial silk and ran a burgeoning research consulting firm in Cambridge. After learning the trade at the huge Cheney Brothers silk complex at Manchester, Connecticut, Royal Little started his own small synthetics company—Special Yarns (1923)—in Providence, Rhode Island, with ten thousand dollars, a partner, and three employees. Little's aggressive salesmanship and astute management brought profit and growth. After five years, the company merged and became Franklin Rayon. Renamed Atlantic Rayon in 1932, the company concentrated on women's "intimate apparel" and cashed in on the rayon vogue.

During World War II, Little won substantial government contracts for parachutes and jungle hammocks. He needed to expand production, and the most expedient way to do it was to buy mills that could feed his sewing machines. The China Mill, Suncook, New Hampshire, was the first. This merger produced "Textron" in 1944. A year later mills at Manchester, Nashua, and Dover, New Hampshire; Manville, Ashton, Albion, and Lonsdale, Rhode Island; and at Lowell joined Textron. Family mill owners, or their trustees, were glad to sell because their interest in textiles had dwindled. Little paid a better price than they could hope for in the slack years that would surely follow.

Little was buying mills so fast that there was rarely time to inspect them before purchase. He did not need to. He knew that they were hopelessly obsolete, and that was what he wanted. Little noted that their "complete inefficiency . . . attracted us as a challenge."

His management plan prescribed modern machinery and total reorganization of each mill following scientific time-study analysis. Simultaneous expansion of Textron in the South followed the same precepts and allowed easy

The Manville-Jenks mill, Manville, R.I., in 1949, a year after it was closed by Textron. Thirty-four hundred jobs were lost. The liquidated mill stood vacant when the 1956 flood did its damage. A conflagration following the flood completed the destruction. (Rhode Island Historical Society)

comparison of the results. As before, fuel and transport prices, taxes, and night shifts all favored the South. Although southern labor costs had risen almost to parity with those in the North, there were dramatic differences in man-hour productivity. Little's new machines and work patterns demanded twice the output per worker. Southern workers cooperated, as did the dependent local labor force at defunct northern mills he reorganized. But workers who came along with northern mills that were still functioning were unwilling to march to Little's quickstep. These old dogs refused to learn Royal Little's new tricks. Little accused them of "living in the past" and shut the offending mills down. Almost ten thousand workers were laid off.

The union condemned Textron's "selfish and cold-blooded plan," and Senator Charles Tobey of New Hampshire began an investigation of the company's transactions at Nashua. The investigation benefited Tobey more than Nashua. There was little anyone could do: Textron actions were legal. Moreover, they reflected sound business judgment. While continuing to profit from its remaining textile division, Textron began to diversify into unrelated fields that were more lucrative and hospitable. Mill liquidations fueled the diversification.

Textron expanded vigorously. By 1953, its textile division—fifteen mills with seven thousand employees, concentrated in the South—represented only half of its various holdings. This recession-sensitive division contributed to the company's seven-million-dollar loss that year. Wanting to expand his more profitable nontextile holdings, but needing a massive transfusion of capital to do so, Little ironically financed his exit from textiles by merging with American Woolen, New England's biggest textile mill holder, planning on eventual liquidation.

American Woolen had aged rapidly since William Wood's retirement in 1924. Wood had become increasingly erratic during his last years—and blew

Nashua Telegraph, September 13, 1948.

Nashua Telegraph, September 17, 1948.

Nashua Telegraph, September 24, 1948.

Editorials in the Telegraph recognized the hardship suffered by the 3,500 workers Textron laid off at Nashua, but called Senator Tobey's investigation of the closing a "three-ring circus," noting that private capital can do as it pleases. It advised its readers: "Textron is going to move out, whether we like it or not, and we must be realistic enough to keep just one objective in view: get new industry here to take over the idle mills." Royal Little finally promised to run the mills at partial capacity for another year and to reevaluate the shutdown decision, but the reprieve was only temporary. Textron left Nashua in 1949.

Hope Company cloth label. The Hope Mill at Lonsdale, R.I., was sold to the Lonsdale Company, which also controlled the mills at Ashton and Albion, just upstream on the Blackstone River below Manville. Textron bought the Lonsdale Company in 1945, and liquidated all the mills and housing before 1950. The Hope Mill was eventually converted into a discount supermarket. (Rhode Island Historical Society)

his brains out two years later. Inept management of the weakened empire he left had pared it down to twenty-seven mills, of which twelve were inactive. Losses of one million dollars per month were continuing. Doomed by over-specialization for the production of blue serge cloth, American Woolen became the brontosaurus of the industry. Articles in *Fortune* magazine called it "a mass producer of staples in an age of style" and described its assets as "inherited cash, staggering losses, the sorriest mills in the industry, and no prospects whatever."[100]

Royal Little wanted the "inherited cash" and the tax relief of losses carried forward. Although he found American Woolen in a "God-awful mess," its directors suspected his intent to liquidate and staunchly resisted his merger offers. It took him a year of maneuvering and arm twisting to force American Woolen into submission. Little called it a "shotgun marriage." *Fortune* dubbed it "Merger by Judo." As finally consummated in 1955, the deal combined Textron, American Woolen, and Robbins Mills, a southern firm, to make Textron American. A wholly owned subsidiary, Amerotron, took charge of all textile manufacturing activities. Textron was free to diversify, its future profits sheltered from taxation by the thirty-million-dollar inherited loss. Amerotron liquidated all its New England mills within two years and consolidated its best machinery in modern southern installations. Amerotron eventually abandoned textiles completely.

Textron had sucked American Woolen dry and thrown its carcass to the scavengers. Although this was neither the biggest nor the last textile closing of the period, it was certainly the most revealing. Little had diagnosed industrial gangrene and ordered amputation. The textile workers' union called him the "grave digger of the industry."

ADJUSTMENT

Unemployment naturally follows liquidation. Dependent communities clustered around the silent mill suddenly lose their reason for being. Union spokesmen for Nashua workers laid off by Textron had condemned management's freedom "to wreck an entire community to further its own narrow objectives" and theorized, "Free enterprise does not mean the freedom to use whole cities as a child uses building blocks—taking one here and discarding another there."[101] Subsequent events proved the union was mistaken. Inspired by free enterprise, industry had created the mill town and, though unable to destroy it, was perfectly free to wean it and force it to learn self-reliance.

The mill town's ability to adapt was limited. Postliquidation mill towns had only two assets: acres of cheap manufacturing space and a desperate surplus of uneducated, semiskilled labor, predominantly aging workers trained only for textiles. The combination had specialized appeal.

Several mill towns organized industrial development groups to manage the vacant factory property and attract new business. Their effectiveness varied widely. Sanford, Maine, which had fifty percent of its employment in textiles before the 1954 shutdown, fought so hard for new jobs that it was labeled "the town that refused to die." *Life* magazine ran a feature on Ware, Massachusetts, "The Town That Can't Be Licked." Concerned citizens of Manchester, New Hampshire, formed Amoskeag Industries, Incorporated, which bought the mills for five million dollars and lured tenants to vacant mill space. Thirty percent of the lost jobs were replaced in two years. New Bedford had a "Help New Bedford Plan" and an "Industrial Development Legion."

Nashua was one of the liquidated mill towns to recover most quickly. When Textron sold its mills there, Royal Little helped set up the Nashua New Hampshire Foundation to manage property and attract new business. Nashua, with 2.5 million square feet of vacant space, was favored also by proximity to Boston, by a tax and labor climate hospitable to industry, and by a relatively pleasant environment unscarred by slums of company housing.

Electronics and plastics firms found these assets especially inviting. Within five years, Nashua gained more jobs in new technologies than it had lost in the old. The city that had condemned Royal Little for unprincipled manipulation of its destiny now hailed him as the "benefactor" who had led them "from ruin to the height of prosperity."

This direct transition from low to high technology, from obsolete to modern, was repeated in several other mill communities. Digital Equipment (Maynard Woolen Mill), Raytheon (Shawsheen Mill, in North Andover), and Honeywell (Wood Mill, in Lawrence) are among the best known examples. Dozens of smaller electronics and plastics firms rented sections of tenanted mill property. An aerospace company took over the isolated and humble factory at Moosup, Connecticut.

Both the old and new technologies shared a common need for cheap space and conscientious, unskilled labor, especially female, for assembly operations. Unfortunately, a third group of industries, labor-intensive "sweatshops" of all

Promotion stickers, Woonsocket, R.I., ca. 1956. These stickers were part of a campaign to bring new industrial development to Woonsocket after the mills began closing in rapid succession. Hurricane-induced floods in August 1955, had destroyed many idle factories. The city responded with a winter Mardi Gras for publicity and tourism. Business Week called "battered, weary Woonsocket . . . the spunkiest city in the U.S.A." (Ray Bacon, Woonsocket High School)

kinds, have the same needs. Many textile mills were converted after liquidation into shoe and garment factories whose technology and working conditions were, and still are, as antediluvian as the textile manufacturing they replaced. Mill town workers had already learned to accept wretched working conditions and, when desperate, would tolerate other jobs that were no worse. Cities like Fall River and Lewiston, among others, became almost as dependent on the sweatshop as they had been on the textile mill.

DECAY

After 150 years of symbiotic coexistence with the textile industry, New England grew tired of the relationship and allowed its senile industrial creation to self-destruct. Although general and irreversible decay began early in this century, slow erosion has made it a lingering death, as each succeeding recession sends another group of mills into liquidation. By 1957, New England's textile capacity had dropped to twelve percent of its peak: its industry was smaller, and far less important, than it had been a century before. The decline continued until the early 1970's. Only the most tenacious companies survived. What had gone so disastrously wrong?

The New England textile industry was a victim of its own research; its mills served as the laboratory where the seeds of its destruction were perfected. During the industry's first decades, New England's mills mechanized all phases of fabric manufacture and perfected the use of waterpower. They also perfected an American version of industrial capitalism. Evolving out of the family partnership, the corporation enjoyed a long adolescence on the mill town playground. Each individual mill was an adventure—*experimental capitalism* at work. Together, the mills formed a regional industry. Investors had built the skeleton for a *permanent industrial environment* expressing the technology available and the business concepts of the times. But soon that same technology became commonplace. Perfected machines banished the "dark mystery" of textile manufacture, making it easy for anyone, anywhere, to buy. The steam engine, which textiles had nurtured, created new optimum locations for industry which were outside New England, many of them overseas. Northern machine builders even provided mill designs to go with their machines. New England technology was for sale, and its export market bought it: first the South, then the developing nations. *Fierce international competition* was the inevitable result. Today, New England mills do not fight the South alone, they fight the world.

New England mills fought their last battles with the industry's most antique equipment. Earlier, for decades, New England textiles had been the quintessence of progress. Most observers at the outset applauded as Yankees proved their strength and individuality, subduing reluctant nature, harnessing its power to machines whose astonishing dexterity would serve mankind, then enclosing it all in a righteous mill village. But progress inevitably leaves *obsolescence* in its wake. The industry had built its destiny into the brick and granite of mills organized around waterpower and the iron of machinery

An abandoned mill at Exeter, R.I., 1907. (Rhode Island Historical Society)

designed for wool and cotton. Times changed. The skeleton did not. Every aspect of the mill town, from concept to execution, represented the status quo of the nineteenth-century industry, so perfectly adapted to the past it could evolve only on a divergent path from the mainstream of progress.

Most mill towns endured long after they had become socioeconomic anachronisms. There had never been anything intrinsically wrong with the idea of a mill town; it simply was not as practical as it once was. Some of the obsolete mills could still survive, fighting their dwindling profit margin, running on their own depreciation. In the meantime, however, the industry was embarking on worldwide expansion, leaving New England burdened with even more *excess capacity* than before. Since mass production facilities run profitably only at or near full capacity, mill owners were forced to operate their mills sporadically—just enough to keep the mill town alive, never enough to nourish it. Each mill sputtered along towards the day when—suddenly—the directors voted for liquidation.

Liquidation put the mill town on the auction block. There were not many bidders. Everything about it was *overspecialized* and out of date. Yet the mills, and their towns, had been built to last: they were permanent, though their industrial life force was not. Vacant or tenanted, hundreds of mills remain today—standing corpses of industrial progress. They die, but remain on their feet.

The Industrial Revolution haunts New England. The carcass of its greatness, in parts, is picked clean to the skeleton; yet it still shows the last isolated twitches of life. It is no surprise that the creature died; it was too big and too old to adapt. The surprise is that so much of its legacy can still be seen.

PART TWO

AS IT IS

THE LEGACY

PHOTOGRAPHS BY THE AUTHOR

VI
Working

Albert Biro, loom fixer.
Wannalancit Textile Co.
Lowell, Mass.

"Every situation in life has its trials which must be borne, and factory life has no more than any other."
—*Lowell Offering*, 1845

The industry is now a mere shadow of former greatness. Employment peaked thirty years ago at 282,000, and slow attrition has whittled it down now to 65,000 workers in 520 surviving companies. Finally, the decline appears to be over. Bottom has been reached. Indeed, as regional labor differences fade, New England may even be regaining some of its earlier competitive advantage.

Today, New England's textile companies, like their employees, show a wide range of personalities, defying simple generalizations. A few flourish, while most struggle bravely on. Some are modern, even experimental. Others are hopelessly antiquated. A handful of companies have hundreds of employees, while most have only a few dozen. The owners may be a family or anonymous stockholders. In two recent cases, the workers themselves have become the owners. While many firms have specialized in one narrow aspect of the trade, there are still quite a few generalists, following the changing winds of fashion and market. Yet these diverse companies do share some common attributes. Each exhibits, above all, a stubborn will to survive. Each shares the bittersweet legacy of textile history. And each inhabits a mill and employs mill workers to get the job done. For most of New England, the textile mill is only a remote memory. But for these remaining workers it is a dominating reality. The mill is the center of their lives.

The mill is the place where the actions of people and machines are orchestrated for the common goal of producing textiles. When mechanical imperatives outweigh human values, the mill can easily become a hostile environment. Often dark, it is usually dirty, hot, and humid. Noise and vibration are inescapable. In the weave rooms, where hundreds of machines march out of step in close, dimly lit ranks, the effect is shattering. Jacquard weave sheds are the extreme, like gymnasiums crowded with dancing mechanical elephants. Many areas of the typical mill are so tightly packed with machinery that the worker is rarely more than a few inches from a machine, and is almost always surrounded by thousands of moving parts, each with its own characteristic sound and cycle. No photographic image can convey the relentless, ear-piercing noise, the constant churning of the floors, or the ever-present danger inside the mill.

Some of the hazards of mill work can have immediate consequences. Unshielded machinery can grab an unsuspecting worker's clothing or hair and pull the person into the works. On occasion, shuttles get deflected from their designated path and, if not intercepted, go hurtling through the weave room. Flying metal chips from grindstones and machine tools are a constant threat to the machinist's eyes. Live steam and caustic chemicals in the finishing room can scald and disfigure the unwary. Although similar occupational hazards can be found in most manufacturing environments, old textile mills have more than their share.

The textile mill also contains a more insidious, long-term set of dangers. The persistent, high-pitched noise of metal wearing on metal is the most obvious hazard. Prolonged exposure endangers the inner ear and hearing loss is commonplace among older workers. The lint-filled air of the typical mill is another long-term threat. This danger varies widely from mill to mill

Alice Veilleux, cotton spinner.
Bates Manufacturing Co.
Lewiston, Me.

depending on the types of fibers and machines used, and is most serious in cotton mills. Cotton dust carries an unknown contaminant with it which causes byssinosis, commonly known as "brown lung" or "cotton death." Untreated byssinosis leads to respiratory disablement similar to emphysema and chronic bronchitis. As cotton fiber is rarely used in New England today, byssinosis is a localized danger. Nonetheless, the air most mill workers breathe can be justly described as contaminated, and can only be harmful in the long run. But while there is always a surfeit of noise and dirt in the air, there is rarely enough light to go around. Poor visibility can cause permanent vision impairment; it also encourages accidents of all kinds.

Both workers and management tend to minimize or deny these dangers. Under recent pressure from the Occupational Safety and Health Administration (OSHA), a division of the U.S. Department of Labor, mills have corrected some of their most immediate hazards. In general, most power transmission belts and gears are now shielded; most looms now have barriers alongside which intercept some, but not all, flying shuttles; most stairs now have railings; and most passageways and fire escapes are now lighted. But OSHA has been quite ineffective in tempering the long-term hazards. Indeed, the mill workers often ignore the safety measures OSHA—and common sense—suggest. Slow accommodation is the most characteristic response to this antediluvian working environment. By the time a recruit has started to climb the long, slow ladder of wage increases, job choice, and tenure, habituation has set in, the mill trapping people like quicksand.

Physical working conditions are but one part of what mill owners call an "image problem" —the fact that no one outside wants to come in. Wages are among the lowest in manufacturing ($4.40 per hour, 1978 average); tenure and advancement seem a lifetime away; job security is nonexistent. Every year a few more companies go under, and all mill workers know their factory could be next; they only hope—often against the dictates of reason—that it keeps running until they reach retirement. Thus industry has little attraction for ambitious young people, who generally regard it as the last resort, and, even then, only a temporary one. Blacks are conspicuously absent. The typical mill is dependent on an aging staff of "lifers," supplemented by Portuguese- and Spanish-speaking immigrants and a sprinkling of the poor of other backgrounds.

Virtually all of the older workers were born into the mill, usually of immigrant parents. They were children of the thirties, when choices were few. Moving from mill to mill as the industry crumbled around them, they have survived. And they are the last true descendants of the mill town era, for few of them encourage their children to follow their footsteps.

The Latin workers are the most recent turn of the immigrant spiral. Mill work, as always, offers a niche for the poor, the illiterate, and the unskilled; and the "greenhorns," perennially, have little choice. At the mill, even an understanding of English may be optional—sign language and rudimentary pidgin English often suffice for communication. Latins are also the last ethnic group left to bring the family into mill work. They are succeeding the old-timers as custodians for the mill work ethic.

Mill work covers a wide variety of jobs and skills—from sweeper to loom fixer, doffer to mender. The lowest jobs can be learned in a day. The highest may take a lifetime. Most mill work consists of semiskilled machine-tending jobs that are relatively easy to master and that have their own demands, challenges, and rewards. Each mill job shapes a different kind of worker. No easy stereotypes can encompass the human diversity found within any given mill. But there is one simple and universal reason most workers have for being there: they think it is the best they can do.

The psychological effects of a lifetime of mill work depend completely on the job. While repetitive menial work eventually stunts the intellect of the unskilled, many mill jobs are neither repetitive nor menial—a ration of challenge and variety is available for those who can reach it. While the unskilled often find mill work empty, alienating, and meaningless, the minority of skilled workers are just as likely to find fulfillment and a sense of self-worth. For those fascinated by machinery and mechanical challenges, the mill can even be a huge playground. Many career mill workers at all levels of skill admit that the factory has become a second home for them. Yet government statistics for the entire industry reveal that less than one mill worker in three would choose the same career if they had it to do over again.

Progress towards the American dream of upward mobility is also job-dependent. All but the most hopeless mill workers want their children to do better than they, and they see their life's work as a springboard for the family, speaking proudly of their self-sacrifice. The plan works best for the skilled workers, for whom life is better in most respects. Children of loom fixers and weavers can and do become teachers, doctors, and engineers. Unfortunately, children of the unskilled—doffers, winders, sweepers, battery hands, and other menial operatives —even today are likely to find themselves following their parents into the mill. A career of unskilled mill work can still be inherited.

Full automation of textile manufacturing is still far in the future. Meanwhile, someone has to keep New England's last machines running. These are the men and women who do.

Vincent "Jimmy" Scarpellino, braider foreman.
Conrad-Jarvis Manufacturing Co.
Pawtucket, R.I.

There are 1,200 braid machines in this room, each with hundreds of moving parts. The noise is deafening.

"The job gets habit forming. It seems to happen automatically. Just like someone pushed a button. The minute you walk in, you turn yourself on. The minute you walk out, you turn yourself off."

"After a while, the noise doesn't bother you at all. You get used to it. If you're out sick for a week, when you come back and open the door it's just like a big roar coming at you."

Charlie St. Pierre, floorman.
Matson Mills, Inc.
North Grosvenordale, Conn.

Packing wool into the baling machine.

Jim "Tiny" Trant, drug clerk.
Quincy Dye Works, Inc.
Woonsocket, R.I.

The drug clerk is responsible for measuring the dyes and chemicals used in finishing. After 12 years as a kettleman at another dye house, Trant came to Quincy Dye Works. He has been there 19 years.

"My father worked 45 years at American Wringer and retired without a cent. I quit school in my junior year. Money was tight and I was looking for a job. I worked in a store until I was 17 or 18, then I went to work in the mill. Woonsocket was the textile capital of the world then. We had 55 mills going around the clock. If you stayed in this area, you worked textiles."

Ted Larter, the owner, stands in front, just left of center. His father founded the company in 1929 at another location in Lowell and moved it into the Suffolk mill complex in 1946. The mill itself was built by its namesake, the Suffolk Manufacturing Co., in 1831, and modified extensively during the firm's 84-year tenure. The Nashua Manufacturing Co. took it over in 1915 and ran it until 1936, when it passed to liquidator Jacob Ziskind. Wannalancit bought the mill from Ziskind.

But Ted spent his youth on the family's farm, not at his father's mill. "I hated the mill," he recalls. "It took my father away from me. Days, nights, weekends—I never saw him." Ted went from high school into the service, returning in 1956. His father died barely three weeks later. Ted inherited his nemesis.

"It was frightening to have this big a thing dumped in your lap. It was either drop the ball or carry it and run with it. I never realized what [my father] was doing down here. Then I came down here and found out. I learned everything about textiles within these walls. The whole damn thing. I love it now, but I had to get to like it. There's a tremendous amount of satisfaction to be gained by taking something someone else can't do, and making it work. Tremendous satisfaction. It is always challenging."

Wannalancit Co. employs about 180 people. Almost one-half of them are Spanish-speaking, primarily recent immigrants from Colombia who already knew textiles when they arrived and were ready to accept mill work Americans refused. "Mill work used to be passed from father to son," Larter remarks, "but not any more. That's the way it always is in mill towns: the third generation wants out. I suppose you've got to be hungry. [Colombians] don't know how to survive without working. They're God damn glad they've got a job."

"If a man works for me, I have a responsibility to keep him working. I've never had a lay-off. I do not believe in the modern theory of laying off as soon as times get hard. I want the employees who work for me to feel secure in their jobs. They can't perform well if they're insecure. We've been through some tough times, but I keep them busy—painting, cleaning, whatever. At least half, if I was forced to the wall, would stand beside me. I know them like I know my own family. You can't let them go. Many of them are happy to work here. They can do the same thing day after day. They're not subjected to terrible changes. The efficiency experts don't come around. The job has to be done and nobody cares how you do it. They're left alone—because of the noise you can't talk—and they do their own thing.

Actually, we shouldn't be here now. It's terribly tough to hang on. As long as I want to play with it, [the mill] will survive. No way in Hell you can sit back and watch it run. It's like treading water: you miss a stroke and it takes five strokes to get back to where you were. You've got to live in it, be right in the bowels of it. You've got to notice everything there is to notice. You listen. You look. Feel the sense, the pulse. You've got to know how everything works and how to fix it. I call the mill 'Mother'!"

Wannalancit Textile Company
Suffolk Mill.
Lowell, Mass.

Genevieve Reilly, narrow-fabric weaver.
Arbeka Webbing Co.
Pawtucket, R.I.

"Make the best work you can, that's all. You can't be careless. Your fingers have got to be limber and your eyesight has to be good. You've got a lot of things you've got to watch. Just like your car, you take care of your loom. They're all different. They say when you don't feel good, your looms don't run good."

She has been weaving since 1928. The mill she started at was nearby:

"Everybody around here seemed to work there, and it was the only place that employed girls. We made satin, and fancy tapes, too, for men's straw hats. It wasn't heavy work, and I guess they figured women kept their hands cleaner, so it was really all women that worked there."

Jenny retired in 1976.

Joe Paniatowski, sample weaver.
Providence Pile Fabric Co.
Fall River, Mass.

His father, brother, and uncles were all weavers when Joe started in the mule spinning room 50 years ago. "But I wanted to be a weaver and make $12 a week like them. I tried to get in as a drop-wire boy. I couldn't. So I snuck in at night to watch and learn. The foreman says, 'If he's that crazy to learn, he can stay.' So I learned from my uncle."

"My wife says I'm a sloppy man, but when it comes to weaving, I just like to look at yards and yards of perfect cloth. It's very difficult to do and that's what I strive for. My job is looking for trouble and eliminating it. That's how I get my satisfaction. All my life, my whole object was to make a piece of cloth that was perfect continuously."

Now retired.

John started in Rhode Island's Manville-Jenks mill as a roving boy. In 1941, he came to Fall River to work as a sweeper at the King Philip Mill, where he met his wife. She is now a weaver at another Fall River plant.

"The first day I went into the mill, the boss says to her, 'Look, I've got your husband here.' Just as a joke. I must have blushed. I was cleaning 5 or 6 months, then I started talking to her. Asked her for a date. I went with her since. When I came out of the service, I married her. She was filling batteries and I was only sweeping the floor.

I got my section in '46 and I've been a weaver ever since. As it turned out, it was the best job I ever had, although it was one of the roughest. There was a lot of responsibility. Quality is the prime subject. You don't want to make bad cloth.

You've got to know your section. When you get close to a loom, it sounds different. It comes to you, the longer you're on. To me, the loom, I can tell if it's functioning right just by the sound. There's no problem learning to weave if you put your mind to it. Basically speaking, weaving isn't the worst job, but you've got to watch almost everything.

I feel proud that people here, or in Providence, or California, all those places, are using what I produced. The way I look at it, I satisfied a lot of people. Not knowing who they are personally, but I feel that it's in their homes. It's not like a newspaper boy. He delivers papers, but then you read it and throw it away. But not what I produce. It's quality that might last maybe fifteen years. That's what people want. Something good. They're using it and they'll keep it. They aren't going to throw it out the window.

It's a long time to weave. Thirty years. I don't regret it."

John Valleriana, weaver.
Providence Pile Fabric Co.
Fall River, Mass.

Frank Roy, drug clerk.
Quincy Dye Works, Inc.
Woonsocket, R.I.

"I used to work in the Packard Mill. We never loafed. I loafed twelve weeks during twenty years, during the changeover from knitting to spinning. The dye house was so clean you could eat off the floor."

Now retired.

Men's room.
Andrews Worsted Mills, Inc.
Pascoag, R.I.

Shortly after this photograph was taken, all obscenities in the mill were painted over with polka dots of industrial green paint. The result was no less nauseating.

"Every apartment (workroom) has its water trough, or what is denominated a sink, for the workers to wash their face and hands in; a most healthy, as well as cleanly, operation, which is punctually attended to before every meal, soap being supplied for this purpose by the proprietors."
—Montgomery, *Cotton Manufacture*, 1840

George Desserren, millwright.
Stamina Mills, Inc.
Forestdale, R.I.

"You can tell I'm a working man. I could retire, but I wouldn't think of it. I work 58 hours a week and that means a lot of overtime. I own my own house and I buy my cars new. I weld, I cut, I rig. You name it, I do it."

Laid off, 1975.

Margot Robitaille, finish percher.
Andrews Worsted Mills, Inc.
Pascoag, R.I.

Margot has been with the company for 22 years, inspecting fabric in the "perch room," one of the quietest and sunniest sections of the mill. Two of her sons worked here, too: one quit; the other was laid off.

"If I had my choice, I'd rather see [my sons] working somewhere else. Being a bobbin strip- per, cleaning looms, it wasn't paying anything. I figure, either learn how to weave or learn a trade in the mill, then it would be all right, you know. Dresser tender, anything. But being a garbage boy for the mill, I couldn't see that."

"I make them for somebody else, plaids, but I don't wear 'em. I get so sick of them. I am beginning to not see any of these things here. It looks all the same, now. I've been doing this job so long that it's automatic. It can get you dizzy. Some stuff we do here, like little checks and that, it goes by pretty fast and after a while everything goes all psychedelic."

Coffee break.
Kenyon Piece Dyeworks, Inc.
Kenyon, R.I.

José Caralho, braider fixer.
Conrad-Jarvis Manufacturing Co.
Pawtucket, R.I.

Francisco Ferrera, slasher tender.
Wannalancit Textile Co.
Lowell, Mass.

José Raposo, loom fixer.
Providence Pile Fabric Co.
Fall River, Mass.

Tattooed while serving as a military policeman
and marksman in Portuguese Guinea.

Leo Maranda, loom fixer.
Providence Pile Fabric Co.
Fall River, Mass.

Retired, because of failing eyesight.

Leo Barton, loom fixer.
C & M Textile Co.
North Grosvenordale, Conn.

He is building timing chains for pattern weaving.

"I'm a loom fixer and ordinarily I wouldn't be doing this. A loom fixer just fixes looms. But in a small place like this, you've got to do a little bit of everything."

Mariano Figueirdo, floor helper.
Wm. Heller, Inc.
Coventry, R.I.

Wm. Heller, a subsidiary of Uniroyal, was closed in January, 1975. Expensive new sewage treatment equipment would have been required for it to continue its dye and finish business.

"Nobody will take us, after this. You get over 60, that's it. Unless you have a college education. I don't have much. I only went up to the fourth grade. I started work at the age of fourteen. Good thing I worked long enough to pay [for] my home."

Narrow-fabric loom fixers.
Arbeka Webbing Co.
Pawtucket, R.I.

Paul and George Thomas, owners.
G. Thomas and Son.
North Grosvenordale, Conn.

George has been around textiles since he was 16 and owned his own mill since 1940. He and his son, Paul, are shown unloading a new loom at their small commission weaving mill.

"It's a rough business. Always has been, but worse now. You've got to keep moving. You can't sit back. Competition is stiff. When times are hard, we cut each other's throats. Either you modernize or you go into a small operation like my son, my wife, myself, and a couple of others. Make it a family affair at which I can earn a living. Right now, I'm putting in 70 hours a week. I'm here 7 days a week."

Paul splits his time between the mill and his MG Midget racing car, stored in the basement of the mill.

"Racing is what I really like doing. But right now, I feel guilty neglecting business and working on my car. I sacrifice almost everything just so I can work on it and race. There's a lot of work that goes into it. I'd say it's 99% work and 1% you're out on the track. You're stuck. You have to sacrifice something. I like working with my hands. I feel more complete, using everything. If you have to think plus use your hands, I like that."

Kasty Simonds, owner.
Simonds Co.
Wilsonville, Conn.

Kasty Simonds is a very tenacious man. For twenty years, he supervised a large woolen mill near Norwich. When it closed in 1973, he decided to run a mill of his own. The abandoned Keegan mill at Wilsonville was the best he could afford. Most of the windows were broken by vandals, the roof leaked badly, and a large section of the floor was sagging towards the river. Icicles covered the machinery inside.

Kasty and his wife, Ida Mae, restored the mill together. They put in over 800 window panes, jacked up the floors, sealed the roof, moved and refurbished the machinery, and converted the guano-laden granite storehouse beside the falls into a home. Three back-breaking years later, they were in business.

"Some folks call us crazy, but we're just determined. Everybody wants to be in busines for themselves. We felt that, too. We've always been independent. If we don't make it, at least we'll have tried."

Leo Benjamin, repacker.
Providence Pile Fabric Co.
Fall River, Mass.

Leo quit soon after his illiteracy was discovered.

Bob Matthewson, assistant percher.
Andrews Worsted Mills, Inc.
Pascoag, R.I.

Laid off.

Louis "Gigi" Klebes, kettleman.
Quincy Dye Works, Inc.
Woonsocket, R.I.

Laid off, then recalled.

Russell Hreczuch, timing chain builder.
Andrews Worsted Mills, Inc.
Pascoag, R.I.

Laid off.

Richard Wilder, chief engineer.
Lawrence Print Works.
Lawrence, Mass.

"I've been a Master Mechanic about 50 years, or pretty close to it. Now I'm getting over the hill. This place here, it's just like being retired. You don't do anything all summer, just get the boilers ready for inspection in the fall. That's all I do. You don't make a helluva lot of money, but I think it's better than the average person. This is a good job. It's all right for a guy that's ready to retire."

Marian Sherman, mender.
Wm. Heller, Inc.
Coventry, R.I.

Marian worked 35 years as a mender, the last 11 at Wm. Heller. She was lucky enough to retire on the same day that the mill shut down. The dog, Mali, is a retirement gift from her
family.

*"If you don't like the work, forget it. But I always liked my work. From the time I started
until today, I still could learn. No matter how experienced you are, you're never experienced
enough. You're always finding something new. I enjoyed every minute of it."*

Shift change.
Providence Pile Fabric Co.
Fall River, Mass.

VII

Villages, Hamlets, and Towns

Teenagers.
North Grosvenordale, Conn.

The isolated textile mill village was both the functioning unit and the emblem of water-powered industry. Here, nineteenth-century manufacturers built their monuments to Capital and Technology. The villages were, necessarily, expressions of high confidence, even egotism. Unfortunately, despite numerous righteous espousals, manufacturers had no special measure of insight or social awareness. Though ambitious, their creations represent limited, idiosyncratic visions of industrial society. Mill villages had to be permanent economic fortresses to justify the long-term investment they required: they were garrisons for a vulnerable industry in the wilderness. Each village was an ordered and purposeful universe with its socioeconomic status quo built in, a universe reflecting a pragmatic, state-of-the-art solution to the challenge of waterpowered manufacturing. Though narrowly limited in concept and never truly utopian in design, these new towns were built to last, and they *have* lasted, long after their obsolescence. Mill villages today mark the frontier of an earlier civilization, one which America has transcended but not completely absorbed.

The mill and its housing were conceived as interdependent: the more isolated the site, the more total the dependence. This symbiosis loosened slowly after the turn of the century as transportation improved and companies sold off their housing, but each mill town's fate continues even now to be linked with the mill that gave it purpose. By design, the mill is a production unit, a container for industry. It has no life of its own independent of the company that animates it. Only a rare handful of village mills in operation today are controlled by the company that created them. The others have been passed from investor to investor; sometimes they are used for manufacturing, sometimes not. As long as there are jobs in the mill—whether in textiles or not—the mill town can survive as an industrial unit. Though the mill no longer draws its workers exclusively from the town, and town residents no longer work exclusively at the mill, the relationship remains. When the mill is vacant, abandoned, or destroyed, the mill town is cut loose. A few of the oldest towns are already in ruins, and several others are reduced to sad and lonely collections of derelict tenements sliding into decrepitude.

Even when the mill is still being used, mill villages generally have a run-down, tawdry appearance. All of them are more than a century old—the first village having been built more than 150 years ago—and only a rare few have enjoyed continuous maintenance. Decay shrouds these communities. They are living anachronisms and, as such, have limited value on the real estate markets where their destiny is traded. Mill town home owners are usually former employees of the mill, or descended from them. Landlords control the rest of the housing. Rents are low—$15 a week is common—but the apartments offer few amenities, and the landlords are correspondingly stingy. Rented mill town housing is always a potential rural ghetto.

The villages have tremendous social inertia even in the face of inevitable decay. Mill workers early in the century sunk their roots in these villages and many families have stayed on long after the parent company is gone. Even ethnic distinctiveness is preserved: the Pawtuxet Valley is still Italian; the Quinebaug Valley still French-Canadian. A high degree of functional illiteracy among adults is also part of the mill town inheritance, and children's opportunities for education are limited.

View from the water tower.
North Grosvenordale, Conn.

While the entire environment is rooted in the past, these mill towns are hardly museums. The television, the automobile, and, to a lesser extent, the school, break down isolation and force them into the present. They are now neighborhoods of the global village and share in its rituals and crises. Their structure is antique and dangerously obsolete, but their citizens live in a reasonable facsimile of the present. Each community, no matter how fragmented and derelict, has a collective will to survive. But it is often a losing battle.

Conceived as a model industrial community, North Grosvenordale still provides one of the best examples of mill town destiny. The company prospered for three generations, surviving the depression to earn praise in 1939 as "one of the busiest concerns in New England, maintaining a high mark for continued operation." At that time, the company employed 2,100 workers making fabric for Arrow shirts. The company had auctioned off part of its housing—the "Three Rows" section visible just in front of the mill—the year before, offering easy mortgages for its employees. But only a few houses were sold to their occupants, speculators taking the others. By 1942, the rest of the company was for sale. Cluett-Peabody, another textile firm, bought it and ran the mills for another dozen years, selling off more of the housing as the company skidded towards liquidation. When the 1955 flood hit North Grosvenordale, the mill was empty. The townspeople bought it thereafter, but their efforts to find a new employer proved abortive. Holding companies and liquidators closed in and took control, passing the mill back and forth.

View from Rt. 12 towards
"Three Rows."
North Grosvenordale, Conn.

The mill is tenanted now. Two small textile firms share it with a furniture company, a firm called "Sanitary Dash," and Colt Plastics, which makes handles for pistols. Together, the five companies employ under 500 workers. As before, the jobs are primarily semiskilled.

The housing auctions split North Grosvenordale into two new castes: home owners and tenants. Those workers who bought mill houses chose the best the company offered, the prim cottages and two-deckers around the rim of the basin. Most of these people are retired now. Unscrupulous landlords have made the run-down tenements below function as a catchall for welfare families, ne'er-do-wells, and the working poor that still depend on local mills for intermittent employment. "Three Rows" is now known locally as "Skid Rows."

The town is almost as isolated now as it was when created, and it is far less self-sufficient. A few stores, a pizza parlor, and a luncheonette meet basic needs. The movie theater has been closed for years. Residents must go to Webster or Putnam for shopping or recreation. Worcester, the nearest city, is 25 miles away, but seems much farther. The most active employer in the region, the Electric Boat submarine yard at Groton, is more than 45 miles downstream. Insulated from American progress, North Grosvenordale struggles along on its predetermined path. The once-prosperous valley is now a backwater.

"Swede Village" mill housing.
North Grosvenordale, Conn.

Pauline and Renee Durand.
"Swede Village."
North Grosvenordale, Conn.

Both born and raised in North Grosvenordale. Pauline and her husband worked in the mill just across the street several years ago. He now does construction work. Several months after this photograph was taken, the family moved to a small house of their own a few hundred yards away.

Leo Bellanceau and his sons; Gregory, Leo, and Andre.
"Three Rows."
North Grosvenordale, Conn.

"I've worked in just about every mill around here. Now I work construction. Imagination's all right, but it's no good in the mill. They put the work in front of you and you've got to do it. That's what they pay you for.

  I've bought some land. Someday we'll move."

Nick came to North Grosvenordale from Yugoslavia in 1914. He was 21. He worked as a weaver until 1939, when he built and opened a small liquor store: "Nick's Package." He has just retired.

"*I never dreamed to stay in this place so long. I like it because, well, the place where I was born was worse than this. We didn't have the convenience we got in this country. We got hot water all year round in the house. We got all electricity. We have automatic washing machine. We have dryer. We have color TV. What I want more than that? And radio in every room.*

I am very glad. When I came here I didn't have nothing. At least now I got my own house. Beside here, I got two old houses in Putnam. And beside that, I put four children through university. They got good jobs. What I want more? I am very satisfied from United States. Very satisfied."

Nick Teguis.
North Grosvenordale, Conn.

Betty Casey Bergeron.
"Three Rows."
North Grosvenordale, Conn.

"This town is still in the Dark Ages. When that mill moved out of there it was hell. Go look at the old people. Vegetables, God bless 'em, who can't talk about anything but what they used to do for Cluett-Peabody. We're hanging on by a thin thread, just living from day to day. We have to. You can't look to the future. The only one I want to look to the future is my son."

Anna and Joe Wojick, retired weavers.
Overseer's house.
North Grosvenordale, Conn.

The Wojicks emigrated from Poland when they were twenty. After weaving in Massachusetts mills, they came to Grosvenordale. They were married at Cluett-Peabody and worked there 37 years. Their house is a duplex and their son's family lives in the other half.

"We started weaving in Blackstone. Low pay, poor work. Here the pay was better and not so far to walk."

Ralph Burnham.
"Hospital Block" tenant.
North Grosvenordale, Conn.

"I've been here too damn long. I had some money when I came, but I haven't any now. I've been trying to leave this place, but it's hard to do. I hate this town."

Mary Wood
"Hospital Block" tenant.
North Grosvenordale, Conn.

"I'm getting out of here. Go somewhere. I don't know where, somewhere I can afford the rent. I'm on social security. Don't get much. The rent is $50, and the heat and lights on top of that. It just isn't worth it. It's so goddamn cold here. Awful cold. I keep waiting for those social security checks. Waiting and waiting. They're never soon enough."

"Swede Village" children.
North Grosvenordale, Conn.

Opposite:
"Salle Union."
North Grosvenordale, Conn.

The French Canadian community built the "Salle Union" in the 1930s as a movie theater and social center for the village. Although boarded up, it is not abandoned. Itek Corporation, creator of optical systems for unmanned exploration of outer space, leases it. They store large-scale models of lunar and planetary terrain here. The lofty theater ceiling allows them to test their cameras at a high viewing angle.

Bruce Tefft, Mary Hesselton, and her children.
North Grosvenordale, Conn.

Separated and moved to Putnam.

Ray Brown
Boardinghouse tenant.
Mechanicsville, Conn.

Ray's family moved from Providence, R.I., to Mechanicsville in 1971. They work in Putnam
at the U.S. Plastic and Chemical factory making buttons. Mechanicsville was once a thriving
village dependent on the French River Textile Company. Fires and hurricanes destroyed the
mill, leaving only the boardinghouse, the post office, and a few mill houses. The boardinghouse is now a shambles of cheaply remodeled apartments. The kitchen was converted into
a garage. The Brown family stayed here four years. A fire in their flat forced them to move.

Quinebaug River.
Putnam, Conn.

The mill at top center occupies the site of Smith Wilkinson's "Pomfret Factory," one of the first mills on the Quinebaug.

Shetucket River and American Thread Co.
Willimantic, Conn.

Riverpoint was the centerpiece of B. B. & R. Knight's Pawtuxet Valley mill system. In the 1890s, Robert Knight combined several earlier mills on the site to make a grand new structure named for his favorite son, Royal, who died in childhood. The new mill was remarkable for its unusually tall, pointed clock tower, which had a four-ton metal sphere poised on top. Royaldale farm was nearby. The Knight kingdom stretched away, both upstream and downstream, into a chain of villages totally devoted to Fruit of the Loom. Early in the twentieth century, a local aristocrat described the valley as "the swamp of Rhode Island, with a great fog hanging over it." Devotion to mill work had made Rhode Island the most illiterate of the northern states, with the highest percentage of young women at work and young men physically unfit for military service. After sixty years of Knight control, the Pawtuxet Valley contributed significantly to the region's backwardness.

Disaster struck in 1919, when the tower caught fire and the ball crashed down, destroying the sprinkler mains as it went. The fire left the entire mill in ruins. Family ownership of the empire ended the next year, when New York financiers took control. One of their first moves was to build the New Royal Mill on the site, with three times the capacity of its predecessor. They tried to replace Knight family paternalism with scientific, efficiency-oriented, absentee management. But fourteen months later, their speedups and wage cuts caused a massive strike, closing every mill in the valley. The national guard had to be called in to stop the rioting. Machine guns atop the towers guarded the mill. Although the mills eventually reopened, the company slid quickly into bankruptcy.

The valley has never quite recovered. The Royal Mill still stands, but most of it is now vacant. Sunbury Dress Company, one of the handful of apparel firms that rent part of it, keeps a sign by the door advertising "steady, pleasant work" at "excellent piece rates" with "music while you work." The three Sunbury employees in the foreground head home after their day's work.

Royal Mill
Riverpoint, R.I.

Bob Watson and Pam Wilder.
Harrisville, N.H.

She is leaving. He is not.

Wilson and Irene Noka.
Alton, R.I.

Wilson Noka worked for several years at the Bradford Dye Association before quitting and switching to Kenyon Piece Dye, a dozen miles upstream from Bradford on the Pawcatuck River. Alton, once a lace mill town, lies between Bradford and Kenyon on a tributary of the Pawcatuck. After Wilson, Irene, and their seven children had been evicted from two nearby mill towns, the family bought this house, built by the factory across the street.

WILSON: *"It wasn't a matter of choice to live here. It was almost like no choice. I went out looking for a place to rent and I saw this place for sale. I bought it and that's why I'm here in Alton. There was very small choice. They didn't really approve of a Black family, seeing as how this is the only Black family throughout this whole area."*

IRENE: *"We had trouble. They figure we were renting the house. So they try to find the land-lord and get us evicted. We own the house, you know."*

WILSON: *"So when they say, 'Who is the landlord?,' I say, 'You're looking at him. I'm the landlord.' I tell 'em, 'No soap. I don't move this time.' For damn sure, I ain't gonna evict myself. If I move this time, it's because I want to."*

Ashton, R.I.

Textron bought the mill from the Lonsdale Co., which had built it in 1867, then liquidated it. It is now occupied by Owens-Corning Fiberglass. Brick tenement blocks are squeezed into the small valley flanking the mill. A mill church sits on the rim of the valley, just out of view on the left.

Stamina Mills,
Forestdale, R.I.

This cotton mill was built in 1860 beside an early scythe works just upstream from Slatersville. The scythe works made sabers for Civil War soldiers. Stamina Mills made garment
linings. It was later converted to produce distress blankets and yarn for baseball cores from
reprocessed fiber known appropriately as "shoddy." When it finally closed in 1975, it was
one of the oldest mills in continuous operation.

In 1875, Forestdale had a population of 361. There were 40 tenements for the cotton mill
and 21 for the scythe works. Eighty percent of the residents came from immigrant families,
most of whom were French Canadian.

Baltic Mill.
Baltic, Conn.

Mill housing.
Sawyerville (near Dover), N.H.

Ponemah Mills.
Taftville, Conn.

Ponemah Mill housing.
Taftville, Conn.

"It's better than some places."
—Danny Zellucci

Millrace.
Wyoming, R.I.

J. J. Brown and his Chevrolet.
Alton, R.I.

The Stone Mill.
Rockville, Conn.

Jean Stanislewski with 5 of her 7 children.
Springville Mill boardinghouse.
Rockville, Conn.

"Nate."
Springville Mill boardinghouse.
Rockville, Conn.

Mike Taylor, retired overseer.
Manville, R.I.

Mike had been working at the huge Manville-Jenks Mill for 37 years when Textron shut it down in 1948. Experienced, capable, and confident, he had risen to overseer of weaving. From Manville, he went on to three other mills—the Merrimack Manufacturing Co. at Lowell, Berkshire-Hathaway's Bourne Mill at Fall River, and the Albion Mill, downstream from Manville—staying with each one until it closed.

"My general manager (at Lowell) told me, 'You should have got out of here long ago, Mike. You could have gone places if you got out of Manville.' I says I was always satisfied to stay here. I don't have any urge to move. I was born in the cottage right behind this house. It's a small town. I know everybody and they know me, so I find it to be a congenial community. This used to be the superintendent's house. It's more than 150 years old. I bought it 40 years ago. I expect to die in this house."

Hamilton Woolen Mill No. 2.
Amesbury, Mass.

Opposite:
The Danielson Inn.
Danielson, Conn.

"It used to be the hub of the town," reports John Polanski, fourth owner of the century-old inn. The front window sill is brass, worn smooth by generations of traveling salesmen who came to Danielson when it was still "Curtain Town"—home of Powdrell and Alexander Co., once the world's largest drapery mill—and propped their feet up while watching the trolleys go by out front. Polanski wove and fixed looms for P & A before buying the hotel in 1940. The mills shut down a dozen years later, but the town and the inn slumber on. He calls it "a Mom and Pop affair" and rents rooms at $15 a week to an aged local clientele.

Housing for Harmony Mills.
Cohoes, N.Y.

VIII
Mill Cities

Joanne Amaral
Price Place
Fall River, Mass.

Hamilton Mills and canal.
Lowell, Mass.

City Hall.
Lowell, Mass.

Lowell, the prototype for all the great waterpowered centers of New England, remains the
classic mill city. Encircled by a polluted river, sliced by idle railroad tracks and stagnant
canals, scarred by parking lots marking the sites of demolished mills, and blighted by
virulent slums, the city has been crumbling for decades. Yet fragments of an earlier age
of pride and prosperity can still be found. Efforts are underway to reverse Lowell's decay
and combine its fragments of grandeur into a National Park. Its sister cities are not as fortunate: their measures of glory were always more modest; their problems were often more
acute; their resources, more limited. Although their problems are shared, each mill city
must find its own solution.

Merrimack St.
Lawrence, Mass.

Most of Lawrence's textile industry folded or headed south in the 1950s, leaving behind ten million square feet of empty mill space. Factories still line both sides of the river, and the city of three-decker tenements is still one of the most densely populated in the nation. Lawrence is primarily an ethnic, blue-collar city—designed for industry, it has to stay that way. Now Honeywell occupies the Wood Mill, at the far end of the street. Prince Spaghetti is in the giant Ayer Mill, just beyond it. General Tire and Malden Mills—the last major textile employer—own large factories across the river. The rest of the space is tenanted by dozens of smaller industries. Some remains vacant.

Placed for a commanding view of interstate Rt. 495, the $$$ sign (backed up by tax deferments and job training programs) tempts industries to relocate. The Economic Development Corporation emphasizes the location, the abundance of semiskilled labor ("They're very dextrous, and good at assembling things"), and the sturdiness of the mills as the city's prime assets, adding that it would be "real suicide" for Lawrence to either destroy the mills or use them for nonindustrial purposes. Lawrence, the queen of industrial cities, will endure.

Eddie Kania's Men's Bar.
Essex St.
Lawrence, Mass.

Frank Albernaz reading his Bible.
East Main St.
Fall River, Mass.

East Main St. connects downtown Fall River with Laurel Lake and the six large mills clustered around it. The Laurel Lake district and adjoining Glove Village are almost exclusively Portuguese.

Reis's Portuguese and American Foods.
East Main St.
Fall River, Mass.

José, Joey, and Fatma de Sousa.
Price Place.
Fall River, Mass.

José and Fatma came to Price Place, an alley behind East Main St., from Sao Miguel, an island in the Azores. José had been a farmer. Now he is an upholstery weaver, and she is a garment worker. Both are laid off. José's two brothers and two sisters work at the same mill he does.

"When I was in Portugal, no good. Too much work for no money. I like over here because of the money. It's better for me. Not yet, because I got no job. No money. Last Friday, my brother came over from Portugal. Three kids. No job."

Manuel Bilhante.
Price Place.
Fall River, Mass.

Freddie Hutchins
and Ed Walsh.
Fall River, Mass.

Ed Walsh runs his Odd Job Shop in the cotton shed of the Borden Mill. He has lived in a house overlooking the mill all his life.

"I worked briefly in the Kerr Mill. Bobbin boy. I stayed three days. Couldn't take it. But I've been in and out of mills all my life. You can't help it here, because that's all there was. Cotton, when they're weaving it, throws off a dust. It makes you gag. That's why they sold so much plug tobacco and snuff, because you had to chew tobacco all the time to keep moisture in your mouth. Otherwise you'd choke. They call it the cotton death."

Richard Borden Mill.
Fall River, Mass.

"One of the most perfect structures
for manufacturing in this country."
—*Lamb's Textiles*, 1916

Borden blocks.
Fall River, Mass.

Built in 1871, the community served the Borden Mill behind it. The streets were named for prominent mill towns: Holyoke, Lawrence, Manchester, Lowell, Lonsdale, Blackstone, Dover, and Nashua. The central block was demolished in 1976 as a fire hazard.

"Colonel Borden transformed a wasteland
into a flourishing settlement and
greatly expanded a prosperous business."
—*Lamb's Textiles*, 1916

Ronald Bouchard.
Borden blocks.
Fall River, Mass.

Recently separated, and just moved in. The view
opposite is from his bedroom window.

Gertrude Ferrara.
Borden blocks.
Fall River, Mass.

Roger Cassidy, loom fixer.
Waumbec Mills.
Manchester, N.H.

"I come up in the mill. I been there since I was 16. My old man is still there. My brother is there. The whole family's there. What are we going to do? All we know is mills. Where the hell would I go for a job? No education. Six kids. The only thing I know is the mill."

Roger Fontaine.
Manchester, N.H.

Roger and his friend Ray share a furnished apartment in the Amoskeag Mill housing blocks. He worked as a cloth doffer for Waumbec Mills, an Amoskeag successor. He was laid off and went to wash dishes at Eli's restaurant.

"For fun, we get a six pack and watch TV. Ain't got no car. If I had a car, I could go to a drive-in, take a ride. It's boring to be in the apartment. Sometimes I watch TV all night.

   My mother was born here in Manchester. My father was born in Canada. I was born here. My father divorced her when I was born. I was living all alone with my mother and had to support her. She was sick and died young. If I win the Sweepstakes, I'll buy my mother a stone. A grave stone. When she died, I couldn't afford it."

Amoskeag Mills and Merrimack River.
Manchester, N.H.

After eleven years at Bates Manufacturing Co.—Lewiston's largest remaining textile mill and the last large mill in New England to use cotton and Jacquard weaving—Julien Cloutier became president of Union Local 462. He has held the position for twenty "very rewarding" years, fighting to allow the 1,200 workers he represents "a voice in their destiny." His wife, Carmen, says, "He's a big, big reader. All he does is read, read, read, read, read, read, read, read, read—all the time." He has 85 college credits from night school—almost enough to finish—and discourses easily on a wide variety of subjects, especially the "lack of purpose" and the "end of honesty" he finds in America, now disillusioned with the national dream.

"If anyone ever represented the work ethic, it's the French Canadians of Lewiston. They work and work and work. They work until the day they die. The French Canadians worked together, they pulled together, to uplift the [family] unit.

Take my father for instance. He could read French. English, he never learned. He was 9 years old, very poor family, 18 kids. They were building the Trans-Canada railway at the time. He went out there, shoveling sand onto the flatcar. Nine years old. He was 11 years old when he came here to Lewiston to work in the mills. Soon, there were 12 people in his family. It was a problem. But somehow or other, before the first of us had started to work, my father had paid for his home—$1,800. Food we had plenty of. A good home life. Wonderful! Every kid in my family went through high school—that was quite a big thing then. When he died, my mother said she couldn't remember one time when he took money out of his pay for himself. Clothes and such, of course, but he never drank or went to the movies.

The aim was to get ahead, to better themselves. That has been the aim of everybody that came to America, I guess. And of course, the whole nation was different—it was the promised land. They came here for a better living, and they worked like hell for it. They built a pretty good place. I'm proud of what the French Canadians have done here: doctors, lawyers; a legacy of honest, hard-working citizens—French Canadians—in the professions.

I can say there are a lot of happy people here in Lewiston. They may not be as sophisticated as a New Yorker, but they've made a much better life for themselves, in my book. It's good. Not the best. And I suppose we're provincial as hell. I've been in big cities all my life. Not a God damn one that I would want to change for this town.

I've been satisfied. I'll be honest with you—I worked like hell, 6, 7, days a week, 10, 12 hours a day. Never bothered me. I'm not a rich man, but I've lived. This place is a house, all paid for. And I hope I can have a few years before I die to do the things I wanted to do. And what else? What more could a guy want, eh? I'm just one of the thousands that have, at some time or another, been on the stage. There's a lot of satisfaction from a lifetime of small gains."

In 1977, Bates Manufacturing Company began a federally-sponsored Employee Stock Ownership Plan, transferring ownership gradually to the mill workers.

Julien Cloutier.
Lewiston, Me.

Androscoggin River.
Lewiston, Me.

Seven-eighths of Lewiston's citizens are French Canadian. They came for textile work and stayed to make a blue-collar city that will outlast the industry. In a recent local survey, one respondent in three rated Lewiston "one of the best" places to live.

Continental Mills.
Lewiston, Me.

The mill is now a shoe shop. St. Mary's Church, center, uses the housing blocks beside it for its rectory and convent. Little Canada begins at the end of the canal. The parish priest guesses that more than half the people in Little Canada still work in local mills, especially the Continental, and adds:

"They're not sophisticated, but decent, hard-working, honest people trying to survive. Those that stay are satisfied. They're content with their quality of life, their family style. They're accepted. They feel they belong. But they're discontented by the fact there is very little chance of being successful. The wages are low. It's a hard life, working in the mills."

259

Rev. Armand Morisette.
St. Jean Baptiste Church.
Lowell, Mass.

Two of Jean-Louis [Jack] Kerouac's novels—*Maggie Cassidy* and *Dr. Sax*—are set in the "Sweet Lowell" of his youth. The spiritual center of Little Canada, where he grew up, was "St. Jean Baptiste church ponderous Chartres Cathedral of the slums." "Father Spike" Morisette was one of the parish priests—at first a friend, then a confidant, and finally the funeral orator for Kerouac. Father Spike remembers Kerouac as brilliant and impatient, in love with superstition and atmosphere, and overly given to drink.

Father Spike grew up in Little Canada, too, eventually transcending the ghetto by advancing through the ranks of the Oblate Fathers, the mission-oriented French Canadian sect centered at St. Jean Baptiste. "I had a very interesting life by staying myself and retaining my identity as a French Canadian," he says. "I capitalized on it. Anyplace can be the center of the world."

Mill tenements.
South Summer St.
Holyoke, Mass.

"Down Riverside and to the right Scotty Boldieu lived with his mother in a wooden tenement, third floor, you went up there via some outside wooden stairs that had the quality of steps in dreams as they rose from ten-foot bushes a jungle of them in the field below and took you swaying up the ladder of flimsy porches with strange-faced French-Canadian ladies looking down yelling to other ladies "Aayoo Madame Belanger *a tu ton* wash finished?"

—Kerouac, *Maggie Cassidy*

Millyard.
Massachusetts Mills.
Lowell, Mass.

Atlantic Mills.
Olneyville, R.I.

The Atlantic Delaine Co. built these mills in 1851 and 1865 to make "delaine," a fabric
with cotton warp and wool filling. It failed in the Panic of 1873. Sold at auction, the factory was reorganized as Atlantic Mills and became one of America's largest producers of
fine worsteds. It had 21 acres of floor space and more than 2,400 looms. Three thousand
people worked here during peak production. The mill finally closed in 1954. It is now a
discount department store.

Ronnie Morin and his father.
Woonsocket, R.I.

Ronnie is a kettleman at Quincy Dye Works. He has been there 9 years. His father has just retired after 28 years as a boilerman at Uniroyal. His mother died recently. The two men share a comfortable tract house in the suburbs of Woonsocket.

"I'm not sorry I never went on my own. I threatened to leave years ago and my parents said, 'If you leave, you can't come back. You can visit, but you can't come back to live.' I never went. I just like being home. I have my own room. I go off whenever I want. I have nobody else to answer to. I like living with my father."

Privilege Mill.
Woonsocket, R.I.

Wamsutta Mills No. 2 and No. 1.
New Bedford, Mass.

Wamsutta No. 1 (1848) was the first successful steam mill in New Bedford. This mill originated the trade name "Percale" and made the city famous for production of fine cotton
sheets. Twenty-three textile companies are still running in the city. Wamsutta went south. Its
mill is occupied by Best Manufacturing, a garment shop specializing in night wear.

J. & P. Coats thread mills.
Pawtucket, R.I.

"It has been the policy of the company from the outset to pay its employees sufficient wages to attract the
best class of help, believing it for its interest to have
efficient workmen. As a result, many of the employees
live in houses which have been built by them from
their weekly earnings, and large numbers of working
men and women reside in close proximity to the mill
property, which is an exceedingly attractive place, and
many of the residences bear evidence of excellent taste
and propriety."

—*Cotton Centennial Guidebook*
Pawtucket, 1891

Grand Trunk Railroad.
Lewiston, Me.

For thousands of French Canadians, this was the portal to Lewiston. Mill tenements mark the end of the line. The Bates Mill rises behind them.

IX
Memories

Nellie Goulet.
Quebec Square.
Danielson, Conn.

Beatrice Rocheford has worked in the mills of Burrillville, Rhode Island, since she was 16. Her father was a pattern weaver; her mother, a spooler. For most of her 46 years in the mills, she has worked as a mender, one of the few skilled jobs available for women. Her last 20 years of mending were spent at the Andrews Worsted Mill of Pascoag, R.I. She retired in 1974.

"I was born in Harrisville. My folks were born here, one Harrisville, one Pascoag. My grand-mother—my mother tells me—was a mender years, you know, way back. She says maybe I went towards that because I took it from her. I've been a mender just about all my life. One of my friends taught me how to do it. It takes a long, long time to learn. It's not only just sewing. It's almost like weaving by hand. You're doing the same thing a loom does, only you're doing it with a needle, by hand.

[She lists some of the subtle defects a mender learns to correct.] Wrong draws, skippy thread. That's a thread that, when it was weaving, it didn't pick up right, so it skipped. That has to be pulled out and sewn back in. Thread out, slack thread, cross thread. That's in the warp. In the filling, there's broken pics, miss-pics, harness skips, cross pics, floats. Floats, that's hard to fix. That's both-a-ways, all messed up. You've got to pick up each one gradually and sew it in its right place. If you put one in wrong, you've got to start over again.

Like I say, it takes a lot of experience before you see them things. When I was learning, they'd say, 'Can't you see that?' I couldn't see it at all, at all, at all. I didn't see anything wrong. And I'd try. When I found it, I was thrilled. 'I see it! I see it!' It's quite a thing to learn.

There would be a thread out in the warp. That comes about 85 or 90 yards long. Well, then I'd have to sew that. You can sew about 5 yards an hour on some material. On finer material, it would take even longer, so you can imagine, sewing about 5 yards an hour, you start off fresh. But then you start tiring. Your eyes get tired. Your hands get tired. Then you slow up. Your hands are all tired from holding needles. That's what you call a long job. You come home at night and everything is all blurred from staring all day.

If we ever lost a needle, we had to find it. You had to look and look and look until you found it, because it would break the machines downstairs and cause thousands of dollars of damage. Sometimes it would slide right out of your hand [and go] into the cloth. Then down-stairs it goes into the machine. Everybody would come to help you find it. When we lost a needle, it was a big deal, I'm telling you. I wouldn't sleep at night if I lost a needle. Some people didn't care and they wouldn't tell anyone. But when you're conscientious about your work, you know, you look. When you'd find it, you'd be so glad. You can't imagine how glad you'd be.

[The long mending needle is held in the crook of the fingers. The grip is tight and awk-ward.] Your hand gets cramped. I've got arthritis now. You have calluses on your hands. You do get awful tired in your hands. Daylight is really the best of all. I wouldn't want to do that job at night. I don't think anybody did do that at night. The kids were always breaking

Beatrice Rocheford, mender.
Pascoag, R.I.

the windows [in her work area] so they boarded them up. There used to be windows. Not as many as there should be. It wasn't made for a sewing room, in other words. When Uxbridge Worsted ran the mill, they had the sewing room upstairs and it was nice.

All of us old help [here], we were conscientious workers. We didn't have a boss over our shoulder. We didn't need to. We always had our heads bowed down. They didn't have to worry over us. But the kids, when they got something done, they'd go sleep in a wagon or sleep in a box. If the boss said go do something, they'd say, 'That's not my job.' There were some good ones. I'm not saying they were all like that. I'm not bragging, but I was never a sloppy sewer. I was conscientious. I had to fix everything. In the end, it pays, because they kept me right until the end. I hope I never have to go back. I hope I never work again, period. I worked enough. From 16 right up to 62. That's enough."

Tom Mulligan, finishing superintendent.
Andrews Worsted Mills, Inc.
Pascoag, R.I.

Tom Mulligan had worked in over 200 mills "from Calais, Maine, to Walla Walla, Washington, from Atlanta to San Juan Obispo." He had worked on and off in the mills all his life. At age 70, he was running the finishing department at Andrews Worsted. He lived with his sister, his brother-in-law, and the most extensive collection of mill post cards in the area. Tom Mulligan died of lung cancer in 1975.

"My father was a loom fixer. My mother was a drawer-in. My grandfather was a boss weaver on one side. My grandfather was a boss finisher on the other side. My uncles were all boss finishers. I was brought up in the mill. I used to go in the mill when it thundered. My mother was a drawer-in. Those days, you had a hander-in, go around the other side, she'd hand the ends. I used to go and hand-in for my mother. I'd hand her the ends and she'd draw them through. I was born and brought up in a mill. That's all you heard talk about.

I started to work at 13. I was carryin' ropin', the yarn that's used on the spinning frame. I wasn't big enough. I got fired. Then I went to work at Stillwater Worsted. Putting on drop wires. I got fired there, too. Then I went to Spinning Room No. 4. Doffing. Then Nasonville. I learned to weave in Nasonville. Then I went to Pascoag, No. 2. I went to Woonsocket. Universal Winding. From Woonsocket I went to Killingly Worsted. My uncle used to run it. And then I went on the bum. I'd work a week, two weeks, weavin'. Central Village, Moosup, Norwich. Then up to Keene, New Hampshire. Pittsfield. Monson. Up into Maine.

Business was bad then. The worsted mills would run maybe 5 months of the year then they would shut down. So the weavers would have to find a job somewhere else. They would go to the woolen mills. Wherever there was a woolen job. That's how they got to moving around the country. When the mills stop, you got to have a job. We'd be in Rockville or Norwich. We'd be getting laid off. Somebody would say 'Geez, they're running in Keene.' So we'd all head for Keene. We usually rode the freight.

Most of the bum weavers were Irish or French or French Canadian or Scotch. Not many Yankees, except the ones from Maine. There were three or four hundred of us. A lot of women. A lot of girls, too. Usually shack up with one, she'd be a bum weaver. She'd get a job, and you'd loaf. Or you'd get a job and she'd loaf. You'd go to Proctorsville or Ludlow.

We used to call it the Bean Line, because when you'd bum something to eat, you'd get beans. You'd leave Norwich. That was the start of the Bean Line. Norwich to Yantic. Work in Yantic a few days. Then you'd go to Jewett City or Taftville. There was a couple mills in Taftville where you could get a job. From Jewett City you go into Central Village. There was three or four mills in Central Village and Moosup. From Moosup you'd go into Danielson. Then up into East Killingly. Then to Dayville. There was a big mill there, the Asawaugan. From Dayville to Putnam. Five mills in Putnam, then. From Putnam to Mechanicsville. Swift River Woolen. Big worsted mill. After you left Mechanicsville you went into Grosvenordale and North Grosvenordale. All cotton. I never worked there. Then to Wilsonville. Keegan's place. From there to the Packard mills and on into Webster. All around Webster was mills. Then Oxford. From there to Worcester, Cherry Valley. You went out to Holden. Holden into Barre, Barre into Monson, Monson into Clinton. You'd come out in Manchester. The end of the Bean Line was Keene, New Hampshire. All the trains came through Keene.

We were called rounders. Cause we traveled around. All the towns had a jungle camp. Do their washing and get cocked. A percentage of them were heavy drinkers. They would work until they'd saved up maybe $100. Then they'd come in and shut a whole mill down. I've seen a rounder come in, stand in the weave shop door, and say 'Come on, boys. I've got $500. Let's drink it up.' All those goddamn rounders would stop their looms and take off. They'd stay drunk for a week. The mill would stay idle. The owner would say 'You'll never get a job here again!' But he had to hire them. They liked to hire them, because they were good.

They had all kinds of names. There was York State Murphy. Gold-tooth Whitey. Reed-hook Harry—he made his own reed hooks. Cowshit Cassidy. Archie Settle-up and Joe Jump-the-freight. They were brothers. Lefty Rondo. Still alive, goddamn it. He was a mean son of a bitch. He could weave anything. He was a real weaver.

You never asked for a job. All the mills, in the morning, anybody wanted a job in the weave shop would go in and stand on the floor. The boss would check all his looms. He'd come over and say 'Go over and take No. 5 loom. Take No. 4.' That's all. Same in the finishing room. The boss would say 'What can you do?' 'Anything.' 'Can you run a shear?' 'Yeh.' 'Can you run the press?' 'Yeh.' 'Run the fulling mills?' 'Yeh.' 'OK, go down to the wet end. You'll see a fat guy. Tell him I sent you.' You had a job. Christ, they wouldn't ask your name for a week."

Nick Langlois.
Taftville, Conn.

Nick Langlois lived in the oldest house in Taftville, on a hill above the Ponemah Mill. He worked for Ponemah as a child, then went on to various other local jobs. He was 65 when photographed, working as a housekeeper for a stereo manufacturer that occupied part of the mill after Ponemah left. Nick is also one of those rare people for whom life has been a long and happy adventure. He retired to Canterbury, Conn., in 1976 after his wife's death.

"I've always enjoyed Taftville, that's why I never moved out. It was a good place to live. Everybody was happy. My grandfather worked in the slash room, on the top floor, until he was 93. He came from Canada. Got a job right away. You see, the big shot that owned the mill would go to Canada. Recruit a lot of people and their families, see. Bring 'em here. Promise 'em a home. Cheap rent. Lights. They'd come. He got 'em in. That's how they

worked it. Didn't have enough help? Go to Canada and recruit a whole family. Three, four families at a time.

Both my parents worked for the mill. My father was a carpenter. My mother worked in the cardroom. Me, I was a doffer. I was only 13 years old when I started and could only work 8 hours. Ten hours, they were working, but I was too young. The whole bunch of us [his thirteen siblings] worked here. My brothers and sisters did the same thing I did. Doffers or sweepers. You started as a sweeper. Then you learned the job doffin'. Then you learned the job band boy or you learned the job fixing. And you'd get the job. Nobody had schooling in them days. When you were old enough to work, you went to work. They'd take you, too. You had a job and that's it. At home, the same way. My job was chopping wood. When we worked, we worked. No bosses came around to tell you to do your job.

They used to hire a lot of people. Oh my God. Everybody was working here. Thousands of them. From Baltic, Occum, you name it. Versailles. Everywhere. This was a big mill. They used to start when it was daylight and work until it was dark. They didn't have all them lights in them days. A lot of people used to walk out of here at night. Later, they used to generate their own power. Furnish all the village, all the barns, everything. Furnish all the power for all the mills. Plus that, they used to furnish all the lights for Lisbon. Yeh, for Lisbon, too. That's how much power they had.

My parents were paying ninety cents a week to live in the tenement block. The company took it out of your pay. They had a great big store. They had everything you could buy. Shoes, socks. Anything you wanted: anybody that worked for Ponemah could go in there and buy anything they wanted. They'd deliver their milk and take that out of your pay, too. We used to make everything. Everything that was needed for the mill, we'd make. If something happened in your home, all you do is call up the office, they send a man over. Carpenter, plumber, tinsmith or blacksmith. They had their own ice house. Used to cut ice on the reservoir, fill the ice house up for summer. They had their own orchards. They made their own butter. They owned all this land, all the way to Occum. Everything in Taftville belonged to Ponemah. Everything! Lock, stock and barrel.

I used to clean cellars, yards, garages and all that. I had a big garbage run. But then my wife passed away. I said to hell with it. I tried to give it to my son. He wouldn't take it. I says, 'There's two trucks. You can be your own boss. Take it!' He wouldn't. Why the hell wouldn't he do it? What do you think he's doing? He works at Plastic Wire in Jewett City and drives a garbage truck in the daytime. That makes sense, huh?

When I first started working in the mill here, I was able to save some money. Gave my mother $5 a week, the rest was mine. When I went into the Navy, I never touched it. It was only $39 a month. I'd keep 10 and send the rest to my mother. I made some and I saved it. Bought some land in Canterbury. It's got a running brook there. I want to make a lake out of it. I have 11 acres. I had more. Gave 6 to my son and he built on it. I said, 'Here, take it.'

Taftville has been good to me. I can't complain."

Lionel Turcotte, loom fixer.
Wannalancit Textile Co.
Lowell, Mass.

Lionel Turcotte has always believed in self-improvement. Born in Quebec province, raised in Lowell's Little Canada, he has used a career in textiles to climb up from the ghetto to the comfort of a prim cottage just across the Merrimack from the mills. Whether at work or at home, everything about Lionel is very proper. In his spare time, he paints in the basement. "Most of them are original," he explains. "Landscapes. Mostly landscapes. I tried to do flowers, I tried to do portraits, but farm scenes work best."

"We lived on Aiken St., where the tobacco warehouse is. We lived there for about 20 or 30 years. It was called Little Canada—from the bridge to Merrimack St., and beyond. Some people, they only spoke French, never knew a word of English all their lives. It was always French in the house. I learned English in school. It took me a long time to grab it, really, because at the school there was French teachers and everything, so you didn't hear much English. Outside the school there was no English whatsoever. Livin' like in a French ghetto, you know what I mean? We started to speak more fluently when we started to work with other people, all different nationalities. It was a slow process.

So anyway, my father worked in the Boott Mills most of his life. My mother worked at Lawrence Hosiery [also at Lowell]. My father was a weaver, then later a loom fixer. His brother, who came here first, was a weaver and showed him how. It was right in the middle of the Depression—1933—so it wasn't a question of where you wanted to work. It was a question of whether there was work. Sons of employees had preference if there was a job open. So there was an opening when I was of age—I was the oldest of 7. My father says 'Things are not too good,' so I took the job. I started sweeping the floor. One year of high school. It was a little bit rough.

I felt the same way as everybody then. You were of age, the opportunity was there, so you just had to go to work. In fact, we thought ourselves to be very fortunate. There was a lot of people out of work. We accepted it. Most of my friends went into the mills: at that time that's about all there was. Most of them, mill work. Some went into the shoe industry. Some managed to go through high school, but the majority, about 16 years of age, they quit. They were all big families, they really had to go to work. When 2 or 3 were working in the family, then the rest could go to high school. None of my family went through high school. We managed to find jobs after 16 years of age and we all accepted it and we all survived. [He laughs confidently.]

At that time, people used to go in there, start out learning the trade, start at the bottom. Promotions, from one job to the next. But it was a very slow process. You had to wait 'til somebody died or somebody quit or somebody moved out of town. People worked themselves sick just trying to hold on to their job. It was a little different than it is today.

Six months after I started sweeping, I had an opportunity to go on weaving. I worked beside my father. He gave me a hand, explained things to me. That lasted a few months then I was on my own. When he got promoted to loom fixer, I took over his job as weaver. I started going to Lowell Tech [the local college] at night. I studied weaving couple nights a week. Then I took another course—loom fixing. Then I took another course—cloth analysis. I worked at the Boott off and on. I worked several places in between when things got slow [Naumkeg Mills, Pacific Mills, and Merrimack Mills]. All told, I worked about 18 years off and on. When World War II started, there was a shortage of loom fixers, so they broke me in on loom fixing.

A textile mill always fascinated me. You have a certain amount of machinery to keep running. If you can do it, you're happy. You go in the shoe shop, you get so much a case to do shoes—if you stop working, you stop making money. Well, in the mills, you could set up your machines and watch 'em work for you. And the less you work, the more money you're making. The machinery was working for you, you see. That's the way I like it. I was skilled enough that I could keep the work going and work half as much as I'd have worked in the shoe shop for the same money. A lot of times, I'd sit by the window for hours at a time—the looms were working. I wasn't overloaded.

In my time, when I started, most of the people formed a certain pride in their work. It was a matter of life and death, pretty close. They had to do a good job. They had to compete with their fellow workers. But I've seen a lot of people for whom work was a drudgery all their lives. They didn't have any ambition or imagination. Never tried to improve anything. They were just there because they had to be there. Forget it!

I always had a certain satisfaction at accomplishing something. That's why I paint. It's an outlet for my emotions. Sometimes I'll paint a very dark picture, because that's how I feel. Another time, it'll be as bright as I can make it. Sometimes, before one is finished, I've started another. When I retire, it will keep me going."

Nellie Goulet came to Quebec Square in 1914 to work for the Quinebaug Company that had built the three-sided block of long, low brick housing units half a century earlier as a model workers' community. Now, only she and another elderly woman remain to remember how it used to be. After the company folded in 1942, the symbiotic link between mills and mill housing was broken. Most of the mills burned soon after, and Quebec Square became just another low rent neighborhood of Danielson, Connecticut, the parent town just across the Quinebaug River. Yet the square still has a faintly utopian charm, surrounded by acres of grass and gardens, with more gardens occupying the interior of the square. Nellie tells her story with a thick Québeçois accent.

"Me, I'm not young. Seventy-seven. I was born in Canada. My mother, she was Irish. She used to work [at Quinebaug Co.] when she was single. She was in there with her parents, too. You know what she do? She do the wrong thing. She go back in Canada, she married my father, and after that, she come back. My father was French. When he was young, he used to work in the tavern [near Quebec Square].

I work all my life. In Canada, I used to work on a farm. At that time, they used to send for the big family to do the work [in the mills]. My mother, she had fourteen kids. Two dead young. Seven boys, seven girls, all mixed up. My mother tell me we go to a free country, that we go to work in the mill, make some money. She don't say too much. Never say too much. You know why? When you grow up in Canada, you work for the rich people in Québec for $10 a month. Rich people—you got to clean their house, and do that work. The rich people, when you're hungry, they don't give you no sandwich, nothing. The rich people are not my people. My mother don't want me to go to work for $10 a month.

When I first come from Canada, it was 1914. I lived over there, you see that block over there? She was hungry, poor Mommy, she send me to work. She says to the boss I was 16, but I was 14. I have no chance to go to school. I used to weave over there. Weaver, oh yeh. My mother had a big family—we all used to work over there. One worked in the spool room. My brother used to weave, like me. Weave, that's a tough thing. Lucy, she used to work in the card room. My brother used to weave downstairs—pillow case. Me, I used to weave upstairs. My mother stayed home. After you have 14 children, there's not much you can do, you know. My father, he's dead long time ago—so much trouble!

My husband used to work over there, too. At that time he used to make $14 a week. He's dead long time ago—1938. So I have three children. I go to work. I have no choice. I can get married again, but I say no. So I bring up the kids myself. It was awful.

You cross the gate, and you in the mill. You never go late. We used to go over there seven o'clock in the morning, and come back for dinner, then go back until six o'clock the night. I can't work any other place because I got no education. So I used to work over there. When I was young, I never complain about tired. But it was hot. In that time, we used to wear a corset—what a difference—it was all wet [by quitting time]. We wear a black blouse. If you wear a white blouse, it was full of holes. And we have sometimes a skirt, and we used to wear

Nellie Goulet.
Quebec Square.
Danielson, Conn.

some sandals. We was not too fussy, because when you go in to work, you don't dress up. The boss, he dress up. We wear the black blouse with the white buttons. In the wintertime, we sometimes wear little skirt with two pocket, you have a little ribbon. We used to go in to work every day.

I moved [to this apartment] when my son was 5 years old. More than fifty years I lived down here. The block was yellow. That's a long time ago. It was nice here. All the people was friendly. It was all French. Everything was clean, everybody had a nice garden. They used to keep the tenements up. Two men came every spring, do the ceiling with a long brush. It was all right. The company paid for that. We used to go to the Catholic school to play whist. We go on a Saturday to Woodward Park. We had a little restaurant, used to serve hot chocolate, you know. We used to have a ball game over there, that's all. The old men used to have a cabin with some candy, something like that. You know how much we pay at that time? For six rooms? Dollar and seven cents! They used to take that off your pay. Bread? Ten cents. Everything was quiet. Nobody drink. It was nice, in a way. It was nice.

During the war, that mill stopped. They threw the loom outside and Arrow-Hart bought that. They make some kind of clothes. It's a different work. I don't know how to do that. I was an old-timer, so I go to Wauregan, do the same job. I used to work at night. Sleep in the daytime. In the afternoon, we warm the stove and get something to eat. I took care of the kids with my pay. Ooohhh. I'd rather die when I think about that. Oh, it was tough. And at that time, the town, the state, don't give me nothing. And I got three kids, two under age. My son started to work when he was 12 years old. It was terrible. His father was dead. We did the best we could.

I'm miserable. The other people, they don't understand me. I don't go outside much. I stay in the house. They don't understand me. I am French. I'm a French lady. That's the best I can be."

X
Epilogue

House for two mill families.
Carolina, R.I.

Most of New England was comparatively deserted before the textile industry came and gave purpose to this barren, rocky, and unforgiving region. Industry brought power, money, and immigration: it was the keystone in the economic arch supporting New England prosperity for more than a century. Filling a void, pioneering manufacturers had license to create a society in their own image, and they produced among the best and the worst examples of industrial civilization. Our present is their creation.

Soon there will be no one left who knows, first hand, what life meant in a company town. The mill era is passing into history along with the old-timers who remember. But New England is left with a permanent legacy—the industrial skeleton and reordered geography upon which the present is built. Postwar development has been little more than a plastic and aluminum veneer over the brick and masonry skeleton of the previous centuries, still incompletely absorbed. Not even utter neglect can obliterate the structure. Fire and flood threaten it, but even these catastrophes leave some remnants behind. The skeleton is too monumental and widespread to succumb quickly to nature. Only total demolition could erase it completely, but much of what has been built is still just valuable enough to postpone this most extreme solution. Commanding their waterfalls, deserted by their young, mill towns endure. Obstacles to American progress, they force highways to go over them or circumvent them entirely. Regional development concentrates elsewhere, diluting the undesirable legacy without completely destroying it.

As manufacturing withdraws from New England, its former life-supporting influence becomes apparent. No comparable regional industry has replaced it. Large portions of the population dependent on manufacturing wages are abandoned to fend for themselves. Many mill villages and cities flounder towards bankruptcy. Welfare and unemployment case loads soar. From inside the mill town, the future looks bleak.

This industrial heritage is in great part dismal, and often tragic. Mills were built for profit, and though they provided employment for thousands of workers, they gave little consideration to the human spirit. Each is a monument to the thousands of lives which animated it. Manufacturers replaced nature with an artificial environment of precarious balance. In some instances, a more contemporary and healthy equilibrium has replaced the original mill town organization. Too often the mill throws its shadow over a stunted community beside it. Indeed, many of New England's most obstinately blighted areas owe their visage to the mill town system.

Living amid such decay can be humiliating. "We came here to suffer our shame alone," one rural mill town wife told me. Another made this statement before slamming the door to deny me entrance to her hopelessly shabby apartment: "I was born in this country and I'm not stupid—we're not all born equal. I'm one of the lesser subjects. I've got enough problems. If we wanted to be photographed or interviewed, we'd write to the paper. And if you had any brains, you would know we don't want that. We like it quiet and peaceful—and *private*." The mill town era has poisoned thousands of lives like hers with unemployment, destitution, disease, and an almost total lack of support or opportunity. Once-proud mill towns breed especially virulent strains of poverty, and they prefer to do it unwatched. New England obliges by spurning these communities. Unwilling to help, more fortunate sectors usually hope to move on unhindered in their transient, throwaway questing for wealth and happiness. The region hosts a collective effort to forget what it is made of, as if the past can be discarded once it is worn out.

There are, however, a few important exceptions to this general public amnesia. Architects, developers, industrial historians, and concerned citizens are now collaborating to save some of New England's most outstanding mills through "adaptive reuse"—the conversion of antiquated structures to meet contemporary needs. Recognizing the latent value of abandoned factories, adaptive reuse is usually less expensive than new construction. Through adaptive reuse, mills are reborn as apartment houses, stores, artists' studios, restaurants, craft cooperatives, museums, offices, modern manufacturing spaces—the possibilities are limited only by imagination and capital. Historic landmark status will save some other mills which are too significant to destroy, but not necessarily suitable or desirable for reuse. In two special cases, the entire village has been designated a historic landmark: Harrisville, N.H., a classic textile community in the family-oriented Rhode Island style; and North Easton, Mass., a shovel manufacturing town whose principal buildings were all designed by Henry Hobson Richardson and landscaped by Frederick Law Olmstead, both retained by the Ames family. Large sections of the city of Lowell have also been protected as historic areas. An ambitious project is already under way to develop the remains of early Lowell into the nation's first urban-industrial National Park.

But most mill towns will never enjoy such attention, for there are simply too many isolated and unwanted sites, and too little interest and concern to go around. Nonetheless, mill towns will survive. They were built to last, and many of them will do just that. They are already becoming less and less recognizable for what they once were, but those willing to look just below the modern veneer will continue to find grim reminders of the forces that shaped local destiny. Communities forever to be haunted by the musty spirit of nineteenth-century manufacturing, mill towns are the standing corpses of industrialization in New England.

Talbot Mills clock.
from North Billerica, Mass.

Crown and Eagle Mills.
North Uxbridge, Mass.

On Saturday night, October 2, 1974, someone set fire to the Crown and Eagle Mills, widely regarded as the finest of New England's surviving textile complexes. Only the masonry shell, the wheelhouse, and the canal system survived the fire. Developers are still hoping to renovate the mill for nonindustrial reuse.

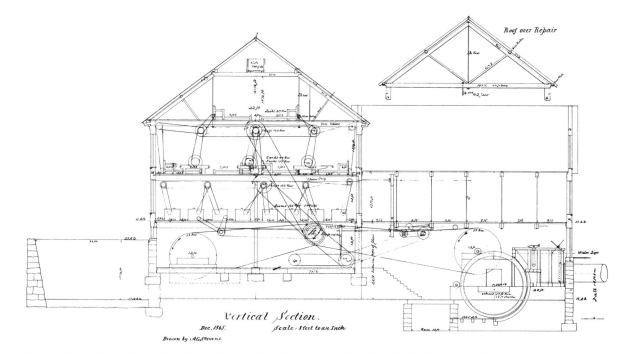

Vertical section of an addition planned for the Stevens Mills, North Andover, Mass., 1865. (M V T M)

Appendices

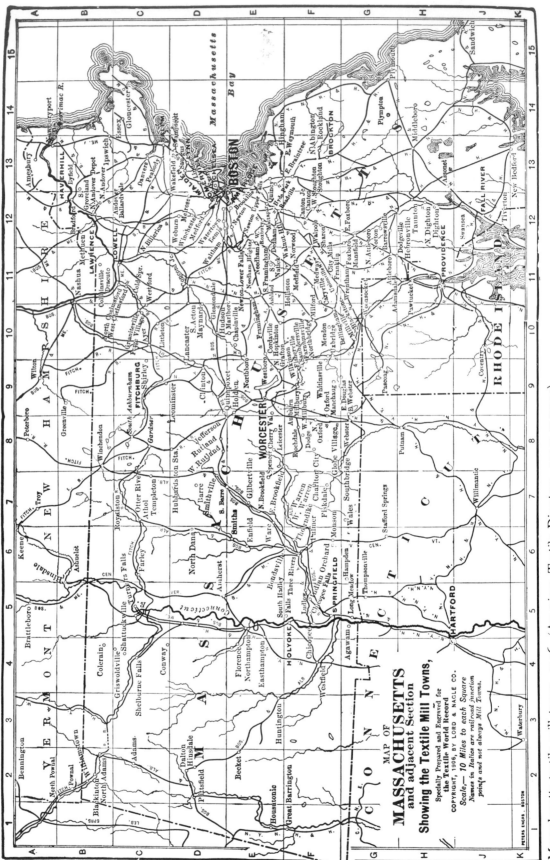

Massachusetts textile mill towns, 1906. (American Textile Directory, 1913; M V T M)

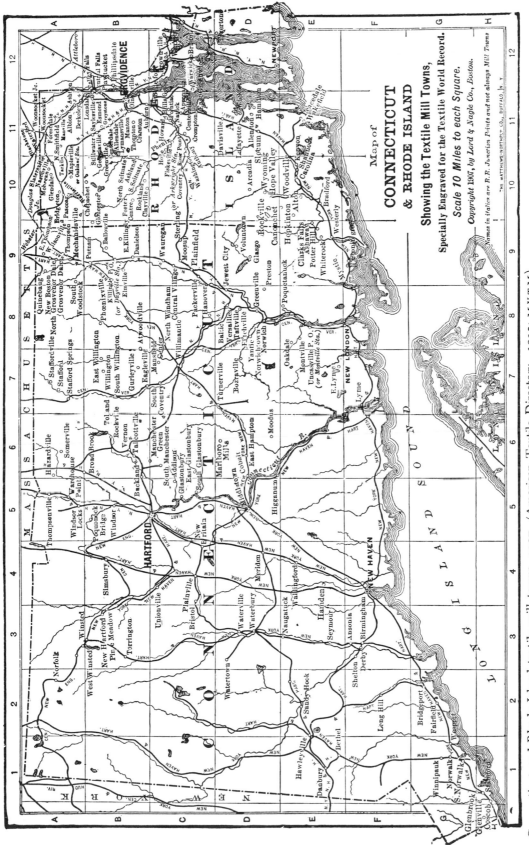

Connecticut and Rhode Island textile mill towns, 1907. (American Textile Directory, 1913; M V T M)

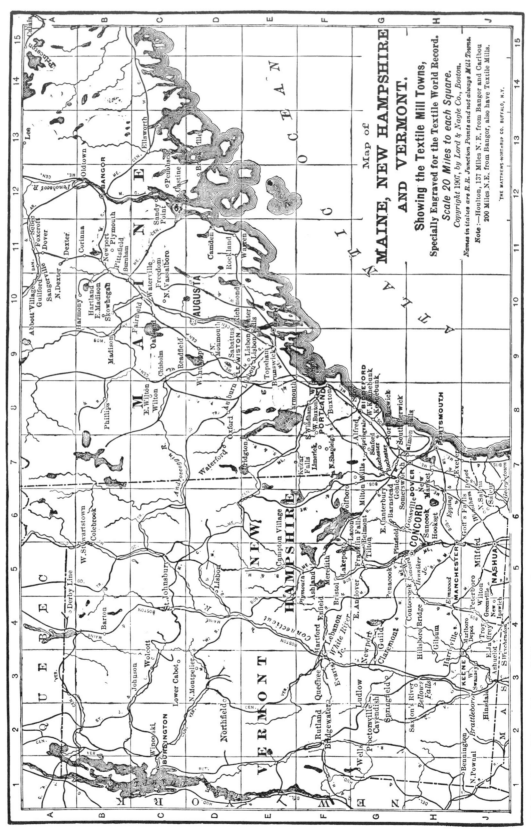

Maine, New Hampshire and Vermont textile mill towns, 1907. (American Textile Directory, 1913; M V T M)

Notes

1. Tench Coxe, "Sketches on the Subject of American Manufactures in 1787," in *A View of the United States of America: Papers 1787–1794* (Philadelphia, 1794), pp. 34–41.

2. Andrew Ure, *Philosophy of Manufactures* (London: Charles Knight, 1835), pp. 15–16.

3. Thomas Jefferson to Benjamin Austin, 9 January 1816. *Writings*, ed. H. A. Washington (Washington: Taylor & Maury, 1853), vol. 4, pp. 387–393.

4. Moses Brown to John Dexter, 15 October 1791, Almy & Brown papers, Rhode Island Historical Society, Providence, R.I.

5. Moses Brown to Samuel Slater, 10 December 1789, Almy & Brown papers.

6. Almy & Brown to Dr. Thayer, 15 March 1790, Almy & Brown papers.

7. Advertisement quoted in James L. Conrad, "The Evolution of Industrial Capitalism in Rhode Island, 1790–1830: Almy, the Browns, and the Slaters." (Ph.D. diss., University of Connecticut, 1973), p. 131.

8. Alexander Hamilton, "Report on Manufactures, December 5, 1791," in *The Reports of Alexander Hamilton*, ed. J. E. Cooke (New York: Harper & Row, 1964), p. 196.

9. Recollections of Mrs. Ann S. Stephens, quoted in F. L. Humphreys, *The Life of David Humphreys* (New York: G. P. Putnam's Sons, 1917), p. 387.

10. Humphreys, *David Humphreys*, p. 378.

11. George S. White, *Memoir of Samuel Slater* (Philadelphia, 1836), p. 120.

12. Patent by de Gennes, 1678. Quoted in Edward Baines, *History of the Cotton Manufacture in Great Britain* (London: Fisher, Fisher & Jackson, 1835), p. 228.

13. Quoted in William R. Bagnall, "Sketches of Manufacturing and Textile Establishments." Typescript, 1908. Baker Library, Cambridge, Mass., p. 1976.

14. Francis Lowell to Patrick Jackson, 7 January 1814. Quoted in Kenneth F. Mailloux, "Boston Manufacturing Company: Its Origins," *Textile History Review* 4, no. 34 (October 1963): 6.

15. Nathan Appleton, *The Introduction of the Power Loom and the Origin of Lowell* (Lowell: B. H. Penhallow, 1858), p. 9.

16. Ibid., p. 12.

17. Harriet Martineau, *Society in America* (New York: Saunders & Otley, 1837), p. 58.

18. *Manufacturers and Farmers Journal*, quoted in Conrad, "Industrial Capitalism," p. 3.

19. Appleton, *Power Loom*, p. 15.

20. Kirk Boott diary, 4 September 1823, quoted in Hannah Josephson, *The Golden Threads* (New York: Russell & Russell, 1949), p. 34.

21. George E. O'Dwyer, *The Irish Catholic Genesis of Lowell* (Lowell: Sullivan Brothers, 1920), p. 8.

22. John Greenleaf Whittier, *Stranger in Lowell* (Boston: Waite, Peirce & Co., 1845), p. 9.

23. Harriet Robinson, "Address," in *Proceedings at the Semi-Centennial . . . of Lowell* (Lowell: Penhallow, 1876), p. 112.

24. Henry A. Miles, *Lowell, As It Was, and As It Is* (Lowell: Powers & Bagley, 1845), p. 75–76.

25. General Rules, Lawrence Company, 21 May 1833, Article 1. Kress

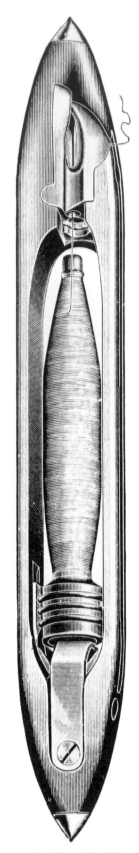

Power loom shuttle with "Northrop" eye.
Draper Co., 1906.

Collection, Baker Library, Cambridge, Mass.

26. Address by Ithamar A. Beard, paymaster, Hamilton Manufacturing Co., 1827. Quoted in Thomas Bender, *Towards an Urban Vision* (Louisville: University Press of Kentucky, 1975), p. 111.

27. Lucy Larcom, "Address," in *Semi-Centennial of Lowell*, p. 95.

28. Henry E. Hovey, "Letter," ibid., p. 125.

29. Whittier, *Stranger in Lowell*, p. 10.

30. Michel Chevalier, *Society, Manners, and Politics in the United States* (1836; reprint ed. J. W. Ward, New York: Cornell University Press, 1961), pp. 104, 130, 142.

31. Harriet Robinson, *Early Factory Labor in New England* (Boston: Wright & Potter, 1883), p. 9.

32. Harriet Robinson, *Loom and Spindle* (New York: Thomas Crowell & Co., 1898), p. 208.

33. John S. Pendleton, *Profits on Manufactures at Lowell* (Boston: Little, Brown & Co., 1845), p. 19.

34. Robinson, *Loom and Spindle*, p. 114.

35. Ibid., pp. 95, 98, 116.

36. Ibid., p. 99.

37. Charles Dickens, *American Notes* (New York: Harper and Brothers, 1842), p. 29.

38. "The Spirit of Discontent," *The Lowell Offering*, 1841, p. 111.

39. Joseph Hollingworth to William Rawcliff, 8 November 1830. Thomas W. Leavitt, ed., *The Hollingworth Letters: Technical Change in the Textile Industry, 1826–1837* (Cambridge, Mass.: MIT Press, 1969), p. 93.

40. Essex (Mass.) *Gazette*, 1825. Quoted in *Semi-Centennial of Lowell*, p. 68.

41. Ure, *Philosophy of Manufactures*, p. 20.

42. John L. Hayes, *American Textile Machinery* (Cambridge, Mass.: University Press, 1877), p. 32.

43. E. H. Knight, "Cotton Manufac-ture," *Harpers Weekly* 50 (December 1874): 89.

44. Henry David Thoreau, *A Week on the Concord and the Merrimack* (1839, reprint, New Haven, Conn.: College and University Press, 1954), p. 76.

45. Zachariah Allen, *The Science of Mechanics* (Providence, R.I.: Hutchens & Corey, 1829), p. iii.

46. American Home Missionary Society, "Manufacturing Corporations and Villages," *New Englander* 7, no. 2 (May 1849): 242.

47. Ibid., pp. 242–244.

48. Thomas Man, *Picture of a Factory Village* (Providence, R.I., 1833), p. 8.

49. Quoted in Joseph Brennan, *Social Conditions in Industrial Rhode Island: 1820–1860* (Washington: Catholic University Press, 1940), p. 38.

50. T. Throstle, "Factory Life in New England," *Knickerbocker Magazine* 30 (December 1847): 516.

51. Ibid., p. 516.

52. Zachariah Allen, "Autobiography." Manuscript, nd. Rhode Island Historical Society, Providence, R.I., p. 45.

53. Ibid., p. 31.

54. Zachariah Allen, "Georgia Mill Diary," 1 September 1855. Manuscript. Rhode Island Historical Society, Providence, R.I., p. 182.

55. James Montgomery, *A Practical Detail of the Cotton Manufacture of the United States* (Glasgow: John Niven, 1840; author's copy with manuscript revisions, 1844, in Kress Collection, Baker Library, Cambridge, Mass.) p. 180.

56. Quoted in Josephson, *Golden Threads*, p. 107.

57. White, *Memoir of Samuel Slater*, p. 267.

58. "Our Manufactures," *Scientific American* 6, no. 12 (7 December 1850): 93.

59. Quoted in Wyatt W. Harper, *The Story of Holyoke: Centennial An-

niversary of the City of Holyoke (Holyoke, Mass., 1973), p. 34.

60. Alfred Smith to George Lyman, 6 March 1858. Quoted in Richard Varnum Spaulding, "The Boston Mercantile Community and the Promotion of the Textile Industry in New England, 1813–1860." (Ph.D. diss., Yale University, 1973), p. 210.

61. Zachariah Allen, "Diary," (1855). Manuscript, Rhode Island Historical Society, Providence, R. I., p. 110.

62. Erastus Bigelow, *Remarks on the Depressed Condition of Manufactures in Massachusetts with suggestions . . .* (Boston: Little, Brown & Co., 1858), p. 12.

63. Ibid., p. 13.

64. Ibid., p. 15.

65. Ibid., p. 14.

66. Elisha Bartlett, *A Vindication of the character and condition of the Females employed in the Lowell Mills . . .* (Lowell, 1841), p. 13.

67. *Massachusetts State Archives*, House Files, 1845, No. 1587, document 9.

68. Henry David Thoreau, *Walden* (Boston: Ticknor & Fields, 1854), p. 30.

69. Cocheco Company (Dover, N.H.) rules (1823). Quoted in Josephson, *Golden Threads*, p. 230.

70. Quoted ibid., p. 232.

71. "House Report March 12, 1845 on the Several Petitions Relating to Labor," *Massachusetts State Archives*, House Files, 1845, No. 1587.

72. Quoted in Norman J. Ware, *The Industrial Worker: 1840–1860* (Boston: Houghton Mifflin, 1924), p. 145.

73. *Voice of Industry* 2, no. 14 (18 September 1846): 2.

74. Petition 1843. Quoted in David Michael Margolick, "Patterns of Change in the New England Textile Towns: A Study of American Industry and Society." (Honors thesis, University of Michigan, 1974), p. 65.

75. Charles Storrow to Horace Mann, 8 February 1848. Quoted in Donald B. Cole, *Immigrant City: Lawrence, Massachusetts, 1845–1921* (Chapel Hill, N.C.: University of North Carolina Press, 1963), p. 23.

76. Quoted ibid., p. 23.

77. Herman Melville, "The Tartarus of Maids" (1855), in *The Complete Stories of Herman Melville* (New York: Random House, 1949), p. 209.

78. Address to Lowell operatives by Mr. Brisbane. Quoted in Bender, *Urban Vision*, pp. 60–62.

79. Lucy Larcom, *A New England Girlhood* (1890, reprint, New York: Corinth Books, 1961), p. 226.

80. William West, *New York Tribune* 10, no. 2862 (18 June 1850): 3.

81. Reported by George Oliver, Lowell agent. Quoted in Ware, *Industrial Worker*, p. 77.

82. Quoted in Josephson, *Golden Threads*, p. 301.

83. Charles Cowley, *Illustrated History of Lowell* (Boston: Lee & Shepard, 1868), p. 60.

84. *Niles Register* 48 (August 1835), p. 397.

85. Frederick M. Peck and Henry H. Earl, *Fall River and Its Industries* (Fall River: Benjamin Earl and Sons, 1877), p. 66.

86. Manufacturers Board of Trade, *Fall River versus the Massachusetts Bureau of Statistics* (Fall River: Board of Trade, 1882), p. 91.

87. William MacDonald, "The French Canadians in New England," *Quarterly Journal of Economics* 12, no. 3 (April 1898): 245.

88. Quoted in George Waldo Browne, *The Amoskeag Manufacturing Company of Manchester, New Hampshire* (Manchester: Amoskeag Manufacturing Co., 1915), p. 202.

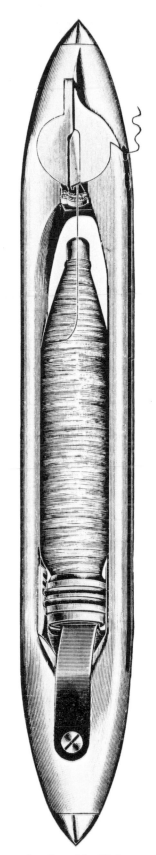

Power loom shuttle with "Stimpson" eye. Draper Co., 1906.

89. Advertisement in a French-Canadian newspaper, 1913. Quoted in Daniel Creamer and Charles W. Coulter, *Labor and the Shut-down of the Amoskeag Textile Mills* (Philadelphia: U.S. Works Progress Administration, 1939), p. 170.

80. "Memoir of James A. Lockwood," in Samuel B. Lincoln, *Lockwood Greene: The History of an Engineering Business* (Brattleboro, Vt.: Stephen Greene Press, 1960), p. 58.

91. Welcome Arnold Greene, *The Providence Plantations for Two Hundred and Fifty Years* (Providence, R.I.: J. A. & R. A. Reid, 1886), p. 250.

92. New York *Daily Graphic*, 4 February 1889.

93. Quoted in Seymour Louis Wolfbein, *The Decline of a Cotton Textile City: A Study of New Bedford* (New York: Columbia University Press, 1944), p. 59.

94. M. D. C. Crawford, "The Early Textile Industry," in John G. Glover and William B. Cornell, eds., *The Development of American Industries* (1932; reprint New York: Simmons-Boardman, 1959), p. 108.

95. *American Magazine*, quoted in Bill Cahn, *Mill Town* (New York: Cameron & Kahn, 1954), p. 74.

96. Cole, *Immigrant City*, pp. 186–195.

97. Quoted in Cahn, *Mill Town*, p. 187.

98. Ibid., p. 212.

99. "Our Manufactures," *Scientific American* 6, no. 12 (7 December 1850): 93.

100. Dero A. Saunders, "Twilight of American Woolen," *Fortune* 49 (March 1954): 200; "The Stormiest Merger Yet," *Fortune* 51 (April 1955): 137.

101. U.S., Congress, Senate, Senator Charles Tobey Committee, *Investigation of Closing of Nashua, N.H., Mills and the Operations of Textron, Incorporated* (Washington: U.S. Government Printing Office, 1948), p. 3.

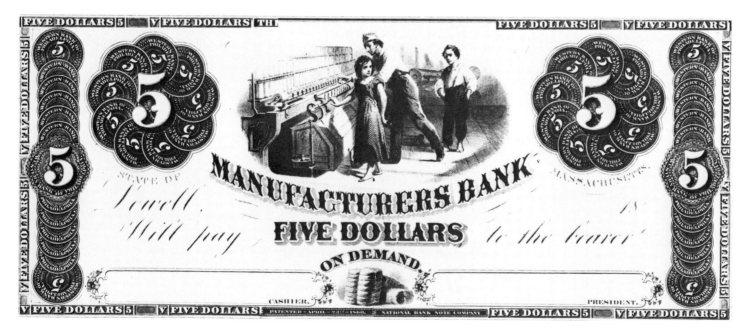

Design for a $5 bill, 1860. Uncirculated. (Lowell Historical Society)

Selected Bibliography

Books of particular interest to the lay reader are marked with an asterisk (*). Complete bibliographies on specialized topics can be found in the appropriate dissertations. Most of these works can be found either at the Boston Athenaeum or at the Merrimack Valley Textile Museum.

BOOKS AND DISSERTATIONS

Baines, Edward. *History of the Cotton Manufacture in Great Britain.* London: Fisher, Fisher & Jackson, 1835.

Bagnall, William R. "Sketches of Manufacturing and Textile Establishments." Typescript, 1908. Baker Library, Cambridge, Mass.

*Bender, Thomas. *Towards an Urban Vision.* Lexington, Ky.: University Press of Kentucky, 1975.

Brennan, Br. Joseph. *Social Conditions in Industrial Rhode Island: 1820–1860.* Washington: Catholic University Press, 1940.

Browne, George Waldo. *The Amoskeag Manufacturing Company of Manchester, New Hampshire.* Manchester: Amoskeag Manufacturing Co., 1915.

Burgy, Jacob Herbert. *The New England Cotton Textile Industry, a Study in Industrial Geography.* Baltimore, Md.: Waverly Press, 1932.

Cahn, Bill. *Mill Town.* New York: Cameron & Kahn, 1954.

Chevalier, Michel. *Society, Manners, and Politics in the United States.* 1836. Reprint, ed. J. W. Ward. New York: Cornell University Press, 1961.

Cole, Donald B. *Immigrant City: Lawrence, Massachusetts 1845–1921.* Chapel Hill, N.C.: University of North Carolina Press, 1963.

Conrad, James E. "The Evolution of Industrial Capitalism in Rhode Island, 1790–1830: Almy, the Browns, and the Slaters." Ph.D. dissertation, University of Connecticut, 1973.

*Coolidge, John. *Mill and Mansion.* New York: Columbia University Press, 1942.

Creamer, Daniel, and Coulter, Charles W. *Labor and the Shut-down of the Amoskeag Textile Mills.* Philadelphia: U.S. Works Progress Administration, 1939.

*Eisler, Benita. *The Lowell Offering: Writings by New England Mill Women, 1840–1845.* New York: Lippincott, 1978.

Francis, James B. *Lowell Hydraulic Experiments.* Boston: Little, Brown & Co., 1855.

Gibb, George Sweet. *The Saco-Lowell Shops.* Cambridge, Mass.: Harvard University Press, 1950.

*Gillon, Edmund V., ed. *A New England Town in Early Photographs – Southbridge, Mass. 1878–1930.* New York: Dover Press, 1976.

Green, Constance McLaughlin. *Holyoke, Massachusetts: A Case Study of the Industrial Revolution in America.* New Haven: Yale University Press, 1939.

Greene, Welcome Arnold. *The Providence Plantations for Two Hundred and Fifty Years.* Providence, R.I.: J. A. & R. A. Reid, 1886.

Hareven, Tamara K. and Langenbach, Randolph. *Amoskeag: Oral History of a Factory City.* New York: Pantheon, 1978.

*Hitchcock, Henri-Russell. *Rhode Island Architecture.* New York: Da Capo, 1968.

*Josephson, Hannah. *The Golden Threads*. New York: Russell & Russell, 1949.

*Kerouac, Jean-Louis (Jack). *Maggie Cassidy*. New York: Avon, 1959.

*Larcom, Lucy. *A New England Girlhood*. 1890. Reprint. New York: Corinth Books, 1961.

Leavitt, Thomas W., ed., *The Hollingworth Letters: Technical Change in the Textile Industry, 1826–1837*. Cambridge, Mass.: MIT Press, 1969.

Margolick, David Michael. "Patterns of Change in the New England Textile Towns: A Study of American Industry and Society." Honors Thesis, University of Michigan, 1974. (Putnam, Conn. Public Library)

Miles, Rev. Henry A. *Lowell, As It Was, and As It Is*. Lowell: Powers & Bagley, 1845.

*Mumford, Lewis. *Technics and Civilization*. New York: Harcourt, Brace & Co., 1934.

Pierson, William H. "Industrial Architecture in the Berkshires." Ph.D. dissertation, Yale University, 1949.

*Robinson, Harriet H. *Loom and Spindle*. New York: Thomas Crowell & Co., 1898.

Shlakman, Vera. *Economic History of a Factory Town: A Study of Chicopee, Mass.* Smith College Studies in History, vol. 20, no. 4 (October 1934–July 1935). Northampton, Mass.: Smith College, 1935.

Spaulding, Richard Varnum. "The Boston Mercantile Community and the Promotion of the Textile Industry in New England, 1813–1860." Ph.D. dissertation, Yale University, 1963.

*Tann, Jennifer. *The Development of the Factory*. London: Cornmarket Press, 1970.

Ure, Andrew. *The Philosophy of Manufactures*. London: Charles Knight, 1835.

*Ware, Carolyn F. *Early New England Cotton Manufacture*. Boston: Houghton Mifflin, 1931.

Ware, Norman J. *The Industrial Worker: 1840–1860*. Boston: Houghton Mifflin, 1924.

*White, George S. *Memoir of Samuel Slater*. Philadelphia, 1836.

*Whittier, John Greenleaf. *The Stranger in Lowell*. Boston: Waite, Peirce & Co., 1845.

*Zimiles, Martha and Murray. *Early American Mills*. New York: Clarkson Potter, 1973.

PERIODICALS

Candee, Richard. "The Early New England Textile Village in Art," *Antiques* (December 1970), pp. 910–916.

Feller, Irwin. "The Draper Loom in New England Textiles, 1894–1914: A Study of Diffusion of an Innovation," *Journal of Economic History* 26, no. 3 (September 1966), p. 320.

MacDonald, William. "The French Canadians in New England." *Quarterly Journal of Economics* 12, no. 3 (April 1898), p. 245.

Mailloux, Kenneth F. "Boston Manufacturing Company: Its Origins." *Textile History Review* 4, no. 34 (October 1963), p. 157.

Nelson, Henry Loomis. "French Canadians in New England." *Harpers New Monthly Magazine* 87 (1893), p. 180.

Shaw, S. Adele. "Fruit of the Loom," *Survey and Graphic* (July 1, 1922), p. 441.

Temin, Peter. "Steam and Waterpower in the Early Nineteenth Century." *Journal of Economic History* 26 (1966), p. 187.

Throstle, T. "Factory Life in New England." *Knickerbocker Magazine* 30 (December 1847), p. 511.

The Lowell Offering. Lowell: Powers & Bagley, 1841–1845.

PAMPHLETS, TRACTS, AND BROADSIDES

Appleton, Nathan. *The Introduction of the Power Loom and the Origin of Lowell.* Lowell: B. H. Penhallow, 1858.

An Authentic History of the Lawrence Calamity embracing a description of the Pemberton Mill, . . . Boston: John Dyer & Co., 1860.

Bartlett, Elisha. *A Vindication of the character and condition of the Females employed in the Lowell Mills . . .* Lowell, 1841.

Bigelow, Erastus. *Remarks on the Depressed Condition of Manufactures in Massachusetts with suggestions . . .* Boston: Little, Brown & Co., 1858.

The City of Holyoke, Its Water Power and Its Industries. Holyoke, Mass.: Holyoke Water Power Co., ca. 1876.

Guest, Richard. *A Compendious History of the Cotton Manufacture.* Manchester: Joseph Pratt, 1823.

Hopkinson, Judge Francis. "Account of the Grand Federal Procession, Philadelphia, July 4, 1788," in *Miscellaneous Pamphlets chiefly on American Affairs.* Philadelphia: Matthew Carey, 1884.

Proceedings at the Semi-Centennial Celebration of the Incorporation of Lowell, March 1, 1876. Lowell: Penhallow, 1876.

Robinson, Harriet H. *Early Factory Labor in New England.* Boston: Wright & Potter, 1883.

SURVEYS, REFERENCES, AND GOVERNMENT DOCUMENTS

Appleton's Cyclopedia of American Biography.

*Asher & Adams. *Pictorial Album of American Industry*, 1876. Reprint. New York: Rutledge Books, 1976.

Beers, D. G. *Atlas of the State of Rhode Island.* 1870.

Chase, David. "An Historical Survey of Rhode Island Textile Mills." Typescript, 1969. Rhode Island Historical Society, Providence, R.I.

Davison's Textile Blue Book. Ridgewood, N.J.: Davison Publishing Co., annually 1936–1976.

Malone, Patrick. *The Lowell Canal Survey.* Washington: Historic American Engineering Record, U.S. Government Printing Office, 1976.

Molloy, Peter M. *The Lower Merrimack Valley: An Inventory of Historic Engineering and Industrial Sites.* Washington: Historic American Engineering Record, U.S. Government Printing Office, 1976.

The New England Textile Mill Survey: Selections from the Historic American Buildings Survey. Washington: U.S. Government Printing Office, 1971.

Rees, Abraham. *The Cyclopedia of Arts, Sciences and Literature.* Philadelphia: Samuel Bradford, 1810.

U.S. Congress: Senate. *Investigation of Closing of Nashua, N. H., Mills and the Operations of Textron, Incorporated.* (Conducted by Senator Charles Tobey.) Washington: U.S. Government Printing Office, 1948.

*Van Slyck, J. D. *Representatives of New England Manufacturers.* Boston: Van Slyck & Co., 1876, 1879.

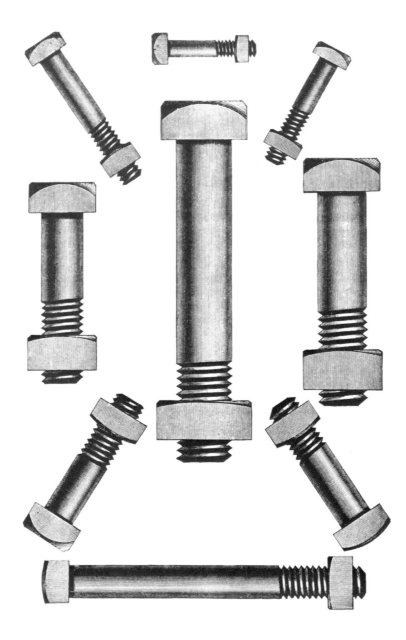

Index

THE RUN OF THE MILL
has been designed by Robert L. Dothard and
composed by American Book–Stratford Press,
Inc. The typeface, Electra, was designed by
W.A. Dwiggins for the Merganthaler Linotype
Company and first made available in 1935.
Electra cannot be classified as either "modern"
or "old style." It is not based on any historical
model, and hence does not echo any particular
period or style of type design. It avoids the extreme contrast between "thick" and "thin" elements that marks most modern faces, and is
without eccentricities that catch the eye and
interfere with reading. In general, Electra is a
simple, readable typeface that attempts to give
a feeling of fluidity, power, and speed. The display type is Perpetua, drawn for and engraved
by the Monotype Corporation after designs by
Eric Gill, the eminent English sculptor, typog-
rapher, engraver, and sometime divine.

This book has been printed offset and bound
by Halliday Lithograph. The text paper is War-
ren's Patina, an entirely pulp- and acid-free sheet.